the PAST gets in My Eyes

Right Brain

Imagery & Hypnotherapy

for treatment of

Sexual, Physical & Emotional

Trauma & Abuse

By: **Dr. Jack Birnbaum**
Interactional Therapy Centre, Canada

Canadian Cataloging-in-Publication Data
Birnbaum, Jack
The Past Gets In My Eyes

Hardcover ISBN Number 0-9681851-0-X
Softcover ISBN Number 0-9681851-2-6

1. AUTOGENIC TRAINING
2. IMAGERY (PSYCHOLOGY) - THERAPEUTIC USE
3. HYPNOTISM - THERAPEUTIC USE.
4. WIT AND HUMOR - PSYCHOLOGICAL ASPECTS
5. ADULT CHILD ABUSE VICTIMS - REHABILITATION

RC499.A8B57 1997   616.85'8223906512   C97-930607-8

Book Design & Photography by Stephen J. Hunter, Kaleidoscope Inc.
First Edition

Reproduction of Peanuts Comic Strip by C. Schulz is reproduced with the permission of United Feature Syndicate

BOOKS
BY DR. JACK BIRNBAUM

Cry Anger, A Cure for Depression

Discovering the Pleasure Principle: Feeling Up Naturally

DEDICATION

To Pat and Molly for new beginnings.

To my patients who had the courage to be in

their right mind.

AUTHOR'S NOTE

The case studies in this book and tape are taken from my clinical practice in psychiatry. Names and details have been changed to protect the confidentiality of my patients.

A special thank you to my editor, Lawrence Jeffrey, author and playwright, who exceeded his role as editor as he coached me in the art of writing. His positive attitude and ongoing encouragement were a powerful motivator for expansion of my ideas.

In the book I have acknowledged the main contributors to my concepts on mental imagery and hypnotherapy. However, there are many other colleagues whose books and lectures have enriched my knowledge. I thank Dr. George Fraser for his excellent critique on the clinical part of my book and his permission to publish his review. Dr. Will Cupchik, Dr. Harvey Freedman, my wife Pat, my children Michael, Leslie, and Peter have read my manuscript and shared valuable reflections. My secretary, Patricia Carter, has worked diligently on the manuscript, often adding her poetic touch. It has been a pleasure to work with my creative designer, Stephen Hunter.

BOOK REVIEW

As a colleague who also includes hypnosis as one of the various approaches available to treat abuse victims, I was pleased to review Part II of Dr. Birnbaum's book which deals with the important area of hypnosis as an investigative technique and a valuable adjunct in therapy. In this area of controversies surrounding repressed memory therapies, it was refreshing to read about successful outcomes that do happen when therapy is properly used to help those with ego state dysfunction. Dr. Birnbaum demonstrates nicely how the cautious and informed use of hypnotic techniques can help those suffering when other strategies have been unable to pass beyond the dissociative barrier. The reader is taken on a tour of many clinical cases and will be able to see how the dissociated mind can be reintegrated using hypnosis. Hypnosis played a key role in the development of psychodynamic theories and Dr. Birnbaum's case studies will demonstrate why the proper use of hypnosis in therapy must never be lost.

GEORGE A. FRASER, M.D F.R.C.P.(C)
Director of the Trauma Study Team
Royal Ottawa Hospital
Assistant Professor of Psychiatry
University of Ottawa

DISCLAIMER

The Past Gets In My Eyes teaches guided imagery and self hypnosis, natural power tools capable of rapidly accessing underlying conflicts, early childhood trauma or forgotten memories. If you uncover personal emotional problems it is recommended that you seek treatment from a mental health professional.

PART ONE
IN YOUR RIGHT MIND

CHAPTERS

In Your Right Mind

Part One

INTRODUCTION

Looking back to go forward

Never in my wildest dreams could I have imagined developing hypnosis as an effective psychotherapy. Nor did I ever see myself teaching self hypnosis and hypnotherapy to you, the reader, for the history of hypnosis, clothed in dramatic extremes from mysticism to magic, is nothing if not tainted and exploited. To my surprise hypnotherapy rapidly uncovered past memories of early childhood sexual, physical and emotional abuse, and opened innovative techniques for healing.

I first discovered hypnosis while still a general practitioner. My dentist had been using hypnosis in his practice and gave me a book on hypnodontics. The basic techniques seemed simple enough and the book suggested that teenagers made the best subjects. The following weekend my family visited our relatives. It was a beautiful summer day and the family was sitting on the porch. My twelve year old nephew was upstairs playing with a friend. I asked him if he would like to be hypnotized. He agreed, but laughed through the whole induction. I was somewhat disappointed until I noticed that his friend had fallen into a deep trance. With excitement I brought the young man down to the porch. I was going to demonstrate to the whole family my new found abilities as a master hypnotist. I repeated the procedure, easily returning the boy to a deep trance. To prove the authenticity of the state of hypnosis I suggested to the young man that when he awoke from the trance his legs would be so heavy that he would not be able to move until I said my name was Jack. Obviously, I rushed the suggestion, for when he awoke he looked up at me and said, "Good-bye, I'm going home." He walked down the stairs, dragging his legs as if they were made of lead. Panicking, I imagined the repercussions of this young boy walking home disabled. I ran down the street shouting, "My name is Jack." He turned around and said, "I know your name," and with great relief his gait returned to normal. This was my first experience as a hypnotist and it haunted me for a long time.

Now, after 30 years as a psychiatrist, I've developed hypnosis and mental imagery into the power tools of hypnotherapy. Hypnosis and mental imagery can help us go deeper into the unconscious mind. Both are tools for accessing the resources of the right brain, the part of our mind governed by the imagination and deep emotions. Paradoxically, these techniques offer safety and protection to my patients, allowing them to process early childhood trauma without re-traumatization. Now a bolder step. I'm going to teach you, the reader, to use the powers of hypnosis. Initially it may appear a hasty journey, but scientific observation offers a more realistic appraisal. Hypnosis is a natural state of consciousness in everyone. The hypnotist is only a coach, helping you access your natural abilities. You and you alone have the power tool of self hypnosis. I, as a hypnotherapist, can only train you to use it better.

Boredom is one of the most stimulating emotions I know. And after practicing general medicine for ten years it was time for a change. My journey has been long, painful and exciting. Going back to training in psychiatry with a family was more stressful than I anticipated. I probably knew less about mental illness than any other area of medicine. I was drawn to psychiatry out of my own pain and search for understanding, and an intuitive ability to relate to people. The vast array of psychological theories felt distant and disconnected from patient's lives. The more I learned, the more questions I had. The satisfactions of psychiatry came slowly, the process lacked the instant rewards of medicine.

My training in psychiatry was Freudian based, waiting for the transference, the childhood conflicts with the parents to emerge in the relationship with the psychiatrist. Focusing on past history lead to analysis, interpretation, and over-intellectualization. The concepts might be valid, but they lacked emotion. The therapist sat like an impressive Buddha, nodding, saying "Ah, ah ...," so as not to interfere with or distort the inevitable transference.

Psychoanalysis matured with the development of self psychology, where the psychiatrist interacted in a human way, empathic to the patient's conflict. My quandary as a psychotherapist emerged from my previous experience as a "real doctor." A "real doctor" examines the patient in the present and looks for clinical findings; a psychiatrist neglects the moment and focuses on the past. I recall a young woman sent for consultation with persistent fatigue and complaints of aches and pains all over her body. Her family doctor, having examined her, found no explanation and sent her to an internist, who completed a full investigation with negative findings. (Negative in medicine means normal. Why don't they call it positive?) As frequently happens when patients have unexplainable symptoms they are automatically diagnosed as neurotic and sent to a psychiatrist. When she walked into my office for consultation she looked depressed. From my family doctor's past experience I've intuitively kept my medical perspective. While she appeared depressed in mood, her gait was heavy and laboured and I was puzzled. During the interview I noticed a small swelling on one side of her neck. I asked permission to examine her neck. I discovered a small lump beside the thyroid gland and sent her to an endocrinologist. The blood calcium was very high, depleting the calcium in all her long bones, leaving empty cystic spaces, that caused pain when walking. This advanced case of hyperparathyroidism was presented at citywide endocrinology rounds to which I was invited. After the presentation the professor of endocrinology asked me the first question, "How did you as a psychiatrist diagnose this case?" Filled with pride and pleasure and sporting a big smile, I responded, "I used to be a real doctor."

Fortunately, in my psychiatric journey away from psychoanalysis, I discovered Eric Berne's Transactional Analysis in *Games People Play*. The parent, adult and child ego states were viable and observable in the present. I could see before my eyes the shifting of different parts of the personality. Fritz Perls' Gestalt therapy added the emotions which blended well with the intellectual concepts of Transactional Analysis. I shifted my focus from the past to the present, fortifying my therapeutic expertise with concepts from communication, family and cognitive therapies. This phase of my psychiatric career peaked with my first book, *Cry Anger, A Cure for Depression*. Boredom returned, as I sensed the intractability of the patients suffering, and the therapist's preoccupation with their suffering. Sometimes the pain continued as a way of life and this disturbed me, for both patient and therapist had lost the ultimate goal of therapy, a return to joy. I shifted my focus again, into the psychology of pleasure and ways to return to happiness from which came my second book, *Discovering the Pleasure Principle - Feeling Up Naturally*.

New therapies continued to intrigue me. But the excitement would soon wane and I would be off exploring again. Finally I discovered Milton Erickson's hypnotherapy and concepts of mental imagery which have lead to my personal model of hypnotherapy. Opening the right brain, the realm of imagination, creative visualizations and feelings was exciting, disorienting and even frightening for the patients quickly regressed, re-experiencing early childhood trauma. I was back in the past and shocked to uncover a much higher incidence of sexual, physical and emotional abuse than I had ever imagined. Physical beatings and childhood neglect exploded in my sessions. Dysfunctional, disorganized families had terrorized their children. Alcoholism, more rampant than I ever imagined was often the foundation of a house of hell. I felt I had new tools to repair the pain and resolve the conflict, but I became overly involved in techniques of psychotherapy. The result was that my caring decreased in quantity but increased in quality. At moments of painful revelations and healing I was more genuinely empathic than I had ever been before. The intensity of the therapy touched me deeply, crossing my therapeutic boundaries to invade my soul. I felt the patients' pain, as well as their joy.

The Past Gets in My Eyes is the culmination of my present psychiatric work in mental imagery and hypnotherapy. It has given me and my patients the power tools to access profound insights, leading to healing and conflict resolution. While it deals with painful and frightening real-life experiences and early childhood trauma, it fills me and my patients with genuine hope for recovery.

I'm glad I became a psychiatrist. The journey has been richly rewarding, for my therapeutic work has helped me and my patients heal and grow in ways I could never have imagined.

PART ONE

In Your Right Mind

Introduction

Mental imagery is a extension of normal daydreaming and fantasizing. When mental imagery is expanded it becomes the building blocks of the natural state of hypnosis. These resources are the keys to the right brain, bypassing the analytical left brain. Create your own entry codes to the right hemisphere, where seeing, feeling, and imagination reside. Bypass left brain critical and judgmental belief systems, build bridges to safe places, green parks, and pleasure zones where the past can be faced and healed.

Humor, the laughter at the absurd, the surprise of the unpredictable, is a universal expression of the right brain. Beyond linear thinking, through imagination, it opens spontaneity, flexibility and playfulness. Let humor expand your range of possibilities, and help you take new directions, and discover the freedom to choose.

If the jokes appear crude or vulgar, remember, their purpose is to explore psychological insights, to look for alternative ways to manage stress, make decisions, and resolve conflict. As a psychiatrist I will analyze popular jokes under various psychological headings to demonstrate right and left brain processing in the search for innovative solutions. Beyond pain, the jokes open joy, laugher, creativity and personal growth. Enjoy them and let them be your guide to the techniques of mental imagery and self hypnosis, the power tools of your right mind. Develop a wide angle lens to see the big picture, and a zoom lens to focus deeper and deeper into your unconscious mind. Uncover past experiences and forgotten memories.

See your reflection in the case studies of the patients in *Part II, The Past Gets In My Eyes.*

Let their insights open yours. Find your way, heal your pain, expand and grow, and let your creativity flow.

CHAPTER ONE

You have your Right brain left!!

Split Brain People

In 1967 a neurosurgeon cut the corpus callosum, the connecting tissue between the two cerebral hemispheres of the brain. It was a desperate and extreme treatment for ten cases of intractable epilepsy. Dr. Roger Sperry, psychologist, studied these "Split Brain People" and discovered separate functions of the right and left sides of the brain. Through the simple use of visual fields he could test one side of the brain at a time. If he showed a picture of a nude woman to the right brain, the male patients would smile and blush, but couldn't express in words what they saw, for the speech center was in the disconnected left brain. After considerable testing he discovered that the right brain was the main center for recognizing patterns, the basis of mental imagery, dreams and fantasies. The left brain was the informational side, where ideas were conceived through logical thinking and expressed with words. The left brain verbalizes through narrative language - "when I was ten years old my drunken father sexually assaulted me." The right brain is experiential, speaking in sensory language - "when I smelt the alcohol on his breath I felt like vomiting. I was terrified, my heart beat so fast I thought it would burst out of my chest."

There was evidence that the right temporal lobe recognized qualities of sound, rhythm and timbre, the heart of the music center. There are cases of stroke victims where the speech center has been destroyed, leaving them aphasic, unable to speak, and yet they could sing. In recent studies with Positive Emission Tomography, a brain scanning technique, the right side of the brain lit up when the music was played and the left side lit up with the lyrics.

The "Split Brain People" suffered Alexethymia (from the Greek - without feelings). They were essentially boring people, unable to fantasize or express emotions. The right parietal lobe may be the solace center of comfort and peace, necessary for nurturing and loving.

Recent research using PET scans by Dr. Bessel van der Kolk [3] at the Trauma Clinic of Harvard University shows startling results. When adult patients re-experienced past trauma or early childhood abuse, the right side of the brain lit up in bright red. The brighter the color on the PET scan, the more activity in that area of the brain, while Broca's area, the speech center in the left hemisphere was suprisingly dim, showing low brain activity. This finding coincides with clinical observations. When you are overwhelmed by an emotional experience, whether it's pleasure or pain, it is difficult to speak. In Dr. van der Kolk's work, when the traumatic experiences were resolved, the right brain colors were subdued and Broca's speech center lit up. Rational thinking prevailed and the patients were able to talk about the memories of the past, without overwhelming emotions.

LEFT | RIGHT

Thoughts   *Imagery*
Thinks   *Sees*
Speaks   **CORPUS CALLOSUM**   *Feels*

                  Imagination
Logic &
Reason
                  Music & Solace Centre

While studies of hemispheric lateralization are fascinating, the brain remains an infinitely complex structure. The terms right and left brain are used loosely, more as a psychological model, rather than as an absolute scientific fact, more as a metaphor for right brain, left brain processing of information, memories and life experiences.

Right Brain / Left Brain Humor

There is a difference between right and left brain humor. A purely left brain joke is Woody Allen's *"Sex without love is an empty experience, but as far as empty experiences go, it's one of the best."* This joke plays with words through reason and logic in a paradoxical way, like Mae West's line, *"When I'm good, I'm very good, but when I'm bad, I'm better."*

Right brain humor deals purely with mental imagery, visualization and feelings. You have to see, feel or experience the joke. A visual joke relates to an old naval battle between the French and the British. *Lord Nelson, on the high seas, was about to encounter the French in battle. He sends a sailor up to the lookout to watch for the enemy. The sailor calls down, "Lord Nelson, there is a French frigate to starboard." Lord Nelson turns to his first mate and says, "Bring me my red shirt." The first mate, somewhat stunned, replies, "Lord Nelson, if you're wearing a red shirt, you'll be an easy target for the French." Lord Nelson replies, "If I am wounded in battle the blood will blend with the red of the shirt and the morale of my men will be kept up." "Aye, aye, Sir," says the mate. A little later the sailor calls down, "Lord Nelson, there are now forty-four French frigates to starboard." Lord Nelson turn to his first mate and says, "Bring me my brown pants."*

Now, here is an integration of right and left brain humor. *A man goes out to play golf on his own and joins up with a stranger on the first tee. As the game continues he notices a rifle in the stranger's golf bag and asks, "Why do you carry a rifle on the golf course?" The stranger apologetically responds, "Don't be frightened. This is an extremely expensive rifle and part of my business. I am a professional killer and this high powered rifle has an irreplaceable telescope. I can hit a bull's eye almost a mile away. It's so valuable I never leave it." The man, fascinated asks, "May I look through it? My home is at the edge of the golf course." "Of course," replies the stranger. As the man gazes through the telescope*

he exclaims, "There's my partner in my bedroom having sex with my wife."
Obviously upset, he turns to his companion, "How much do you charge
to kill someone?" "My fee is $20,000 a person," responds the stranger.
"OK, go ahead, I want you to kill both of them, right now." The rifleman
picks up his rifle, looks at the target. Just before he's about to fire he turns
to the man and says, "You know, I am a professional killer. With me it is
an art. For the price I charge I can kill people in any way you want." The
man says, "My partner has the biggest mouth I have ever heard. Shut
him up forever. My wife, she's been cheating on me for a long time, blow
it out." The gunman slowly picks up his rifle, aims it, and then turns to
the golf companion saying, "I think I can save you $20,000."

Right Brain Personality

The histrionic personality is predominately right brain,
overflowing with feelings, intensely self-centered, their style is
flighty, dramatic and playful, yet rambling and unreasonable. The
roller coaster of intense emotions quickly shifts from sadness and
anger, to laughter and joy. Intensely outgoing and verbal, they
ramble over many topics within the same sentence. Overloaded
with stress, their judgment leads to unrealistic solutions. Very
attractive, they make rapid attachments to the opposite sex, where
the initial excitement explodes into destructive interactions.

Left Brain Personality

If highly intellectual, rational people could shift from their
introspective, analytical, left brain, to experiential, right brain imagery,
they could open up absurd life humor and have some fun. From the
rigidity of rationalization they can shift to flexibility, expansiveness of
imagination and feel truly free. Perhaps they can even find more
innovative solutions to life's conflicts and discover as Fritz Perls, the
Gestalt therapist said, *"Lose your mind and come to your senses."*

Fuzzy Functioning

Some of my patients are surprisingly in their "wrong brain." Oh, I don't mean they're crazy. They're simply on the wrong experiential tract. They may be primarily visual in experiencing life but extensive education has lead them to approach life entirely through rational thinking and words. While they are bright and even right, they actually feel in the wrong personal space, like people with sexual identity conflicts who feel in the wrong bodies. It shows in communication and relationships where their thoughts ramble and are hard to follow or understand. They may appear phony, lost in a misplaced mental track of fuzzy functioning.

Can you imagine the conflicts this must cause in relationships? A left brain thinking reasonable man, discussing an issue with a possibly right brained feeling woman, they are literally on different wave lengths. The man complains, "I haven't had sex for seven days." The woman replies, "I don't feel like it." Could humor help this couple? Of course. The man switching over to humor might say, *"You know, seven days without sex makes one weak."* If they both started laughing or playing, it could lead to sex and they would both be on the same wave length again.

The different sensory tracts for experiencing life are visual, auditory (listening and reasoning) or kinesthetic (sensations and feelings), derived from the field of neurolinguistic programming. If you lead with your primarily experiential tract, the other pathways follow naturally. Let me give you a few examples. A young medical student was doing a histology bellringer test. In a room with twenty or more microscopes he would have two minutes to look down the lens, examine the slide, answer the question on the paper then move on to the next microscope. While bright and knowledgeable, he barely passed. His approach was to look down at the slide and quickly analyze what he saw. In a sense he didn't really see. In a brief exercise I suggested he look down the microscope, then turn his head away and see the picture in his mind's eye, before he thought about the answer. He opened up his visual channel and the knowledge was quick to follow. He aced the next test.

A high school student in his final year was diagnosed with a learning disorder. On further testing he was found to be a purely visual person, with little development of his thinking processes. Surprisingly he had passed all these years in high school by simply recalling the pictures of the page. Finally, when he was challenged, he couldn't understand. After extra training to improve his concentration and stimulate his rational thinking, his auditory track became well conditioned and he passed the year easily. In university a teacher asked him a question in the class. He stood up and paused for a moment. The teacher asked him to hurry. The young man responded effectively, "I have to see the words in my mind before I can give you the answer." He recognized his primary experiential track was visual. If he saw first then he could explain, he was truly a "good looker."

A woman finally saved enough money to attend the opera. Buying an expensive seat she looked forward to her special night. Arriving at the music hall she found a man lying across her seat. "That's my seat!" she angrily protested. The man looked up and responded, unintelligibly saying, "Ah, ah, ah." She called the usher who threatened the man with eviction if he didn't leave the seat immediately. Again the man looked up uttering, "Ah, ah, ah." A policeman finally came to remove him and got the same response. "Where are you from?" asked the policeman. Slowly lifting his head, the man, pointed his finger upwards and said, "The first balcony." The woman, the usher and the policeman filled with righteous indignation missed the big picture.

I met an American master painter at an opening of one of his exhibitions. I told him how much I enjoyed his work, but had difficulty understanding the description of his paintings published in the catalogue. He acknowledged that he had written the description of the paintings but did not understand what it meant. He said, "I paint what I see but the public demands an explanation so I give them one, even though it has no meaning to me." I realized he was a purely visual, right-brained person. Jokingly, I offered him help to open his left brain auditory track. He graciously declined answering, "Why tamper with success."

A primarily cognitive, logical, reflective lawyer found his visual side in a group therapy session when he responded to another member by saying, "When I listen to you I feel like I'm seeing myself in a mirror." He opened his right brain. With excitement he could now shift from emotional flatness, deadness and anhedonia (absence of pleasure), to seeing, feeling and wholeness.

A compulsive rigid businessman, anxious about what might go wrong in the future, found his realistic adult by "standing back and taking a look at the situation."

Is career selection rigid? Are left brain people destined to be bankers, lawyers, accountants and doctors? And are right brain people architects, artists and musicians? I recall a successful accountant who had developed a large trust company. As we talked he said, "I hate accounting and can't stand the boredom of all the figures. I've been successful because I can SEE THE BIG PICTURE in business and make plans for the future. A truly visual man in a analytical field.

In right brain/left brain concepts people who are primarily visual and emotional are right brain people and have easier access to mental imagery and self hypnosis. As children they were more likely to fantasize or have imaginary friends. Under duress they could escape more easily into the daydream state of self hypnosis and dissociate, leaving the unpleasantness of reality. A survival technique in a powerless situation.

Most children are initially right brain oriented and emotionally responsive before their left brain matures. As they grow they shift, as education stresses reasoning and thinking. This is how we begin to lose our more imaginative side. Children who are primarily visual may initially appear to have learning disorders. But fuzzy thinking has nothing to do with intelligence. In mental imagery and hypnotherapy I often find rigid, compulsive thinkers blossoming as they rediscover creative imagery abilities. Primarily left brain people, who hear, listen and reason, are initially difficult and resistant to using imaginative techniques. With perseverance they develop a whole new side of their personality, discovering visual ability and emotions, perhaps initially as some pain and sadness, often followed by playfulness, sensuality, intimacy and loving. The rigidity of their lifestyle transforms to flexibility, choice and personal freedom, as they find their right brain left.

Is Your Left Brain Right?

The ultimate goal of therapy or maturity itself is the integration of right and left brain abilities, a free and open exchange between the two, responsive to life's experiences. The left brain person can expand his logical, analytical mind to levels of abstraction and get more joy out of living. The right brain person, ruled by emotional reasoning, can develop more realistic thinking and reduce anxiety of living, for it is rewarding to find their left brain is right. With both hemispheres integrated, resonating in harmony, you're truly in your right mind.

The Psychiatrist's Mind

Are all psychiatrists analytical, constantly introspective, probing the unconscious? Can they read your mind, predict the future, know what's best for you to do?

Two psychiatrists pass each other and say hello. They ask themselves, "I wonder what he meant by that."

"Sometimes a cigar is just a cigar."

Generalizations never fit. Each therapist is custom made. I swim each noon hour at a health club. Surprisingly, six other swimmers are psychiatrists: an analyst, a psychopharmacologist, a child psychiatrist, an eating disorder specialist, a Gestalt therapist, and me, a hypnotherapist. Are we simply loners seeking peace and quiet, or expressing pent up hostility through upper body thrashing? Fortunately we kibitz around and avoid professional talk, for we each speak in different tongues.

Dr. Harold Greenwald, a prominent New York psychologist, developed a comprehensive humor psychotherapy. He said that there were basically two kinds of therapists, the district attorney who says "what do you mean by that" and the co-sufferer who says "ain't it awful." He described therapy groups as a place where psychopaths teach obsessive compulsives to act like schizophrenics. When I met Dr.Greenwald at the Humor Symposium at the American Psychiatric Association Convention we talked about some of the ideas in my book, *Discovering the Pleasure Principle*. When I expressed my surprise at discovering many taboos about the natural pleasures of life he quickly replied, *"I think it all happened when Moses came down from the mountain and found the Jews were having a party."*

Group therapy has always been my major interest. I find it fascinating that ten to twelve people can sit down as strangers, form unique family trust and share intimacy. Each brings his own music and I, as the conductor, join the different themes into a symphony. A patient confronted me, "You don't listen." After my embarrassment passed I admitted it was true. The reality is that it's impossible to listen to everyone carefully, yet group therapy works. Beyond the principle that sharing is therapeutic, I hope my psychiatric presence is useful.

Words alone are a small part of communication. My right brain, visual and emotional, predominates and is the worker. I watch the posture and body movements. Hands speak volumes; as the patient points the authoritarian finger or clenches the angry fist, I sense the feelings in the tone of the voice, the moisture in the eyes and the changing colors of the skin. I encourage the lyrics to fit the music.

I never realized that my right brain was the work horse of therapy and my left brain the driver. If at times I miss the trees, I hope I see the forest. For one look is worth a thousand words.

A psychiatrist wished for his son to become a psychiatrist and join his practice. However, the son became a colon/rectal surgeon. Out of respect and admiration for his father, he shared his Dad's office. The sign on the door read, "Dr. A. Jones and Dr. P. Jones, Psychiatrist and Proctologist, Odds and Ends, Rears and Queers, Nuts and Butts. (It's a "punning joke" where the cognitive left brain and the visual right brain coalesce into a groan).

Psychotics build castles in the sky. Neurotics live in them. Psychiatrists collect the rent.

Psychiatrists, as well as many other professionals, may suffer work addiction and subsequent burnout. Giving so much at the office leaves only fatigue for the home. A psychiatrist's young daughter was asked what she would like to be when she grew up. She responded "a patient."

So remember this:
Your left brain may not be right
But you have your right brain left.
Integrate both sides and be all right.
If you're well balanced
Your legs are stronger
For at last you have
Good under-standing.
See what I mean?

The language of the talented poet, writer, or dramatic speaker flows back and forth from right brain experience to left brain understanding. Skilled in the use of metaphor their eloquence combines the concrete and the abstract in the same words, like Richard Loveless's poem.

To Althea From Prison

Stonewalls do not a prison make
Nor iron bars a cage
Minds innocent and quiet take that for a hermitage
If I have freedom in my love
And in my soul am free
Angels alone that soar above
Enjoy such liberty

Use humor to tap right and left brain resources and develop a simple, but not easy way, to manage stress and resolve conflicts.

CHAPTER TWO

Doing Psychotherapy

How difficult is psychotherapy? Most people think it's simple, especially other doctors. I've heard many physicians say that when they retire they'll take up psychotherapy because it's easy, "You just listen and give advice."

A young psychiatrist finishing his first day of practice is exhausted. Going down the elevator he meets his senior colleague looking fresh and dapper. After a few weeks he says to the older psychiatrist, "You look as good in the evening after a day's work as you did in the morning. I'm exhausted after listening to my patients all day. How do you do it?" The colleague responds, "Who listens?"

The following anecdote reveals the complexity and stress of being a psychiatrist.

A young woman, suffering from anorexia nervosa, a psychological starvation disease with a high mortality, had been in intensive therapy for years, without any improvement. Her psychiatrist, concerned that she was wasting away, on the verge of starvation, desperately yells out, "You've got to eat something or you are going to die!" The patient responds, "Okay, I'll eat worms." The psychiatrist brightens up and says, "We're in luck, I'm going fishing this weekend and I have some fresh worms in my fridge." He takes out the worms, puts them on a plate and presents it to the patient. She says, "You don't expect me to eat them raw?" "Of course not," answers the psychiatrist. "I'll cook them on my hot plate in the back." He fries the worms and presents them to her, "Here, they're all cooked." She says, "I'll eat one." He throws away all but one. "Here it is. Eat it." She responds, "You eat half first." He

reluctantly cuts the worm in half and eats it and then he says, "Now, eat."
"No," she says, "you ate my half." (Left brain deductive reasoning!!?)

Sometimes doing psychotherapy is like, "Spitting into the wind." (Right brain image, one picture is worth 170 words of the last joke).

The term "shrink" is one of the more offensive names psychiatrists are labeled with and a total misnomer, for if any effective therapy takes place, the mind expands. Repressed memories, feelings and experiences are discovered. Conflicts are resolved and unfinished grief is completed. New or undeveloped parts of the self are found, reowned, healed and integrated into the rest of the personality. More than relieving the neurosis of anxiety and depression, the personality grows and matures to become autonomous, independent and free.

When patients are asked their purpose in coming to a psychiatrist the most frequent answer is, "I want to understand myself." When I ask, "When you fully understand yourself, how do you want to be different?" they are perplexed, for they have learned the popular dogma of psychiatry - that understanding makes everything better. (This is a simple and naive, rational approach common even in highly educated people). This intellectual approach is basically an expectation of magic. First, you think the psychiatrist, in a very short time, will know more than you know about yourself. When he tells you what he or she knows about you the explanation alone will cure you, and you will become the person you want to be. Could you imagine someone falling down a flight of stairs, breaking his ankle, looking at his ankle and saying, "If only I could figure out why I fell my ankle would be all better." If you believe that simply understanding your problem will make it go away, then you believe in magic. You are waiting for "Santa Claus," whose marvelous gift of interpretation will change your life forever. Once you've told your story all you have to do is sit back and wait, in a dependent victim role, for the rescue to work. This is transference, wishing that the psychiatrist will become the wonderful magical parent you never had and are still searching for. Effective psychotherapy may emerge if this replay of the search for "Santa Claus" is accompanied by the resolution of the transference.

When patients gain true insight they often complain of the slowness of change. Perplexed, they are either angry at themselves or at the psychiatrist. This is the time for therapeutic humor. I ask, "Have you ever been to New York City?" Regardless of a yes or no answer the next question follows, "Do you know how to get to Carnegie Hall?" And again regardless of their answer, my response is *"practice, practice, practice."* In one of his movies Woody Allen was asked by his lover, *"How did you become such a great lover?"* He answered, *"I practice a lot when I'm alone."*

Currently there are at least 400 different psychotherapies, and the field continues to grow. During my psychiatric training there was a disruptive, violent young man in the hospital tearing up the unit. Despite the sophisticated approaches of the senior therapists nothing changed. A new young resident came on the service and took charge of this difficult young man. Within a short time he became a model patient. At staff rounds we inquired into the new approach of this young psychiatrist. Embarrassed, he admitted he had taken the patient aside and said, "If you keep breaking up this place, I'm going to kick your ass." He was the founder of "Tough Love Therapy."

Change May Be Simple, But Not Easy

A married couple, both psychologists, had two young boys. One was an extreme pessimist and the other was an ultimate optimist. It was

Christmas time and the parents were going to conduct an experiment to change the children's basic personality. In the pessimist's room they put a magnificent electric train, knowing this could only bring a smile to his face. In the optimist's room they put a pile of horse manure. The next morning they entered the pessimist's room. He was sitting glumly and hadn't even unpacked the train. When they asked what was wrong, he said, "I like the gift, but if I plug it in the wall, it might break, so I'd rather not unpack it." Discouraged at this failure they entered the optimist's bedroom. Much to their surprise, this child was full of excitement, playfully digging through the pile of horse manure. They asked, "How can you be so happy with all this horse manure" and he said, "With so much horse shit, there must be a pony nearby."

One of the most difficult personality styles to change is the obsessive/compulsive. Very bright and driven, the perfectionist (business person, lawyer, accountant or doctor) uses his superior left brain for the most complex intellectual work. But he's a workaholic, driven by the curse of perfectionism and rarely gets any lasting satisfaction from his achievements. He continues to be driven by the future anxiety of the next piece of work. Overburdened and stressed out he is a "Triple A" personality, impatiently racing to early burnout. I've developed an easy cure, a simple prayer. *"Please God, give me patience, but hurry."*

Another great therapeutic technique for compulsives, is "try harder not to try so hard." One of my patients put this sign up on her fridge door. After looking at it day after day with growing frustration and anger she finally realized her marriage was over, and left. As Milton Erickson said, *"If your house is too dirty, move out."*

For the perfectionist who cannot settle for good enough, I say, *"The only perfect thing I've ever seen was a perfect asshole."*

Occasionally when one of these intellectuals backs me into a corner I respond by saying, *"Your problem is that you vacillate from sensibility and procrastinate from thought, and lose your power of action in the energy of resolve."* Impressed by my linguistic brilliance, they finally accept my authority and expertise. I usually sit in a "bigger chair" with all my degrees lining the wall behind me as backup.

Many clients expect the therapist to provide answers and speak. I've gained the reputation of being talkative. Believe me, to talk without saying something significant, without giving direction or advice, is not easy. Even if my advice was good, the very relationship I would create of *rescuer to victim* would only propagate the patient's sense of inadequacy. Should my rescue fail I would probably switch to persecuting them for not following my advice. It's an ongoing challenge as a therapist to relate to patients without falling into the vicious circle of rescuer/persecutor, becoming or creating a victim. So I live by the ancient Chinese philosophy - *"if you give a man a fish you feed him for a day. If you teach him how to fish you feed him for life."*

Generally, I have a number of psychiatric clichés readily available for patients who demand some interaction. I would hate to be the psychiatrist whose reputation is for saying only "ah, ah," like psychoanalysts. In all fairness, they deal with early childhood conflicts affecting the present. They focus on a transference, where the patient relives his/her early childhood conflicts with his/her parents through their relationship with the therapist. Resolving the transference cures them??! Paradoxically, the psychoanalyst hardly speaks to avoid distorting the transference - get it??

A psychoanalyst starts seeing patients at 9:00 a.m. Every hour his secretary sends in another patient. When the secretary went into his office at the end of the day, she found the psychiatrist dead. The coroner established the time of death as 9:30 a.m. that morning.

Trying to avoid a reputation as a silent wall, I have learned to say things appropriate to specific situations. If a patient is having a difficult time and exaggerates catastrophe to disaster, I say, *"One swallow does not a summer make."* If a patient is in the midst of dilemmas and crisises and asks for advice I respond with Peit Hein's *"Shun advice at any price. That's what I call good advice."* If a swinging hippie needs an answer on the meta psychological level, I usually say, *"The wet bird flies at night."* If they say, *"What, the wet bird flies at night?"*, I plead ignorance and ask, *"Doesn't the wet bird fly at night?"*

As patients recover, they often poke fun at me, their therapist. They laugh at my verbal slips, groan at my jokes and ridicule my multi-tone green rug. Am I offended? On the contrary, I'm pleased. For "taking me on" are signs of their new found confidence and assertiveness. Their sarcastic, humorous interactions are signs of emancipation and resolution of the transference. With tongue-in-cheek, I moan and complain "why are you picking on me?" One patient with glee and great timing, responded *"you make it so easy."*

Motivation

My initial approach as a psychotherapist is to stimulate motivation, to help the person find a goal for change. If a reluctant husband appears in my office saying, "I'm here because my wife says it's my fault," therapy is doomed to failure. I explore and stimulate and help my patients discover and articulate their personal desire for change.

"How many psychiatrists does it take to change a light bulb?" The answer is, *"One, but the light bulb has to want to change."*

The ultimate motivation to learn and change is "contagion." You have to catch it. The information alone is insufficient for it only touches the cognitive left brain. The drivenness of *"musts"* and *"shoulds"* are self defeating as the rebellious inner child resists authoritarian demands of the internal and external parents. It's the right brain experience of feelings that stimulates the motivation to change. Emotions energize thought to take the journey into discovery. Often, anxiety and depression are the pain that provokes action. The fever of contagion takes you past enthusiastic beginnings to fire the "staying power" of perseverance.

When the patient finally establishes a goal and takes responsibility I accompany them on their journey as their coach. As the coach, I simply help them do what they want to do better. I travel a very fine line to avoid inserting my own values and respecting theirs. I follow Milton Erickson's philosophy, "Accept the patients where they are and help them take another step forward." I am always careful to avoid the vicious circle of the drama triangle, so that neither I nor the patient become a victim, nor their rescuer/persecutor. If they seduce me with words of helplessness, "I don't know," I reassure them that they know a lot more than they think they know, and that the dirtiest word I've ever heard is "can't." Perhaps this is where religion and psychiatry differ. Religion says that I am my brother's keeper and psychiatry is like the gorilla in the zoo that says, "I am not my keeper's brother." One of the most satisfying gifts I've received from my patients is a T-shirt saying, "I'm the coach."

When I began right brain psychotherapy using mental imagery, I was thrown back to the past. Not to Freudian dynamics of the *id* with suppressed unacceptable desires, but to genuine childhood trauma that had been suppressed and dissociated. I saw again and again that inappropriate reactions in the present reflected the intrusion of an unresolved past. The delay of yesterday's unresolved pain can be triggered by an indirect or symbolic incident today. Paradoxically, at times, the past is in the present.

My job is to help my patients function as realistically as possible today. Say no to past regrets and the ain't it awful of lost relationships, disappointments and missed opportunities. But recognize and explore the intrusive past.

A Peanuts cartoon by Charles Schulz beautifully illustrates the insight.

PEANUTS reprinted by permission of United Feature Syndicate, Inc.

Lucy's comment is the basis of Dissociative disorders. These range from amnesia, fugue, psychosomatic illness, post traumatic stress disorder to the ultimate of multiple personalities. Multiple personalities result from early childhood physical, sexual, or emotional abuse; or adult catastrophic experiences that haunt the present. Fortunately, The American Psychiatric Association has recently changed the name from "Multiple Personality" to the more appropriate Dissociative Identity Disorder. Multiple personality is not many people in one, but a seriously fragmented single personality. The treatment is integration of these fragments into a single whole.

Multiple Personality has become a popular catchword with broad extremes. Are they iatrogenic, self induced, encouraged by the media and talk shows? In a small town of five thousand an over enthusiastic, obviously inexperienced therapist, diagnosed nineteen cases, a gross exaggeration from a normal range of about one in ten thousand. There's a patient attraction to this illness because dramatic and effective therapy exists. A cartoon shows a psychiatrist responding to a patient, *"Be realistic. If you had Multiple Personality, why would you use this one?"*

I look at individual personalities as made up of different parts called ego states, each in a different stage of development, from immaturity or complexity, from wholeness to fragmentation, from damage to health, from suppression to repression or dissociation. The term *child ego state* refers to early parts of ourselves that are still present in the adult, perhaps in a more grown up form. I know the term inner child is overused and dramatized into disbelief, but believe me, the child ego states exist. Don't throw out the baby with the dirty water.

On the Shoulders of Giants

I would like to share the stories of some of the therapists who have influenced my professional and personal growth. Before I went into psychiatry I read a book called *Listening with the Third Ear*. In one of the stories the psychiatrist began treating a very talented scientist who was no longer able to work. He sat at his desk wrapped up in daydreams. In the interview the psychiatrist determined that the man was living in a fantasy world. He had created an interstellar planetary system where he was king and spent most of his days running his kingdom. The psychiatrist, looking for an innovative approach, decided to join the man's fantasy and took on the role of prime minister. Together they spent the psychiatric sessions managing outer space. One day the scientist told the psychiatrist, "This is crazy. I'm going back to work." The psychiatrist was pleased by the patient's recovery and his creative therapy, but could not emerge from the fantasy. In fact he said, "Wow, now I'm king!" Trapped in this imaginary world he eventually sought therapy for himself. Don't be discouraged. If you think your psychiatrist is more disturbed than you are, it may be a good sign. He may be more sensitive to your needs, having experienced your conflicts. When the psychiatrist needs treatment it is euphemistically called, "personal analysis."

Some years ago I was at a Transactional Analysis conference in California. Eric Berne, the founder, was standing at the back of a packed room, listening intently to each speaker. When one paper discussed combining Transactional Analysis with Body Touching, Berne became agitated. As soon as the paper was finished he jumped up to the podium, grabbed the microphone and said in an angry voice, *"We're here to fix cars, not go on trips."* His message was clear, psychiatrists, psychologists, all mental therapists must respect personal boundaries of patients. Touching, under the guise of body therapy or "sex therapy" is unethical. The very nature of the therapeutic relationship puts the psychiatrist in the position of power over vulnerable patients. Unfortunately, a few psychiatrists have crossed the line to the sexual abuse of patients. Groucho Marx might have said, *"good example of shrinks probing where they shouldn't."*

When Eric Berne focused on the individual as being made up of many ego states, Parent, Adult and Child, Berne gave an observable tool to the therapist. The psychiatrist could go beyond deduction to here and now observation. The harsh voice of the demanding parent was suddenly different from the adult ego state that dealt only with the facts in a realistic and logical way. Then there was the child ego state, the center of the emotions of the original child that are still present in the grown up today. This simple but marvellous tool allowed the individual to experience himself in different ways. Patterns of communications were easily observable and destructive games became apparent. With his innovative approach in Games People Play, Eric Berne gave psychiatry more than he expected.

Nevertheless, an over intellectualization of Transactional Analysis brought the focus back to the left-brain, with a loss of feelings. Fritz Perls' Gestalt Therapy was purely experiential and blended well with Transactional Analysis. He invented the "empty chair." When his patients spoke of others he said "put them in the chair and talk to them directly." The patient who had spoken of anger at his mother now burst out crying. He expressed his love and wanted hers in return. Perls felt that the dramatic shift in emotion brought the past into the present. But it was more subtle than that. Imagining his mother in the empty chair had opened the right brain fields of visual and emotional experience. Resolution was now possible through dialogue with the patient playing both roles. Perls' entrance into patient self-awareness through ego state thinking became accessible when he suggested the patient put part of him or herself in the empty chair and dialogue. He described the encounter between internal ego states as *Top Dog and Underdog*. Talking to different parts of the self exposed the internal conflict and opened ways of resolution. The chairs around the room would often be filled, dramatically, as different ego states appeared in the patient. It was ludicrous as the patient quickly moved from chair to chair to dialogue with their internal self.

Milton Erickson was one of the most imaginative hypnotherapists. His innovative approach was positive reframing; when you're stuck with a lemon, make lemonade. The following anecdote is funny and powerful. A university student was writing on the blackboard when she dropped the chalk. As she picked it up she expelled gas. The other students burst out laughing and she ran from the room, humiliated, vowing never to return. She sought Dr. Erickson's help. In the interview he discovered she was a recently converted Catholic and orthodox in her beliefs and practice. He then opened his anatomy book and said to her, "I want to show you a picture of the anal sphincter. This sphincter can distinguish between solid, liquid and gas and has the ability to expel air downwards against the force of gravity. This is an engineering feat that has never been reproduced by any human being. This is a perfect valve, God's creation. Your attitude of shame and humiliation is degrading God's work." Stunned by this different way at looking at flatus she asked, "How can I atone?" He gave her a simple prescription. "Go home. Cook up some navy beans and onions. In the privacy of your own home eat them, then dance, completely nude, emitting small ones, big ones, yelling, hallelujah."

Most people who are stuck in psychiatric conflicts and are unable to make decisions are usually preoccupied with the grand solution, the big step. It may be the right one, but the anxiety of taking such a giant leap is overwhelming and paralyzing. The clue to movement is to find the next small step, where the anxiety is low enough to begin the journey. Surprisingly, only the creative mind can see the next small step.

Like a mother warning her son that if he continues to masturbate he will go blind and the boy responds, "Can I do it till I need glasses?"

Milton Erickson was called in by the American Olympic Musketry Committee to help them improve the team's performance. While they were an outstanding team they always lost to the Russians. Erickson explored their strategy. They had a fifty shot competition and would start by saying to themselves,

"Bull's eye, forty-nine shots to go" and then "Bull's eye, forty-eight more shots to go," and so on. Milton Erickson, in his gently hypnotic and strange voice, said "You don't have to make fifty bulls eyes. You don't have to make forty-nine or even forty-seven, or thirty-five. All you have to do is make one bull's eye, the next one." And of course, as with most of Milton Erickson's stories, the team was successful and won the next competition. Milton Erickson's cases were always successful. When questioned about the failures, Dr. Erickson responded, "I only talk about my successes because I've learned so much more from them, than from my failures."

In a crisis, a conflict, a decision or a change there's always realistic anxiety or fear, even if the change is positive, like a promotion or moving into your dream home. There is always anxiety of the new or unfamiliar. No one can function or take action if anxiety is too high, for the fear becomes paralyzing. As Erickson suggested, pick the smallest first step and when you think you've found that one, look for an even smaller one. Obviously it's much easier to get one bull's eye, the next one, than fifty. Or as the following ditty says, *Inch by inch, life's a cinch. Yard by yard, life is hard.*

There are times when real life stresses are much too much. The plate is full and overflowing. Compartmentalizing is necessary. Deal with one thing at a time, not all at once. The major overflow of anxiety is often not from external reality but from internal distorted thinking. "What if it happens again?" Anxiety of future worries and past regrets compound realistic stress into panic and paralysis. Stay in the now. Feel and think at this very moment. This is crucial for stress management, for we rarely stay in the present. To access realistic thinking and bypass exaggeration, imagine objective observers watching your dilemma. What would the general consensus, assessment and opinion be? Remember you can deal with the future today, for future planning is today's action.

I have studied more psychological models than I can remember, yet sometimes I have to fly by the seat of my pants. I recall a elderly Greek woman who could not speak English. Her family would bring her in periodically for treatment of a recurrent psychotic depression. Always dressed in black, she was a private, quiet, reclusive grieving woman who would not talk about her problems. I couldn't reach her even with translation by her relatives. Fortunately, antidepressant drugs helped, but some therapeutic intervention was necessary. One day I discovered she was a marvelous baker and I shared through the interpreter how much I loved baklava. Before each visit she would stay up most of the night baking. In the morning she would bring me a box of freshly baked Greek pastries. In the therapeutic ritual I would open the box, have a cup of tea with a piece of baklava. She would not join me but would watch with a smile as I enjoyed her baking. She beamed all the way into the next the session. The ritual went on for many years and each time she recovered from her depression. Years later the family moved to a new city and missed the early symptoms of recurrence of their mother's depression. She committed suicide and was found hanging in her closet.

Black humor is a mixture of tragedy and comedy. In a movie a flamboyant, dramatic writer felt he was at the end of his career and decided to hang himself. Standing on a chair with a noose around his neck, he is talking with dramatic flair. Looking at his successes and failures he suddenly comes to the conclusion that life is worth living. At that moment his big sheep dog runs into the room. Pleased to see him, the dog accidentally upsets the chair and the final decision is made.

Suicide is one of the major risks every therapist faces. Paradoxically, psychiatrists have one of the highest suicide rates in the medical profession. Psychotherapy is heavy duty stress, for the only tool the therapist has is himself.

Besides being stressful, the practice of psychiatry can be dangerous. A friend of mine was knifed in the chest, and a distressed woman, obviously dissatisfied with the therapy attacked me with a large hair pin. I was forced to wrestle her to the floor to prevent her from stabbing me. My secretary called the neighboring psychoanalyst for help. In a quiet unruffled voice he asked me if everything was all right. The scene probably confirmed his previous impressions of my unique psychotherapy. I replied that it was under control. He turned and walked away.

One day as I was out walking and had just crossed at the light I heard a screeching of brakes. I looked around to see a big old cadillac screech to a stop in the intersection. A rough, tough looking young man well over six feel tall rushed towards me, yelling and swearing, "You fucking bastard. You fucking bastard." I looked around and I was the only one on the sidewalk. As he came closer he yelled, "You fucking bastard. You ruined my life." Stunned, I responded, "I don't even know you." He screamed even louder and shook his fist, "And you don't even know me. You sent me to the hospital and they committed me." I yelled back even louder, "What, they committed you! I'm going to get to the bottom of this!" and he yelled back, "You better!" and then he yelled, "You call me!" and I yelled at him, "No, you call me!" This went back and forth for a few moments and suddenly my left brain took over saying, "Stop this yelling" and I ended the conversation replying, "Yes, I'll call you." A very threatening incident, yet I intuitively responded on his wave length averting a violent situation where somebody could have been hurt, mainly me. When I returned to the office I remembered him and read his chart. He suffered from paranoid schizophrenia and at the moment was probably off his medication and out of control.

My interaction with this potentially violent patient was a right brain encounter. My automatic response was a "mirroring of his behavior." Unconsciously I responded to him as he was relating to me. Seeing himself in my eyes had a controlling effect on his anger. One patient, suffering from a rage disorder and physical abuse of his children, complained in my one of my therapy sessions of my rough and tough manner. When I explained that I was responding to him in the very same way he was relating to me, he was visibly shaken. For the first time he saw a picture of himself that he abhorred. This was the best therapeutic experience he has ever had. And certainly a strong motivation to change.

Interpreting Dreams

Interpreting dreams is easy. *A patient said to me, "Doctor I have troubled dreams. Sometimes I dream I'm a wigwam and other times I'm a teepee.* What's the problem?" My interpretation was fast and simple, *"You're just too tense."*

I don't interpret dreams. With mental imagery I have the patients imagine themselves back in the dream. As their movie director I help them complete the dream. A bright professional man seeking treatment for impotency felt inadequate because he couldn't function sexually with his wife; paradoxically he could masturbate to orgasm. He had an anxiety dream in which he and his son, while sitting around a camp fire, were surrounded by a pack of hungry wolves. He picked up his son and ran with the wolves chasing close behind. He awakened from this nightmare sweating, in a panic. When I first asked him to go back to the dream and imagine an ending, he sarcastically responded, "Sure, the wolves catch up and eat us." I encouraged him to relax, put his thoughts aside and see himself back in the dream the moment before he awoke. As he entered the meditative state he began to re-experience the dream, crying out in fear, "They're chasing us." As he and his son were about to be caught he imagined himself turning around and with his bare hands breaking the fangs of the leader of the pack. The wolves stopped in their tracks, turned around, and ran away. He awakened from his day dream, smiling with satisfaction. He said, "Deep down I know I'm more competent than I believe."

In good psychotherapy, the patients, not the psychiatrist, make the correct interpretation. In right brain mental imagery therapy, the left brain understanding usually follows spontaneously.

Sigmund Freud discovered that dreams were the royal road to the unconscious. Dreams are pictures or images in the mind. As Freud encouraged free association and interpreted dreams he switched from right brain visualization to left brain analysis and failed to develop the dream in its natural visual form. Carl Jung, through amplification, stayed with the dream image and let it have its own development. Fritz Perls bypassed the interpretation of dreams and encouraged their completion visually. "Add an ending to the dream," was his therapeutic direction. Simply, the dream remained an unfinished movie, searching for a final scene.

Changing Belief Systems

Helping people change basic belief systems is one of the most complicated parts of psychiatric treatment. It is the basic script that runs your life. If you have an "I'm stupid" or a "fuck up" script you're a loser. These basic beliefs are rigid, inflexible and difficult to change.

A young man seeks psychiatric treatment for sexual problems. The psychiatrist gives him a Rorschach Test. The psychiatrist draws a simple horizontal line and asks the patient what it is. The patient responds, "That's a nude woman lying down." The therapist draws a vertical line to which the man responds, "That's a nude man standing up." Finally the therapist draws an X and the patient, with a grin on his face says,

"Now they're having sex." The psychiatrist says, "The test proves you're a sex addict." The patient protests angrily, "You have the sex problem. You're the one who drew those dirty pictures."

It's crude, but please accept the following joke for its psychological insights, for it reveals the intensity of belief systems, developed at an earlier age and the need to rationalize rather than change them.

An adolescent, with his first love experience, is on the verge of intercourse. He becomes acutely anxious, sweating profusely. The woman asks, What's wrong?" and he responds, "I'm frightened, I've heard there's teeth down there." Young men grow up consciously or unconsciously with castration anxiety and the myth of genital damage by vaginal penetration. This is not uncommon although often an unconscious belief. *The young woman bursts out laughing and says, "Of course there's no teeth. Take a look. He looks down and then replies, "Of course there's no teeth. Look at the condition of the gums."*

Even if you do change the old behavior always comes back first with each new experience.

A pirate, after a long time at sea, returns to his favourite bar. The bartender, surprised to see changes, remarks, "My God, what happened, you've got a wooden leg." The pirate responds, "I was fishing in a small boat and a shark bit it off, but I feel great." The bartender says, "But look at your left arm. You've got a hook on it. You lost your arm." "Oh, I was in a duel in India and lost my left arm. But the hook works fine. I'm okay." "But look what happened to your eye. You have a patch on your left eye." "That was when I was on the ship looking into the sky and a bird shit in my eye." The bartender surprisingly remarks, "I can understand the shark biting off your leg, or losing your arm in a duel. But how can you lose an eye because of bird shit?" The pirate answered, "That wasn't the problem. It happened when I tried to wipe it off."

Gallows Humor

A gallows laugh is diagnostic of an underlying loser script. The term originated in the French Revolution. *A prisoner leaving his cell for the guillotine asks the guard, "What kind of a day is it?" The guard responds, "It's warm and sunny," and the prisoner laughs, "What a beautiful day for a hanging."* The laugh is often spontaneous, beyond awareness. For example, one patient laughs as he tells the group of losing fifty jobs and another is smiling as he shares how he got drunk again after years of sobriety. If they're made aware of their laugh and helped to put lyrics to the sound of their laughter then, "I failed again," or "I'm a fuck up," or "there I go again," rings true.

Comedians get paid for laughing at themselves. When Woody Allen says, *"The only thing in life that I regret is that I wasn't born someone else."* Or when accused by his boss of being incompetent, he defends himself by saying, *"I don't know enough to be incompetent."* When ordinary people laugh at their troubles it's not through nervousness or to make life easier to bare. It's usually a hidden form of self ridicule, a personal discount and a sign of an underlying destructive lifestyle. I rate mental signs from one to four plus. The four is an uncontrollable burst of laughter when the words fit, like "Life's a bitch, then you die." Ha. Ha. Ha. Ha. But the "fuck you" to the internal and external *"shoulds"* leads the pack. The universal protest, when healthy, leads to emancipation. Where the goal is revenge, its vicious circle of opposition to authority leads to stuckness. The passive aggressive behavior becomes the foundation of neurosis, personality disorder and failure. Belief systems are the foundations of personality and a false or self destructive one leads to a personality disorder. A competent, handsome, well-educated young man lived with an "ain't it awful" script. An expert in negative thinking he was always looking at the blackest side of life. He failed in work and love and eventually added a second line of "poor me" to "ain't it awful."

Treatment is difficult when patients believe these false systems. They have lived with them since childhood and they are the only ones they know. Therapeutic entry through the present helps, by gaining conscious insights into these hidden life plans. With further treatment past origins are brought into awareness. The "ain't it awful" patient was given a poem and a picture of a little sulking boy saying, "Nobody loves me, everybody hates me, I'm going to eat worms." When he finally understood the way he was living, he recognized his early childhood sadness of searching for a father's love. Now, as an adult, he was still waiting for Santa Claus, hoping that someone special would recognize the pain and suffering of this little boy and look after him. The painful search still goes on in the grown man of today.

The turnaround came by understanding that he maintained this loser lifestyle by continually thinking of past regrets and future worries. He was always looking at his past failures and predicting lousy outcomes with "Here we go again," and "It will never change." He missed opportunities in the present. This deeply embedded cognitive script was very difficult to shift through his left brain. Fortunately the visual pathways of the right brain were open. The thought of living now, opened a new script of *"See the positive."* It immediately transformed the negative thoughts of his boring, poorly paid job and he became friendly with new people who crossed his path. Surprisingly they liked him and he beamed with joy as he began new relationships. I warned him, as I usually do, "The old stuff always comes back briefly." Then I suggested he take a mental picture of himself with his new script, which he stored in his head where it was easily available for recall when the next "ain't it awful," thought came back. The positive self images in his imagination were a series of circular pictures in a view finder with many different scenes of his happy, "up face", connected with his new life plan. His face glowed with excitement and pleasure as he conditioned himself to a new positive attitude towards living. Too embarrassed to sing it out loud, he quietly sang the personal song that fit his new self image. A great new beginning, not an ending, for a new life journey.

When the patient with the "I'm a fuck up" script put music to his words he heard the scream of a little boy yelling, "Fuck you," to his violent father and an older brother who frequently beat him. With left brain understanding, integrated with right brain experience of the past trauma, the patient went beyond pure intellectualization and rationalization, to insight and was ready to begin the process of change. Reliving of early childhood conflicts through past imagery and hypnotherapy helps the child face, accept and reown the reality of his past and recognize the false belief systems he made as a child and carries with him as an adult. Now, knowing it was "not his fault," he is free to accept more realistic beliefs. The power of imagination transgresses time, space and reason and helps the grown up put an end to his inner child's trauma. Even though it's pure fantasy, if it fits and feels right the healing begins. In most early childhood abreactions the adult today rejects the abused child of the past, because the trauma was too painful or shameful. Being powerless to stop the abuse, the child blames himself with a label of weak and inadequate. The movie of the mind allows for reowning, protecting and healing of the child ego state. When the movie has been completed, it can be put away, and the patient is now free from the past, to live fully in the present. A "fuck me" script can become a "fuck you" and release the energy of action to get on with a rewarding life.

Converting the gallows laugh to absurd life humor can shift the self destructive lifestyle. When Groucho Marx first applied for membership in a Beverly Hills golf club he was rejected with a letter saying, "We don't accept Jews." Years later when he was a successful comedian he was invited to join the same club. He replied, *"I refuse to join any club that accepts members like me."*

People do not change with new information, or the right answer. Milton Erickson was the master of this insight. He always accepted a person's belief system or their view of life and helped them, simply but not easily, find another step, a new direction. One of the most touching stories happened when he was invited to a mental hospital to give a lecture on hypnosis. He found a nurse whom he was going to use for demonstration. When the director heard of his choice he said, "You can't use this nurse. She's going through a major depression and she's suicidal." Of course, Dr. Erickson knew that and that's why he chose her in the first place. He refused to give his demonstration without her, for she would feel more rejected and worthless. The director agreed and Dr. Erickson introduced the faculty to hypnosis. As the nurse sat on stage he told her a simple and rambling story of a flower blooming, something like this: Imagine yourself walking in the woods. You find a beautiful flower. Smell it, see it, and enjoy its beauty. Imagine this flower changing as summer turns to autumn, the petals fall and the leaves turn brown. Winter comes, the flower disappears beneath the snow. As winter passes, spring returns and the flower blooms again. Notice the new stems and extra flowers. See the different colors on the petals. Rambling, he continued his simple story, then brought the patient out of the trance. Asked how she felt, she replied, "It was very relaxing and comfortable." The audience saw a very simple induction into hypnosis which they couldn't understand. The nurse left the hospital, never to return. They thought she had killed herself but no body was ever found. Some years later Dr. Erickson received a letter from her saying, "I don't know why I'm writing this letter but I just wanted to tell you what happened after my hypnotic experience. When I left the hospital I felt different. Walking down the street I saw an army ad for women in the army. I immediately joined and within a week I was shipped off to the Pacific where I became a surgical nurse in an army hospital. I met a surgeon, fell in love and now I'm happy and have a beautiful family. Thank you." Milton Erickson accepted her wish to die. Most psychiatrists would talk the patient out of it. In his philosophy the patient had a right to be where she was. His job was to help her find the next healing step. In his hypnotic induction the flower wilted away, then grew again next season, giving the nurse the hope of psychological rebirth. Fortunately she chose the option to live again.

Comparative Analysis Of Belief Systems

Judaism	Shit happens to us.
Islam	If shit happens to us, it is the will of Allah.
Protestantism	Shit won't happen if we work harder.
Catholicism	Shit happens because we deserve it.
Evangelism	Shit happens but we can save you.
Tele-Evangelism	Send money, or shit will happen.
Hare Krishna	Shit, Shit, Shit, Shit
Fundamentalism	Holy Shit.
Capitalism	Shit happens, so let's make a pile and sell it.
Socialism	Shit happens and we are all in it together.
Marxism	Shit happens, but we must share it.
Nazism	We are the super race, everyone else is shit.
Xenophobia	I'm OK, you're OK, they are shit.

Individual belief systems are more relevant to the study of mental illness. In Freudian psychiatry neurosis is seen as *"repressed shit"* while humanistic psychology says *"I can feel your shit"* The goal of psychotherapy is to *"get rid of all that shit"* or paradoxically to *"get all your shit together."*

Psychiatrists may have to break through the mechanism of denial that says that there is *"no shit"* or the Masochist who *"takes *all the shit"*, the Nihilist who says *"it's all shit"*, or the sadomasochist who *"loves this shit."* Hypnotherapists like myself focus on positive reframing to *"transform that shit"* or *"with all that shit there's got to be a pony nearby"* to something useful. Cognitive therapists convert thinking distortions to realistic thinking, *" if it looks like shit, feels like shit, smells like shit, it is shit!"* Is *"we are in this shit together"* the basic belief of a true love relationship? In the corporate ladder *"shit rolls downhill"*, Internal Revenue Service *"you're in deep shit."*

Discovering the basic belief system is only half the battle. For if it is false you need to make a new one. In political ideology, the American foreign policy from McCarthyism to the Vietnam War was *"get rid of the commie shit."* In Post Vietnam *"it is not our shit."* Is the Canadian ideology *"fence shitters?"* Changes in belief systems are simple but not easy. In the compulsive personality, with the script of *"control your shit or it will hit the fan"*, the critical parent *shoulds* beats the frightened internal child (less he/she go wild) into exhaustion, burnout and depression. They are the biggest *"shoulders"* I have met. They need to go to the right brain, find their feelings - see the world and become *"free."* I help my patients shift from negative thinking to optimism *"that shit happens but they can rise above it."*

Can Mental Imagery Therapy Drive You Crazy?

Sometimes I ask patients to focus internally and identify different parts of themselves as if they were made up of many different people, (ego states), an inner child, a lonely child, an angry teenager, a harsh judge, a loving parent, or a realistic adult. "See and hear these parts," I tell them, "and give each part a voice." I suggest dialogue with each ego state, doing internal group therapy to resolve their conflicts. Is it pure fantasy? Isn't that psychosis, living in an unreal world? Am I creating Multiple Personality Disorder? If the patient is talking about a conflict with another person, I use Fritz Perl's Gestalt Technique, "Imagine that person in an empty chair and talk to him directly." I say. Now if you see people talking to an empty chair you might think they are a little weird. This is the basis of imagery and hypnotherapy. Can it drive you crazy??

I was treating a woman in her sixties who had been a patient of mine some years before. She had been in a hypertensive drug study at the local hospital where she had a major confrontation with the doctor in charge. She quit the study but was haunted by recurrent attacks of anxiety and ruminations where she would continually review the confrontations she had with this doctor. She was unable to stop these obsessions, even though she wanted to. After brief traditional psychotherapy where she faced the anger underlying her humiliation she improved. However, a year later she returned with a flair up of anxiety and the same obsessions concerning the doctor. Using mental imagery I helped her relax, asked her thoughts not to intrude and let her imagination take over. "Where do you feel this anxiety?" I asked. "In my stomach," she responded. "Focus on your stomach and imagine yourself there," I suggested." Within a few seconds she exclaimed, "There are butterflies in my stomach." "What's wrong with the butterflies?" I asked. "Nothing, they can't get out." She was puzzled and tried to figure out what this meant. Her thoughts had intruded, so I asked her in what part of her head did she experience her thinking. "In my left brain," she answered. "Be in your left brain and tell me what it is like." "It's a very clear place," she answered. Looking out from her left brain she saw a bridge to the right brain. Visiting her right brain she found a beautiful park with the sun shining, but the papers from the drug study were falling down like rain and she was upset and wanted to leave. I took her down the hallway of her mind to her past. She discovered past experiences of effective assertion when she had sucessfully stood up for herself in many different areas of life. This was the end of our first session. In the second session she shared with me her past week's review of good old experiences with friends and family. Remembering times of effective protest, especially one where she, as the head of a woman's group, actively and successfully campaigned for changes in the community hospital. As she realized how well she spoke, she saw her mouth and acknowledged that she could protest in the present as well. Visualizing her mouth, spontaneously led to a connection with her stomach. With excitement she exclaimed, "The butterflies are now free in my mouth and they are flying into the park in my right brain. They're thrilled to be out in the sunshine." She was very comfortable and happy, but frightened that these fantasies were getting out of control. In the third session she pulled together all her symbolic discoveries. In the left brain, understanding, she recalled all the doctors who had helped her in the past. She found in the center of her brain a control room filled with computers. Unfortunately, the nasty doctor's face kept intruding and she quickly went to relax in her right brain park. From here she looked into a future of new doctors who could help her and she vowed to be more assertive. At the end of the third session she was puzzled, asking me more questions about drug studies.

On the fourth visit she stated, "I'm all better. I finished the fantasy at home. I was walking down the beach in my park in my right brain and I saw my father's face behind a rock. He was alcoholic and violent when drunk. As the eldest of four children I was the only one who could manage him. The aggressive doctor was like my father. I had to handle him in deceptive ways, just like I had to control my father. Now I understand that what I did with this doctor was necessary, as it was with my father." She never did tell me what she did with her father or the doctor but it obviously caused sufficient guilt when the past and the present collided. All was finally resolved when she accepted what she did was necessary for survival, then and now.

This psychiatric model of mental imagery for conflict resolution is called Transformational Fantasy, [4] developed by a friend and colleague, Dr. John Shaffer. Dr. Shaffer is a minister, not "a real doctor" like me. As a brilliant, imaginative, creative and enthusiastic psychotherapist he developed an innovative conflict resolution mental imagery using the body areas as symbolic stages of mental life.

Looking for the dramatic conflict in the imagery like the trapped butterflies, then finding possible solutions or resolution through body imagery resources, becomes a right brain theatrical play or movie. Frequently, the body image conflict has the potential for transformational resolution. The image of being locked in a dark cave could transform into a safe place, or an attacking beast could switch to a protector. As in Greek mythology the Phoenix could rise out of the ashes. I frequently see the sun burst through the dark clouds of depression enveloping my patients. Imagination opens many new directions for change, much beyond those of logic and reason. When the fantasy is complete the left brain insights or understanding follow spontaneously (a paradox, since insights are basically a right brain experience).

Stigmata

There is still bias and prejudice towards mental illness.

A man driving his car past a mental hospital has a blow out. The inmates behind the fence watch as he repairs his tire. Three tire nuts fall into the sewer. He's frustrated, pacing around with a look of desperation. One of the patients says, "Why don't you take one nut off each of the other wheels and then you can put on your spare tire." The man, pleasantly surprised at this creative suggestion asks, "Are you a patient in this hospital?" The patient responds, "I may be crazy, but I'm not stupid."

In a recent survey by the National Institute of Mental Health - titled *American Attitudes About Clinical Depression and its Treatment*, some of the key findings reflected today's attitudes. More than half of the respondents believed that depression was a sign of weakness, not an illness. If suffering from clinical depression, more than half would seek treatment from someone other than a health professional including friends, family and clergy. One fourth would handle it themselves. The major barriers to seeking treatment were denial, embarrassment and shame, not wanting or refusing help and lack of insurance or money. Women are twice as likely as men to suffer from depression and the survey results indicate that African Americans and those aged 65 and older are less likely to seek treatment for depression from a qualified health professional.

If you had the choice between an emotional illness like depression or a physical illness, which would you choose? I recommend depression. First, most depressions recover with or without treatment. Secondly and most important, there is no residual damage. All your abilities and personality strengths return intact. You might even learn and grow from the experience.

I am amazed in group therapy that strangers can come together and within a short time open up, share their most intimate life and reveal their secrets. They risk exposure of their vulnerability, guilt and their shame. Why? First, there is the principle of universality, that many of us have in common the pain of loss, death and disappointment. Sharing is releasing and healing. It is a relief to know that you are not alone, that the way you feel or think is not "crazy." As my patients see and hear the coping and survival of others, hope is rekindled.

The stigma of "going for therapy" is slowly vanishing. Hopefully to be replaced by the curiosity for discovery, the joy of learning about yourself, the excitement of change and expansion and last, but not least, developing the bonus of creativity. *If your stuck with a lemon, make lemonade!*

The most difficult step in psychotherapy is making the first appointment. The newer voice mail menus have lessened the initial anxiety. The modern psychiatric message may be, *"If you are obsessive compulsive, press one, repeatedly. If you're co-dependent, ask someone else to press one for you. If you're Multiple Personality, press two, four and six, simultaneously. If you're schizophrenic, listen, and a little voice will tell you which button to press. If you're paranoid, we know who you are and what you want, so please stay on the line."*

Repetition

The trials and tribulations of doing psychotherapy are repetition. Psychotherapy is repetitive as patients go over and over the same thing and the therapist repeats his wisdom ad nauseum. The nature of depression is to brood and ruminate over inadequacies, guilt, and failures, over and over again. The worst obsessions are over the loss of a love relationship. The rejected lover who is totally preoccupied with the details of "he said/she said" drive his/her friends into a frenzy. The therapist caught in this vicious circle is often brought to task by the frustrated patient, "You keep repeating the same thing." Reluctantly I admit that I can be verbose, repetitive, circumstantial, redundant, bordering on pomposity and pontification. Surprisingly, at times the repetition works. As one patient said, "You've pointed out a hundred times how I'm always future worrying and living in past regrets, but it wasn't until you drew it on the board that I realized how I miss the present. As I look at the three columns with the past and future surrounding the present, I can see the present shrink as the future worries and past regrets expand. I feel stupid that it took me so long to learn." My response was, "You're not stupid. You're a visual rather than an auditory learner. My words didn't register until you could see the picture." The patient responded, "Now I know why I hated school. I had so much trouble understanding the lectures." I responded, "Congratulations. You now have your right brain left."

The Psychiatric Hour

The most distorted, immature concept in psychiatry is the psychiatric hour. Paradoxically, it was conceived by the brightest, most highly educated psychologically sophisticated group, the psychiatrists themselves. Imagine a surgeon removing your appendix. He books the operative hour from seven to eight a.m. After a smooth and rapid anesthetic induction the surgeon deftly makes an incision and the inflamed appendix is fully exposed. Quickly clamped, incised and stitched the operation is successfully completed. The surgeon calls out, "Begin closure," so the anesthetist can relax the abdominal muscles. A head nurse yells, "Stop, it's only seven thirty. You have a half hour to go." Apologizing, the surgical team patiently waits beside the open abdomen for the next thirty minutes. Absurd, isn't it? Well it's even more ridiculous in psychotherapy.

The psychiatric hour is a lie, for it was never sixty minutes. The fifty minute hour was a rationalization, giving the psychiatrist ten minutes to complete his notes, more often, time to recover. With inflation the psychiatric hour has shrunk to forty-five minutes and the psychiatrist now gets four hours out of three. Deception, deception, deception. At least my approach is more direct. Let's go back to my original consultation. When I ask the patient why they've come and the reply is, "I need to talk to someone," my response is, "I'm sure your friends would be better listeners. They're probably nicer and care more about you." Perplexed, they may answer, "But

I need professional help." "Oh, what do you want to change about yourself?" When they describe the goal I respond, "Great, I'll take the job." Now therapy begins. If a session ends before the forty-five minutes, the patient complains, "Dr., I have five minutes left." (It's really the inner child yelling and demanding, "I want more, too much - now!") Now I expound and pontificate on my unique, creative and realistic approach. "We are not here to fill time, but to do something constructive, take a step, make a decision, add a page to your book of life, complete a scene in your movie and find another piece to the puzzle." The psychotherapy session is time for action and one step forward is progress. If the patient can take home one idea, thought or image, reflect, explore and expand it, the session was worthwhile. Change is process, so many want the final destination and miss the journey. (For the trip to go faster, like the hare and the turtle, slow and steady, wins the race.)

If you think I'm a frustrated surgeon, you're probably right. If you think that most psychiatrists are, *"Doctors who can't stand blood,"* you're probably right. Realistically, each psychotherapy session is like a surgical procedure. The tools are the psychiatrist's response and in my case, accompanied by surgical slices with my hands and movements of my arms. My purpose is to accomplish something, an insight, a recognition, a correction of a distorted thought, a shift in the false believe system, find an ego state, a new direction, a new beginning, make a fresh start, turn a corner, or take another step forward in saying "goodbye" to the past.

Yes, protest, not for the length of the session, but for quality, for time in itself is a mental distortion. Under hypnosis it moves faster than it does in full consciousness and with hypnotic time distortion you can shift the passage of time to slow or very fast. It is the patient's job to make the psychiatrist work harder as guide, director or coach. Give him some food for thought, for "I don't know," "can't," and "yes, but," only defines you as a helpless, passive aggressive victim wasting the long years of training and expertise of your therapist.

A man sees his friend running down the street and calls out, "What's wrong?" The man shouts back, "I have a two o'clock appointment with my psychiatrist. If I'm late he'll start without me!"

The Patient's Viewpoint or Why Psychiatrists Don't Get Christmas Presents

- He knows everything about me, so why won't he tell me?
- He doesn't care, he just does it for the money.
- Is he bored or sleeping with his eyes open?
- Anyone happier than the psychiatrist is called manic.
- His book was great, it cured my insomnia. Every time I read it I fell asleep.

The caption I've adapted summarizes the patient's attitudes to psychiatrists. *Two bears captured a psychiatrist and have him hanging from a tree. One bear is talking to the other. "He says I come from a dysfunctional den and have suffered early cubhood abuse. He says my inner cub needs nurturing, comfort and repair and that by capturing him I'm acting out hostility directed towards my parents. He says this is transference, not reality. He urges me to heal my inner cub. .... I say we eat him!"* [5]

CHAPTER THREE

Be a Man/Be a Woman

Homosexual Panic

There were three bulls in a pasture, having an animated discussion. They had heard that a massive, prizewinning bull was coming to the pasture. The larger of the three bulls spoke first, "I have twenty cows and he's not getting one of them." The medium sized bull said, "I have ten cows and he's not getting one of them." The small bull said, somewhat pathetically, "I only have two cows. I can't afford to give him any." The next day the truck drove into the pasture, the ramp came down and this enormous, snorting, powerful bull descended. The large bull immediately responded, "He can have all of my cows." The medium sized bull said, "He can have all of my cows." The little bull silently put his head down and began to snort and stamp his feet as if he was going to charge. The other two bulls looked at him and yelled, "You must be crazy! You can't fight this bull." The little bull replied, "Hell, no. I don't want to fight him. I just want him to know, I'm not one of the cows." (The humor in this visual joke is the surprise switch to left brain realistic thinking.)

The bull joke reflects fear of homosexuality. While there is more openness and acceptance today, heterosexual males are often homophobic, avoiding and disliking homosexuals. Gay bashing by heterosexual men is a defense to ward off their own hidden homosexual impulses. The worst anxiety, called homosexual panic, occurs in heterosexual men when their subconscious homosexual impulses surface.

A famous male celebrity is found guilty of sexually assaulting women and committed to a VIP country club correctional facility. The prisoner in charge explains the daily routine. "You're lucky you came today. It's a tennis day." "Oh, I love to play tennis," responds the celebrity. "Great, tomorrow is our golf day." "Well, I'm an excellent golfer. It is my favourite sport." The man asks the celebrity, "Are you heterosexual?" and the new arrival responds, "of course," and then the inmate says, "Well I guess you're not going to like the next day."

The Myth: Penis Power

Male genitalia are a symbol of power. Not only the penis, but the testicles as well. Women have difficulty understanding men's preoccupation with its size and function and frequently ridicule them by exclaiming, *"So much fuss over such a little thing,"* or the ultimate insult, *"He can't even get a smile up."* Little do women realize the castration anxiety provoked by the threat of harm to this sacred area.

Two men wake up in their hospital room after a recent operation and one man says to the other, "What kind of operation did you have?" "Castration," he responds. The first man replies, "I had a circumcision." The other man screams out in panic, "That is the word I was looking for!"

Male circumcision at birth, originating from the Covenant between Abraham and God, has been a recognized Jewish ritual that paradoxically and tragically identified the Jewish man for extermination by the Nazis during the Holocaust. Infant circumcision has increased throughout all cultures based on the belief of health, cleanliness and possible prevention of rare cancer of the head of the penis. Fortunately the previous myth of absence of pain during circumcision of infants has been exposed. Local anesthetic to the foreskin now compliments the ritual sipping of wine by the infant. Perhaps the low incidence of alcoholism in Jews in the past was the initial painful association with losing part of the penis. *Jews are optimists, they cut off twenty percent of the genitals at birth without even knowing the eventual size.*

53

While doing a hemorroidectomy the testicles are frequently taped up for a clear surgical view of the operating site. After one operation, the surgeon failed to remove the tape. When the man awoke in the recovery room he inadvertently reached down to his groin. Unable to feel his testicles he screamed out, "Where are they?" An alert intensive care nurse responded immediately to the desperate cry, thinking he was looking for his glasses, "Don't be upset, sir. They're in the drawer beside your bed." [1]

A severely depressed male patient had been through several mutilating operations for cancer of the prostate. The last one was removal of the testicles. Before the surgery he asked the surgeon to replace the testicles with implants. The surgeon, with a derogatory laugh replied, "At your age you don't need those things. At your age they don't serve any purpose." Subsequently the man was tormented by severe depression and his most poignant concern was not cancer of his prostrate but the loss of the masculine line in his trousers. Are the testicles mainly sperm factories or are they equal to the penis as symbols of masculine strength and power?

A man in great financial difficulty decides to wrestle the champion for the $100,000. prize given to anyone who can stay six rounds or break his famous Pretzel hold. His friend warns him of life-threatening consequences, "No wrestler has broken the Pretzel hold. After all the twisting of their bodies many have never been the same." "I need the money," says the man. I'll run around the ring until it is over." The fateful night arrives, the match begins and the friend surprisingly evades the champion until the middle of the third round when he is trapped in the deadly, torturous Pretzel hold. The crowd gasps with horror until suddenly the man breaks the Pretzel hold and the champion is thrown into the air. The crowd cheers and the man wins the match. Later his friend asks in amazement, "How did you do it?" He replies, "When I found myself tied up in knots, I felt I was going to die. Suddenly, in front *of me, I saw the biggest pair of testicles I had ever seen and with my last breath I took the hardest bite I could. You can't believe the surge of power I got from biting my own testicles."*

This is a purely visual right brain joke. If you laughed immediately, your visual track is primary. If it took you a few moments to get it, you were busy figuring it out, in your thinking left brain before you crossed over! *SEE WHAT I MEAN!!*

I found its female visual counterpart.

A man after many years alone in the wilds returns to civilization. Sexually frustrated he asks his friend for the town prostitute. "There is only one left and she is not very good - she never moves." Nevertheless, he seeks her out. "Do you have any money, "she says." No, but I'll give you my pair of moccasins." She accepts, and they go to bed. In the middle of sex one arm swings around his body and then she flings one leg over him. Pleasantly surprised, he believes he has "turned her on." Sensing something wrong, he looks over his shoulder and sees her trying on the moccasins.

Male impotence with the loss of recital power, or the inability to ejaculate may be devastating. Unfortunately one of the newer classes of antidepressants called S.S.R.I., of which Prozac is the most popular, has a side effect of suppression of sexual drive, ranging from delayed, or absent ejaculation, to impotency. In mild cases it is welcomed as a cure for premature ejaculation, unless the delay continues, turning sexual excitement into physical exhaustion. Surprisingly, many men, tormented by the terror of depression accept the side effect of impotence as a trade off for the relief of depression. Another excellent antidepressant discovered some years ago, called Desyrel, in seven percent of cases produced priapism, an intense and prolonged erection. While this sounds like every man's dream, in a third of these cases the erection persists with excruciating pain, requiring surgical intervention, to return it to its comfortable, but shrunken state.

There are anecdotes about a primitive tribe which has castration anxiety phobia. Under extreme stress they notice a shrinkage of the penis and become panic-stricken, a visual misinterpretation that the penis will be sucked into the abdomen. This is a cultural fear, and is called, as I recall, Koro. Should a warrior be afflicted he would rush through the village screaming "Koro" and the villagers would rush out and grab on to the vanishing organ.

The supremacy of the penis is clearly described in the following joke: *Angus MacDonald spent Saturday night, as usual, at the local pub. Angus MacDonald, as usual, had too many pints of beer. However, this Saturday night, sleep overtook Angus before he could make his way back to his cottage. He simply lay down in the ditch by the road and went to sleep. As he slept the wind blew up his kilt revealing that he was a true Scotsman. As he lay in the ditch two village lassies passed by on their way home. They noticed Angus and his exposed parts. Since he was a popular lad they were concerned that the chill of the night might damage him. While they didn't have any extra clothing to cover him, one woman untied the red ribbon from her auburn hair and delicately wound it around Angus' exposed penis, gently tying it with a bow. When he woke in the morning Angus looked around groggily. His eyes settled on the red ribbon around his penis and he slurred, "Agh, laddie, I dinna know where you bin but wherever it was you won first prize."*

With such a valued organ it is amazing the risks men take, and the poor judgment they show. Oral sex may be exciting but you'd better trust the person at the other end. There have been accidents where it has been inadvertently or purposely bitten off. Be sure your partner does not have suppressed hostility. Emergency rooms have many stories of personal abuse of this tiny and sensitive organ. A colleague's patient called him in the middle of the night saying he had been playing with a ring at the base of his penis and developed an erection trapping the ring at the bottom of the shaft. The erection was enlarging, painful; the penis was turning blue. The patient asks the psychiatrist to call the emergency room, not only for immediate care but to treat him gently since the humiliation was as intolerable as the genital pain. It's surprising where some men will put their penis. Some have tried a vacuum cleaner, seeking new excitement. Others, failing to understand the mechanics of an electric broom have inserted their penis into the opening and found it mashed beyond repair.

I was a general practitioner for a beautiful young family. I had delivered three healthy children and did their pediatric care as well. One day the husband complained of recurrent pain in the left testicle. The physical examination was normal. As we discussed his sexual activity I learned that it was infrequent, once every two to three weeks. The love was there but they were tired after the day's work and sex suffered. With some hesitancy I suggested the pain could be what college boys describe as "blue balls" with D.S.B. (Dreaded Sperm Backup). I recommended the obvious - increase sexual activity. About a week later he had another attack of testicular pain that radiated to the left kidney. The x-ray confirmed the now obvious diagnosis of a stone in his left urether, which fortunately passed spontaneously. Embarrassed, I apologized for my diagnosis of sexual frustration. With a pleasant smile he forgave me, stating he and his wife enjoyed the prescription immensely.

A woman complained to her doctor of terrible pulsating headaches after intercourse, lasting an hour or two. The doctor's physical examination found nothing wrong. Fortunately he had been treating her husband who was suffering from angina pectoris. He had prescribed nitroglycerin paste, a vasodilator of the coronary arteries, he applies on the skin for the prevention of chest pain. As the physician questioned the husband, he revealed with embarrassment that he had rubbed the nitroglycerin paste on his penis and found it produced an enormous erection that enhanced his performance. Nitroglycerin not only dilates the vessels of the heart it also dilates other small vessels throughout the body, especially vessels of the brain causing headaches. During intercourse the nitroglycerin was absorbed through the woman's vagina producing a pounding vascular headache. The doctor deserves credit for his fine detective work. The woman insisted on settling for headache free intercourse with a smaller penis. Headache may be a popular excuse to avoid sex but an unusual one to follow sex. [1]

With advancing age the intensity of sexual response diminishes in males. The height of erectile power is probably between thirteen and twenty years of age when erections are popping out all over the place.

A young man preparing for his first sexual encounter with his girlfriend seeks advice from a more accomplished friend. "What do I say when I make love?" The friend says, "Just say you love her over and over again." During sex the young man repeats, "I love you. I love you," and the young woman passionately responds, calling out, "Deeper, deeper." The young boy lowers his voice into a deep bass and repeats, "I love you. I love you. I love you."

All joking aside, be affectionate, speak the words of love until they fit and feel right. Too often in love relationships, we voice the criticism and complaints and take the love for granted. The more difficult words are beyond sexual, into the realm of attachment pleasure, the joy of caring, trusting, sharing and mutual recognition.

The days of female rigidity are declining as women reown their sexuality and find their sexual powers stronger than men's. Some women have multiple orgasms, one after another while the man is limited to a single experience with increasing refractory periods from minutes, to hours, to days, to weeks, increasing with age.

Sex is like shopping. A man quickly gets in, buys what he wants and gets out. Women like to browse for hours.

The act of intercourse seems like the dominant male penetrating his sword-like protrusion into the passive female pouch. This sexual metaphor translates into male dominance over women, a power struggle that is reflected in many areas of life. Unfortunately it's true, for in most cases of physical and sexual abuse it's a violent man attacking a weaker woman. This stereotype extends into sexual ethics for the promiscuous male is regarded as macho while a sexually active woman is a whore or nymphomaniac. With the rise of the women's movement female sexuality has become accepted. A most dramatic positive reframing occurred in another of Milton Erickson's famous cases. A prostitute had a major phobia. She was terrified of the erect penis. She came to Milton Erickson's house saying, "Dr. Erickson, when I was a child I was sexually abused by my father. This went on for a number of years. I felt it was my fault and I was a bad person. I tried to make up for this by working very hard at school. I succeeded and was an A student. I continued my education into university and achieved a professional degree. I still felt like a bad person, I couldn't go out and work at my career. I became a prostitute to earn a living. Now I come to you for help. I know I'm a bad person but I just want help to carry on with my profession. Help me get rid of the terror of an erect penis?" Milton Erickson used indirect hypnosis with subtle talk that I summarize. "Not only are you a bad person, you're a stupid person for you do not know the power of the vagina. You see, there's no erect penis, no matter how big or powerful that can stay erect for more than a few minutes in any vagina without collapsing into a helpless dangling mass." This powerful statement, one of the most creative therapeutic moves I have ever heard, allowed her to reap vengeance on her father and other men who had penetrated her, and respect her power as a woman. As most of Dr. Erickson's stories go, the patient made a dramatic change, gave up prostitution and probably became an outstanding psychotherapist.

Have we exposed the myth of penis size? Can men who are not as well-endowed give up the search knowing bigger is not better.

A man at a urinal observes a man beside him. He says, "Excuse me, sir, please forgive me, I can't help noticing how well endowed you are. As you can see I've not been as fortunate. How did you get to be that big?" The man responds, "I'm not offended. I got this way by dipping my penis in beans." The man, surprised, says, "What kind of beans"? The man responds, "Human beings."

Give up the obsession with size, don't be threatened by shrinkage after a swim or cold shower. Scientific studies show that most penises when erect are within a functional range. As you've seen by Milton Erickson's story, sexual performance depends less on the size of the penis, but more on the power of the vagina. The muscles of the vagina expand or contract to make a good fit. So, men, relax and let the anxiety of performance shift into the excitement of making love.

When men were invited into the delivery room, marvellous things happened. Watching the birth of their child and handing it to the mother, produced intense feelings of excitement and instant bonding. The father/child relationship which previously took months or years to develop now fused like metal under a welder's arc.

A secret pact between the gynecologist and the husband has been recently exposed. It became an almost universal request in the delivery room for the husband to whisper into the doctor's ear *"put an extra stitch in for me."* One husband spoke too loudly and was overheard by his wife, who was fully awake under spinal anesthesia. Hearing his request, she lifted her head and said to the gynecologist *"for him, you better put in two extra stitches."*

While men may be ready to perform at any moment women often need romance. A warm and caring relationship is crucial and men need to become more expressive and add talk to the art of making love. Words of passion can be the foreplay of arousal. Increase your abilities as a raconteur and become a cunning linguist. Use your words carefully for they can hurt.

A caring lover asks his mate after intercourse, "Did it hurt?" and she responds, "No, I didn't feel a thing."

There are hardly any references to jokes on the tenderness of lovemaking and the only line that comes to mind with a chuckle is that some couples, after enjoyable lovemaking might quietly say to each other, "Was it good for you?", embarrassed to talk about orgasm lest the failure to have one reflects the failure of the other. Totally unrealistic, for the final satisfaction does not depend on the mate but your own participation and mental set. Take responsibility for your orgasm. Take matters in hand if you have to and stop blaming your partner.

One famous comedian said that his wife kept her eyes closed during sex. She couldn't bear to see him having a good time.

Use your right brain, open the mental imagery of making love. Talk during sex, use visual language of body sensuality. Touch, smell, taste for they complete the right brain experience of lust. In the privacy of togetherness, be free and open. What may be crude and obscene in public may be a turn-on in the bedroom. Leave embarrassment, guilt and shame outside the bedroom door. The excitement wave of intercourse crests with orgasm then flows to the trough of tranquillity. The post orgasic relaxation is a time for intimacy and caring. Express your feelings of love and reach another orgastic experience, ecstasy, the happy sad of love. *If you don't want to stay for breakfast, it isn't love.*

One of the most tender words I've ever heard was "fuck" in the movie Shirely Valentine when the Greek lover first invites her on the boat and says, "You don't have to be frightened. I won't make fuck with you, even though I'd like to because you are a beautiful woman." She does go on the boat and they do make fuck.

On the first night of his marriage a man begins to undress. As he takes off his shoes there's a deformity of his toes. His new wife looks on, somewhat aghast. He explains that as a child he had this terrible disease called toeleosis. He takes off his trousers and he has swollen knees. He explains that this is the equivalent to measles called kneesles, leaving him with these bulging knees. And when he takes off his shorts she quickly interjects, "Don't tell me. You had small pox."

Women, go easy on men for penis size. A small penis inferiority complex leads to men who devalue themselves, feel inadequate, and strive to prove themselves. Men need to compete, win and dominate, to prove they are Big and Powerful!

Why does it take 1,000,000 sperm to fertilize one egg? Because no man will ask for directions.

Psychiatric Denial of Woman's Rights

Breasts epitomize female sexuality. A T-shirt saying, *"Don't stare. Grow your own,"* reflects women's frustration at men who see women as sexual objects. The swing to lumpectomy, rather than radical mastectomy for cancer of the breast, has reduced mutilation, and subsequent psychological trauma. More than 50% of all women who suffered the removal of a breast experienced years of prolonged depression. While men are preoccupied with the size of their penis, women focus on the size of their breasts and breast implants have been popular even though slippage, leakage, and the hardening of implants has made women think twice.

There are many jokes about men's fear of castration, but few about women's. Female castration continues in some underdeveloped areas of the world. This barbaric custom involves the removal of the clitoris. Is there room for humor here? No, for we handle the horrors of female castration with denial. Humor would force us to acknowledge its existence.

Emotional denial is looking with a blind eye, a primal and fascinating defense against pain. We can understand something intellectually but remain blind to its consequences and the emotional impact on our lives. Alcohol and drug abuse are often denied. "I can handle my liquor. I simply drank too much on the night of the accident." "All my friends drink." Society too often encourages the denial of alcoholism by excusing the alcoholic from personal responsibility.

The Supreme Court of Canada recently carried this to "reduction ad absurdum" when it freed a man charged with sexual assault on the basis of extreme drunkenness. The argument was that he was too drunk at the time to know what he was doing and he's therefore not responsible for his actions. Where does responsibility begin and end? Certainly, under the influence of drugs or alcohol a person is mentally impaired. But that does not excuse or explain the decision to take that first drink.

Don't confuse denial. It's not the largest river in Egypt.

One of the most flagrant examples of psychiatric denial occurred early in the career of Sigmund Freud. The damage to women has only recently been acknowledged and redressed. The psychological nature of mental illness was discovered through hypnosis in 1880. Dr. Charcot, the founder of the Paris school of hypnotherapy, attributed hypnotic behavior and its bizarre mental and physical activities to "Animal Magnetism." In 1883, Pierre Janet, a philosopher turned physician, studied Charcot's patients and developed the first sophisticated psychological insights into these altered states of consciousness. Janet was the father of modern psychiatry, and developed the Theory of Dissociation.

* *"Patients suffering from Fugue (sudden unexpected travel away from home with loss of one's identity), or amnesia (loss of memory) or successive existences (alternate personalities) and conversion symptoms, (psychological paralysis or movement disorders) were attributable to split off parts of the personality capable of independent life and development. These symptoms and behaviors had their origin in past traumatic experiences and could be treated by bringing into consciousness the split off memories and affects (emotions) which were then transformed by further therapy."*

* Pierre Janet's words, the brackets are mine

The wisdom of Pierre Janet is as valid today as it was in 1883. Ninety-five percent of all cases of Multiple Personality Disorder have a childhood history of repeated sexual abuse, almost all with accompanying physical and emotional abuse. Females are five times more likely to be sexually abused than males. The ratio is evening out as cases of sexual abuse of boys in training schools, orphanages, religious institutions, and athletic training are being uncovered.

Unfortunately, Janet's work was overshadowed by Sigmund Freud's psychoanalysis and later interest in schizophrenia. In 1905, Dr. Freud, working with Dr. Bruer, published a study on hysteria based on the treatment under hypnosis of the famous patient, Anna O. Under hypnotic abreaction (reliving the experience), she recalled and relived childhood sexual abuse by her father. From this case Sigmund Freud developed the Seduction Theory of Neurosis - that sexual abuse in childhood was the cause of neurosis.

Shortly after, and without any explanation, he abandoned the theory and developed the principles of psychoanalysis, claiming that the memories of early childhood sexual abuse were Anna O.'s wish fulfillment fantasies coming from her unconscious mind. Basically, he felt she desired a sexual relationship with her father. Freud's development of psychoanalytical theory followed, with the unconscious mind made up of the *id*. The *id* contain sexual drives or forbidden wishes, and caused the *Electra* complex of the daughter, and the *Oedpedal* complex of the son.

Why did Freud change his ideas on the sexual abuse of Anna O? The mystery remains. Was it beyond Dr. Freud's belief that respectable Austrian gentlemen could commit atrocious acts of incest on their helpless daughters? Some rumours suggested that Anna O was the daughter of a psychiatric colleague. Or did

Freud's own unconscious sexual urges for his daughter Anna cause him to reject the Seduction Theory of Neurosis? Anna Freud became a famous psychoanalyst. She never married and remained totally devoted and dedicated to her father's work and life.

Perhaps Freud felt the suggestible state of hypnosis had induced the sexual memories. Whatever the explanation, a grave injustice was done to women. The existence of female childhood sexual abuse was denied. The dominance of psychoanalysis as the primary movement in psychotherapy pushed the subject back further still. Pierre Janet was forgotten and early childhood trauma and abuse, primarily of women, was dismissed or ignored. It wasn't until 1954, with Thigpen and Clekley and their book *The Three Faces of Eve* that childhood abuse returned to modern psychiatry. In 1980, the American Psychiatric Association finally included Dissociative Disorders in their diagnostic manual of mental disorders. The veil of denial surrounding childhood sexual, physical and emotional abuse has finally been lifted. Recently Dissociative and Post Traumatic Stress Disorders, based on realistic trauma in children, and catastrophic events in adult life, have also been accepted and incorporated into modern psychiatry. Welcome back, Pierre Janet! Long live the women's liberation movement.

The Female Protest

Women have reowned their sexuality and aggressiveness. It's good news/bad news.

Bad news, *"Why does it take five women with PMS to change a light bulb? "Because it does! Want to make something out of it?"*

The good news? Women are standing up and directing their

anger into personal and professional power, effectively asserting themselves against oppression.

This guy is going to visit his friends in a high rise apartment building. He parks in the parking lot. As he's walking towards the front door he gazes upwards. He sees a gorgeous woman on the tenth floor, stark naked, with breasts hanging over the balcony, motioning to him. He can't believe it, he looks around; there's nobody else. He points to himself and she says, "Yes, you, come up to my apartment, 1004." He races up to the tenth floor. The door is open at 1004. He goes in. This beautiful woman is standing naked. She says to him, "I'm so glad you came up. Please take off your clothes, you'll feel more comfortable. I'll be right back." He takes off his clothes, paces around the living room, sexually excited. This is his lucky day. She comes back, walks up to him seductively, reaches down and grabs his testicles, squeezing them tightly. As he's screaming in agony she says, "Don't ever park in my parking spot again."

The Sexual Evolution

Woody Allen's famous line, *"Sex without love is an empty experience, but as far as empty experience's go, it's one of the best"* is the philosophy of a previous generation. Many years ago free love was in and casual sex rampant. Today it's a new "ball game" and AIDS changed the rules.

A middle aged man coming on to the single's scene after leaving a long marriage has to think of safe sex. He enters the drug store to buy one of those dreaded things he hasn't used for years, a condom. He's shocked. They're displayed openly in the middle of the store, not hidden behind the counter. That's a relief. At least you don't have to ask a female clerk for condoms, although you still have to put them in front of the cashier for everybody to see. As he looks at the rack he is overwhelmed by all of the different makes and brands. Suddenly, his eye catches something in the small print. He's perplexed. He's never seen this before. He says to himself, "What, they come in different sizes?" Reluctantly, and with embarrassment he approaches the pharmacist. "Excuse me," and in a clumsy attempt at a brief explanation about such ignorance at his stage of life he says, "I haven't used condoms for a long time. You see I was married and now I'm separated." The pharmacist cuts the conversation short and says, "How can I help you, sir?" The man says, "Well, I notice there are different sizes of condoms. How do you tell what size you need." "Oh, that's no problem. We have a special board. Take it into the dressing room and test out your size." A few minutes later the man emerges and the pharmacist asks, "Is everything satisfactory, sir?" "Oh yes," says the man with a smile. "By the way, how much is the board?"

Pleased with the purchase of his new board and condoms that fit he buys a typical male T-shirt that says, "So Many Women" and on the back, "So Little Time."

Are religious fundamentalists rejoicing at the AIDS epidemic? Do they think that this is God's final answer to sexual promiscuity and sin? "For was not Onan struck dead by God for withdrawing at the time of ejaculation to cast his sperm upon the ground?" Is not the ultimate goal of sex procreation? Has the righteous pendulum swung from free and open sex, to restricted sex where even talking, or telling one of my jokes, may be sexual harassment? In a recent incident, a university professor was thrown out of the university pool for swimming too close to women. He was accused of voyeurism. In the past few years there have been numerous cases of physicians, and more notably psychiatrists, being charged for having sex with patients, a terrible abuse of power. Has the pendulum swung too far when a medical ethics committee reprimands a physician for sexual language (such as a gynecologist at the moment of delivery saying, "Look what penis power can do!") Sexual inappropriateness is a form of sexual abuse, punishable by professional misconduct. Is the pendulum now swinging towards personal oppression?

I treated an orthodox rabbi for severe depression. He failed to respond to psychotherapy or antidepressants. However, he had a powerful visual side to his personality that was demonstrated by his interest in photography. Looking at nature and its beauty would brighten his mood and he would shift for brief moments out of his depression. By lifting up his head to see a clear blue sky, he would open his visual track and his capacity for joy and pleasure. But he walked with his head down, staying in his depressive state. When I explained that "looking up" could be a cure, he said, "I keep my head down to avoid looking at women, and sexual temptation," a belief system that contributed to his depression. In Orthodox Judaism there is separation of men and women. At wedding celebrations they sit separately to eat and don't dance together. The dance floor is separated by a partition. Women dance on one side and men dance on the other, with the bride and groom alternately visiting each side to be entertained. *A young orthodox man is having a prenuptial discussion with his rabbi. "Rabbi," he says, "Can I have sex lying down?" The Rabbi says, "Fine." "Rabbi, can we have sex with the woman on top?" "Of course," responds the Rabbi. "How about oral sex?" "Why not?" "Anal sex?" "No problem." Finally the young man says, "Rabbi, can I have sex standing up?" The Rabbi says, "Oh no, that is forbidden. It could lead to dancing!"*

Sex without love is an empty experience, for it's the intimacy, the closeness and sharing, that brings sex to ecstasy. It was over attachment, not intimacy, that we heard when Prince Charles said to his girlfriend, "I wish I was a tampon so I could be inside you all the time." Are sexual morays changing? Is penis power shifting? Will intercourse change as the preferred way of lovemaking? Some jokes might indicate a shift. There is certainly an increase in oral sex jokes. *What's better than roses on a piano? Answer: two lips on an organ?*

Who knows how the sexual act will evolve. These anecdotes about Martians may be helpful.

A spaceman lands on Mars and finds a Martian woman stirring a huge cauldron. "What are you doing" he asks? "Making a baby" she replies. "How do you do it on earth?" she asks. "This way," and he makes love to her. When it's over she asks, "Where is the baby?" "Oh, it takes nine months to develop" he says. "Then why have you stopped stirring?" she asks.

There are anecdotal reports on a new antidepressant drug that causes orgasm when the patient yawns. A psychiatrist observing the phenomena might respond, "Are you really happy to see me or do your want your prescription refilled?"

I've had a bulimic patient give up Prozac because she couldn't reach orgasm. A surprising contrast to depressed men who sacrifice their sexual potency for the relief of depression. Hurrah for the new short acting S.S.R.I. antidepressants! As depression lifts and the libido returns I recommend sex holidays. Stop your antidepressants for a few days and "celebrate." Lovemaking becomes a self rewarding ritual for recovery from the black hole of melancholy.

CHAPTER FOUR

Love Relationships

Now I've Got You, You Son-of-a-Bitch:

On their wedding night a husband says to his wife, "Dear, put on my trousers." She puts them on and exclaims, "There're much to big," and he responds, "Don't you ever forget it. You're not big enough to wear the pants in this family." That night, after exciting sex, she says, "Dear, put on my pants." He tries and says, "There're much too tight. I can't get into them," and she responds, "If you don't smarten up, you never will."

The power struggle begins, with sex the ace in the hole. Why do people in a love relationship compete for power? Why can't they simply love each other? Intimacy, sharing and trust are difficult. The risk of pain and the memory of broken love relationships still prevails. What a waste, to let past regrets and future worries interfere with loving. Genuine power is great; it enhances life with vitality and the desire to explore and discover. The fine line between dominance and strength, can easily slip into domineering and control. Two dominant people can stimulate each other with their personal discoveries, but domineering people can fall into the daily game of "Now I Got You, You Son-of-a-Bitch." Let's hope your love relationship avoids the route the following young couple took.

While courting they screwed everywhere, even in the kitchen. When they married they screwed only in the bedroom. A few years later the only screwing is in the hall when they pass each other yelling, "Screw you, screw you."

Love Bonds

Oscar Wilde said, *"Sometimes the bonds of marriage are so heavy it takes more than two to carry them."*

'Love bonds' is an interesting term. The word 'bond' as a noun describes the connection between two people, the attachment bridge. As a verb it's a process of attaching, which becomes "crazy glue." Even if the love relationship is seriously damaged, the glue has set and it's excruciatingly painful to break. A flagrant sexual affair is often the precipitating factor in a marriage breakdown, but it begins with a breakdown in communication and the failure to grow and thrive as a couple. It takes an average of two to four years to separate emotionally, twice the time of grieving a loss through death.

The foundation of a love bond is trust.

A husband plays golf every Sunday, diligently leaves at 8:30 and is home by 3:00. One day he arrives home at 9:00 at night. His wife is concerned and asks what happened. He tells the following story: "I was heading home and there was a lady with a flat tire. I stopped to help her change the tire. It was raining and my clothes were soaked. Her apartment was nearby and she invited me to freshen up. She washed my clothes while I took a shower. Since they were still in the dryer, she gave me a bathrobe to wear and invited me to have a drink. She then appeared in a see-through negligee. I lost control and made passionate love to her. That's why I was late. His wife burst out laughing, "You're kidding. You played an extra nine holes of golf."

Denial is a powerful defence. Love is blind and only the neighbors can see. Sometimes psychiatrists are blind. I was treating a woman who was resistant to every therapeutic technique, continually complaining of emotional pain and distress. Despite many extra sessions she deteriorated. One day walking down the hall I heard two cleaning women talking as my patient entered my office. One said to the other, "There's a love sick lady." They made the diagnosis I had missed. The patient had formed a positive love transference and the only way for her to maintain the closeness with me was to stay ill.

A man was sent by his wife for psychiatric help because he had yet another sexual fling. When I brought in the wife on the second visit, I saw a strong, domineering woman who treated her husband like a little boy. She put his indiscretion into the perspective of their relationship by saying, "He's a good man, but occasionally naughty and mischievous. Boys will be boys. Once he's put in his place, he's okay." It was obvious that this was a mother/child relationship requiring the punishment and reprimand by a visit to the psychiatrist. She was willing to forgive and forget. Recognizing a well balanced attachment bond I agreed, "Boys will be boys."

One of my colleagues, a sex therapist, would describe the above relationship as pseudo-incest, which is one of the common causes of loss of sexual interest in a marriage. The couple shift to a parent/child relationship, with the loss of sexual excitement. I recall a bright, creative woman with her own business who was sexually promiscuous outside her marriage and frigid within. The question of leaving was always dismissed since her husband was her best friend. He cared deeply for her in an over-protective way. Men, too, can act like mothers.

Many dysfunctional relationships are, paradoxically, stable. Unfortunately, if neither party changes they live harmoniously, but in a rigid, limited and boring way. Observe a rescuer/persecutor/victim relationship. The rescuer thrives on the power of protecting the weaker mate, which outweighs the loss of personal identity. Deep down he/she is avoiding his/her own vulnerable internal needy self. In this kind of relationship, there is a basic shift when the rescue fails and victimhood persists. The rescuer gets mad and persecutes the victim for not changing. Sometimes the roles change and the victim becomes the persecutor of the original rescuer. The only movement in a rescuer/victim relationship is circular. The victim's payoff is being the "center of attention," even if it is through pain and suffering and self-devaluation. Constant recognition and protection from the anxiety of aloneness make it worthwhile. The disadvantage is dependency and loss of autonomy. The relationship is inflexible and any significant movement immediately threatens its balance. The attachment bond is only broken if the anger builds up enough to really blow them apart. The pleasure of individuality and freedom must outweigh the pain of standing alone.

Woody Allen's movie, Annie Hall, was his first foray into the complexity of relationships. It was beautifully done. At the end of the movie, Woodie Allen turns to the audience and tells a joke,

"This man went to a psychiatrist and said, "Doctor, my brother's running around the house clucking like a chicken." The psychiatrist said, "He's very ill and should be hospitalized," and the man responds, "Oh, we can't do that. We need the eggs!"

Over-attachment can be seen when a physically abused child is taken out of a dysfunctional home and placed into a foster home where there is genuine tender loving care. What do you think he does? Well, if he's old enough he runs back to the home where he was mistreated. Of course he doesn't like the beatings, but he has emotional attachment to his brutal parents, not to the new foster parents.

Crazy Glue

Strip layers from an excessively nice person and you will find a passive/aggressive. The hidden anger emerges indirectly, disguised by sneaky, manipulative behavior. It is a destructive, critical, oppositional personality, which has the creativity and genius of a chemist who can, *"Can turn anything good into shit."*

The histrionic personality is a chameleon, the bright colors charm, seduce and attract like the pull of a powerful magnet. Once trapped in the spider's web, the colors darken and venom slowly poisons its victim. The entrapment has occurred, the negative strokes begin. Perceptive, visual, they see everything and their critical zoom lens focuses in on the *"One black spot on a beautiful white chicken."* Transforming the positive, accentuating the negative, exaggerating trivial issues, they convert disaster to catastrophe. Their realistic judgment is blinded by their self-centered jealously and search for personal attention at any price. The power of control is exerted through the myth of protection of the loved one. They rationalize their criticism as vigilance and care for the weak, ineffective, immature or bad other. The relationship is enmeshed, over-attached and strangulating. The way out is to break *"The Pretzel hold,"* to escape from the vicious circle of rescuer/persecutor/victim.

It's not easy to break the bonds of attachment once the crazy glue has set. The anxiety of leaving the painful but secure, and the anxiety of facing unfamiliar territory alone, makes the journey painful and difficult. If compounded by past regrets and future worries, the anxiety becomes unbearable. The paralysis of dissociation, or a spill over into depression, relieves the acuteness of the fear, transforming it into withdrawal, passivity and helplessness.

Once the bonds of entrapment are broken, the victim is free. Emancipation occurs with self-confidence. Paradoxically, the same people may come together again, hopefully with new boundaries that are well defined and separated. Tolerating aloneness may be necessary until new relationships are created.

When marriage breaks down a separation phase begins. The nicest people do the strangest and nastiest things to each other. Here's a typical scenario. A sophisticated, well educated, professional couple decide to end their marriage. The causes are realistically mutual and multiple, yet each one blames the other. If I see one party at a time, the other is invariably described as an awful human being. But when I interview the other party, they appear intact and human, but paint a horrible picture of the one I saw first. This is a typical scenario if children are involved: The man arrives to pick up the children for the weekend. The wife argues with him at the door. He pushes the door open and she falls. She calls the police, pressing an assault charge and they take him to the station. Humiliated and raging, he counter-accuses her of mental instability, demanding psychiatric assessment of his damaged children. She counter-charges that he is a violent father who has beaten the children, and demands he have psychiatric treatment. The court stops his visiting rights until the assessment is complete. The children are the painful pawns in this ongoing sideshow. The emotional pain is pervasive, the financial cost is prohibitive, and the process, fueled by legal process, goes on and on and on for many years. Believe it or not, this crazy behavior is considered normal in love relationship breakdown.

The crazy clue of attachment produces the most bizarre, erratic, unrealistic behavior as it is torn apart, like the man who left his home yet spends each evening walking around it.

The Stockholm Syndrome is a more recent example of the bizarreness of attachment. When hostages of a terrorist group are released their major concern is the welfare of the very people who threatened their lives. Attachment process is extremely rapid under life threatening or dramatic situations. Ask any father who's been present throughout labour and holds his child immediately after birth. Instant bonding occurs, where previously it took years for father/child attachment to develop.

Attachment defies logic, superseded only by emotional bonding in humans and animals as well. In Harlow's experiment with monkeys, a baby monkey is separated from its mother and placed in a cage with two poles. One pole was for feeding and the other was covered with a cloth monkey. The baby monkey hung on to the monkey doll and reached over periodically to feed. Attachment overrides the physical need for food. It is the food of survival. In lower animals, the attachment reflex clicks in like an electrical switch shortly after birth. Konrad Lorenz, the famous zoologist, stayed with a flock of baby geese shortly after their birth. Now they follow him for life. I always smile when I see the photograph of this prestigious scientist walking the banks of a river followed by his line of geese. The attachment bond in humans is more complicated but just as irrational. Let's face it, your kid is not the best even if you think he/she is.

Dr. John Bowlby was a famous British psychiatrist who devoted his career to the study of the mother/infant attachment bond. Revealing the anxiety of separation and the pain of loss, he wrote three major volumes called *Attachment, Separation,* and *Loss,* that were acclaimed by the psychiatric community for their innovative scientific observations of this basic and most important human relationship. When I read his work, a whole new way of viewing adult relationships exploded in my mind and in my work.

Realistic separation anxiety and the breakdown of love relationships with the need for grieving were clearly visible.

The mother/child relationship required gradual emancipation for the child to grow up independent, and eventually leave home to begin its own life. Dr. Bowlby meticulously documented the pain of separation. He described how the young child, sitting with its mother in the park, would gradually wander further and further away as it grew older, yet always looked back to check that she was there. While he discoved the pain of separation he barely explored the exciting human desire, curiosity, to discover the external world, even more powerful than the need to be securely attached to mother. I expanded this drive for exploration into my book, *Discovering the Pleasure Principle*.

Dr. Bowlby was invited to a Child Psychiatry Convention held in the country, which I attended simply because I wanted to meet him. For the first few days he was surrounded by admirers. Early one morning as I was setting out to play tennis, I saw him sitting alone in the lobby. I cornered him and thanked him for his work and began sharing mine. He was puzzled with the concept of the pleasure drive, having spent the major focus of his life on the pain of separation. A female physiologist had joined our discussion. She had a young son, about 1 1/2 running loose around the hall, who would periodically come back to her. Without any embarrassment she would pull up her sweater and nurse the baby. After feeding, the child would once again run off and play. It was during one of these feedings that I turned to Dr. Bowlby, pointed at the child and said, "Why would anyone leave that?" He might not have agreed, but he saw my point.

A gorilla escapes from the zoo and climbs into the apartment of an elderly Jewish lady and rapes her before he is caught and returned to the zoo. She stays closeted in her apartment for weeks. The neighbors are concerned. When she finally emerges one of her neighbors asks, "How are you?" She responds, "How can I be? He doesn't write, he doesn't call."

Most of the original research on separation came from Harvard University where they studied 150 couples who had left their marriage. A fascinating study in many ways. They found that divorced people were likely to divorce again. Contrary to public opinion this was not a sign of instability, but an act of personal maturity, for they had learned that ending an unsuitable love relationship was a realistic option to staying in a bad one. The high divorce rate in Nordic nations is basically a sign of women becoming happier. A professor of psychology from Oslo University stated that welfare benefits and increased sexual equality made woman less willing to endure loveless marriages and more able to overcome the trauma of divorce. The rates of divorce in Nordic countries is likely to continue to rise in line with increased happiness in women's lives. Women have become happier because they say what they want and take action. "If your house is too dirty move out!" (Milton Erickson)

Here's an easy formula for intimacy, four simple words, I, Thou, Here and Now. If two people together can share as separate unique individuals they create intimacy. One grandiose self centered male in a group therapy session would respond to others by saying, "Me too." Whenever someone talked about their experience he would give a speech about himself. There's nothing wrong with saying "Me too." The problem was that he forgot the other person. When he recognized his self centeredness he asked for help. I gave him a simple formula, "Whenever you talk to somebody, always ask about them as well." His new beginning was somewhat awkward, as he said, "Well, I talked a lot about myself, so let's talk about you. What do you think about me?"

A man delighted with the growth of his love relationship said to his mate, "You've ruined me - I can't have sex with you; I can only make love."

Transform the role of rescuer, persecutor or victim, into a healthy love relationship of caring and empathy for your partner. A wise Rabbi said, "If not for me who will be. If only me, who am I?" Two men in my group, both dominant, bright, verbal, authoritarian and narcissistic, attack each other verbally, dueling for points and escalating into threats. As they recognized the persecutor/attack position, each of them spontaneously switched to humor which surprisingly solved the power game. The joke took them out of the drama circle of rescuer/persecutor/victim. They both laughed, the people around them joined in and the rage dissolved.

Negative stroking is the mark of over-attachment. The onslaught of controlling, blaming, criticizing, compounded by past regrets, failures and future worries, may be more emotionally intense than a healthy bonding, but it is also strangulating and inhibits a healthy independence.

I recall parents saying, "I love my child so much, I'll spoil him." You cannot spoil anyone with positive stroking, for love, caring and recognition, comes from healthy attachment. Individuality, personal freedom and mutual respect are its essence.

Trial Separation

Love relationship breakdown heads the psychiatric list. The separation anxiety, compounded by the sadness of loss, is an excruciatingly painful, yet normal process. My patients often ask, "When will it end?" I tell them two to four years. I expand this to say that this is twice as long as the average grieving over the death of a loved one. One woman, in the midst of separation anxiety from a husband who left the marriage for another woman, exclaimed "I should have killed him, it would have been less painful."

A patient of mine and I laughed as he shared his trial separation. For years the marriage was dead, no sex, poor communication. He complained that his wife was too quiet, too nice, inhibited and not exciting. He compensated by having many affairs. Recently, after the loss of his last lover, he confronted his wife and expressed his desire to leave. His wife cried, her pain compounded by the recent loss of her job. A short time later she made a turnaround and said to her husband, "You know, this marriage has been empty for a long time and suddenly I feel free, even a little excited, looking towards a new beginning. I'm even feeling sexy." Surprisingly, he responded with excitement himself and he felt attracted to her strength. This trial separation might be the best thing for their marriage. His absurd life humor shifted his pain and fear of loneliness to pleasure, opening him up to fun and playfulness. They might start talking again, discussing their frustrations and anger with the empty years. They could stay stuck in past regrets, or now I got you, you son-of-a-bitch. Hopefully, they recognize the repetitive and circular accusations and move on, using a statue of limitations to close the door on the past. Focusing on their life today, they can use their anger for the resolution of realistic conflicts and differences. Through his mischievous, sarcastic child, he may open up the opposite to his anger, love, empathy and intimacy, rekindling sexual desire. *Make up sex is great!*

THE GESTALT PRAYER
BY: FRITZ PERLS

I do my thing and you do your thing.
I am not in this world to live up to your expectations
And you are not in this world to live up to mine.
You are you and I am I,
And if by chance we find each other, it's beautiful.
If not, it can't be helped.

CHAPTER FIVE

Cry Anger Louder

Anger is the most misused, ill-used, over-used, under-used, repressed emotion in psychiatric illnesses, especially depression. Yet it is the most powerful energy available for conflict resolution and personality growth. If I were to rewrite my book *Cry Anger, A Cure for Depression,* I would hold to all the principles I said then and add a few new ones. If you're very angry don't go to a respected authority to acknowledge it, for most psychiatrists, still fearful of anger, see it as a symptom of illness rather than as the energy of repair. People in authority need to maintain power and someone else's anger is a threat. Some religious groups including AA see anger as bad, evil or self destructive. "Turn the other cheek" is their motto. Forgiveness is the only way to resolution for personal injury, insult or assault.

FORGIVENESS[2]

The friend who ran off with your wife
Forgive him for his lust;
The chum who sold you phony stocks,
Forgive his breach of trust;
The pal who schemed behind your back,
Forgive his evil work;
And when you're done, forgive yourself
For being such a jerk.

A young man goes the monastery and takes an oath of silence. At the end of each year he is allowed to speak only two words. At the end of the first year he says to his priest, "Food bad." The priest gives him the blessing and tells him to go into his second year of meditation and search for inner peace and tranquillity. At the end of the second year he says, "Bed hard." The priest gives him the benediction for personal health and search for God and dismisses him with a fatherly touch. At the end of the third year the man says, "I quit," and the priest responds, "Good. Ever since you've been here you've done nothing but complain."

In our society it's difficult to protest, to raise our voice in anger, without it being interpreted as belittlement, complaining, overreaction or loss of control. Many of us suppress our discontent, trained by early childhood scripts or belief systems of "try to please, don't make waves, don't be angry." Under the sanction of society's "correctness" and complacency we drop into the dungeon of depression. When the boiler of suppressed anger bursts into rage attacks we react by over control, rather than by seeking ways of effective assertion. This vicious cycle of locking up our anger until it explodes and then suppressing it to avoid loss of control, stunts our growth and creativity. One of my patients, desperately trying to control his violent temper, succeeded by converting it into realistic effective assertiveness. He was proud of a recent experience in a bar when a loud drunk came up and threatened him. Usually, this would have been instant provocation to rage, and throwing a punch the ultimate satisfaction. Instead, he bent over, kissed the man on the forehead, made a joking remark and walked out. The whole bar burst out laughing and he felt more gratification than if he had knocked him out.

Guilt and Shame

Guilt and shame both share misdirected anger - anger turned in upon the self. Guilt is the feeling that you have done something wrong and shame is the humiliation you feel when others find out about it.

I grew up feeling guilty about everything, the things I had not done, the things I should have done, and things I wanted to do. Thank goodness for a lecture I heard by a female New York Rabbi who said that we can think anything we want, we are only guilty when we do it. I felt the beginning of freedom, where my Catholic friends were trapped in remorse for their thoughts. I realized then that *Jews were born with guilt and Catholics go to school to learn it.*

Paradoxically, Catholics have an easier load to bear because they can empty it weekly at the confessional. Jews must carry it for at least a year to Yom Kippur, the Day of Atonement. Catholics are much higher in shame for their rigid code of sexuality is modeled on their religious leaders. A celibate Priest contrasts with the prolific Rabbi. In ancient times, this rigid code of sexual morays became the ultimate absurdity. For the clergy attracted the most intelligent and promising young men. The Catholics wiped out their brightest lineage, the Jews increased theirs. The myth still exists today that "Jewish Doctors are smarter."

Show compassion for the inter-marriage between Jew and Catholic for they have the double burden of guilt and shame.

A woman returning from a visit to her elderly mother shared her "good news" and "bad news" with me. Her mother again referred to her former husband as such a great guy. She spoke up, "It hurts me when you continually praise him, I wish you would stop." The mother appeared stunned and withdrew. The bad news, "I feel guilty, I hurt my mother," said the woman.

This is a common myth that words of anger can "hurt." *If you get angry, and they cry, did you make them cry? If they get angry, did you make them angry? If they burst out laughing, did you make them laugh? If they shift their thinking to new understanding and respond with more empathy, did you make it happen? No, you cannot make other people feel or think anything.*

People respond from who they are, their own personality and personal belief system. You are not that omnipotent and they are not that inadequate that they are devastated by your words. As Eleanor Roosevelt said *"No one can make you feel inferior without your consent."*

The next time you speak up and observe the other person's behavior, don't "MIND READ." For as one group member said to this woman, "Your mother may have been surprised and her quietness may be because it was the first time she understood your pain."

When in doubt, check it out!

Depression

A major cause of depression is self-directed anger. Self-blame is wrought by a critical, punitive internal parent ego state, continually attacking and belittling the internal child into worthlessness and melancholy. The curse of perfectionism, the mask of the internal, critical parent, drives the patient to exhaustion with *should, got to, must* and *have to.* The failure to live up to unrealistic goals, often internalized in childhood by parental, cultural and religious demands, causes guilt and shame. They exact the toll of depressive burnout in adult life.

"I am angry and I am not going to take it anymore" is the way out.

As Dylan Thomas said:
Do not go gentle into that goodnight
Old age should rage and burn at close of day
Rage, rage, rage at the dying of the light.

Anger is a natural response to conflict and frustration and if repressed or held in, you either click out and dissociate, or turn the anger against yourself into a self blaming depression. When patients begin to externalize their righteous indignation they may go through many stages. First there is blame, anger at someone who harmed them. If you continually blame then you're waiting for them to improve your life. You're giving up independence and power for your hopes for resolution lie in the other person's hands. Blaming anger is one of the first stages of emancipation but to continue the journey of self fulfillment you need to go to the next stage, self assertive anger. Regardless of who did what to you when, you need to use the aggressive energy of protest to take action and make decisions. The journey of self assertion leads to personal freedom. It has dangers, like any move or change, but the benefits outweigh the risks. I recall Thomas Wolfe's book, *Sea Wolfe*. Billy Budd, the young sailor, is continually harassed by the first mate. He says nothing. Towards the end of the trip Billy Budd explodes and kills the first mate. When the captain questions his violence he responds, "If I could have used my tongue I would not have struck."

Frequently, the most painful risk of expressing anger is discovering the underlying sadness. The pain of a traumatic childhood, a lost relationship, loss of self through illness, the wasted years and disappointments and the dream of what it could have been. Grieving is more painful than depression but it is healing. At times it is difficult to know the fine line between sadness and depression. A famous poet said it well, *"A feeling of sadness comes over me that is not akin to pain and resembles sorrow as mist resembles rain."*

Timing

When patients become aware of their suppressed anger, timing becomes an issue. When they find the right words it's usually much too late. It's great satisfaction to get the right line at the right time.

Lord Chesterfield was walking down the muddy streets of London with a pompous, arrogant and ignorant colleague. They were on a wooded sidewalk while the common people walked in the mud. The pompous man said to Lord Chesterfield, "I wouldn't give up the sidewalk to a pig." Lord Chesterfield, as he stepped down into the mud, said, "I would."

I met an old childhood acquaintance I hadn't seen for many, many years on a bus. As we talked he said, "When we were kids I used to steal from your father's store." When I asked why, he responded, "Well, we were poor." I answered, "Well, we were all poor." As the conversation continued I asked what he was doing today and he replied, "I'm in the house renovation business," and with much glee I responded, "I guess you're still stealing."

Sometimes my timing is off. I was shopping for an air conditioner and two neighboring stores displayed the same machine at much different prices. I spoke to the owner of the cheaper one and said, "How can you charge so much less than your competitor?" He checked his invoice and said "Wow, I made a big mistake. Thanks very much." "Does this mean I don't get the sale price I asked?" "Of course not," he replied, "I would lose money!"

As you test out new assertive techniques be very patient for it takes a long time to get the right words at the right time. Don't forget how to get to Carnegie Hall - *Practice, Practice, Practice.*

Effective Assertion

Few patients realize that the raw aggressive anger they feel can be expressed in quiet, but firm, language of self assertion, like, "No thank you." It's even more difficult to accept that creativity is the next level up, and is the force that shapes humor.

A lawyer goes out with a high class prostitute. After the sexual encounter he asks if she would mind if he sent her the cheque through his office. The next day the cheque arrives with the following letter, "Dear Madam: Re the rental of your apartment. I am reducing the fee from $200 to $100 for the following reasons. One, there was insufficient heat in the apartment. Two, it was much too large for my purposes and three, the apartment looked like it had been over used." She responded quickly and curtly, demanding her full fee with the following explanation, "If there was insufficient heat it was because you didn't know how to turn on the switch. If you found the apartment too large it's likely you didn't have enough furniture to move in. Last, but not least, an apartment as good as mine should not go empty for very long."

Creative Assertion

Hostility expressed through humor, borders on sarcasm, a Jewish cultural trait of survival. Jews have suffered centuries of oppression. They have fought back mainly with words, transforming their discontent and anger into a humor of double entendres.

A Rabbi and a Priest meet. The Priest, criticizing the rabbi says, "At your services you people are so messy. Your prayer books and shawls lie all over the place. We keep our church neat and tidy." The Rabbi, in a contemplative manner, quietly responds, "Well, you have the Virgin Mary to clean up." The priest goes on, "You're services are loud and irritating. We speak quietly, and often remain in silent meditation." The rabbi responds slowly, "You're right, we do speak loudly, for our God is old and hard of hearing." The priest finally says, "You know, at your funerals you people are actually disgraceful. You scream and yell and go hysterical. Our funerals are held with quiet dignity and sometimes we even celebrate the passing of our loved ones into the Lord's hands." The rabbi, again contemplating his answer, responds, "You're right, and that's why I prefer to go to your funerals."

A Rabbi and a Priest meet at a civic event in some Eastern European town. The Priest says to the Rabbi, "When will you give up your old prejudice of not eating pork?" and the Rabbi responds, "At your wedding, your Excellency."

When Mr. Kissinger visited the Pope as the representative of the U.S. Government he was given a gift of fine Italian cloth. Going to a tailor in Rome, he found there was not enough material to make a suit. While he was negotiating in Israel he decided to approach an Israeli tailor. The first one said, "Mr. Kissinger, we can make you a suit with an extra pair of pants and a vest." Mr. Kissinger, delighted, asked, "In Italy they couldn't even make a jacket and a pair of pants and here you can make me two pair of pants and an extra vest?" The tailor answered, "Well, Mr. Kissinger, in Israel you're not such a big man."

Mother Superior wanted to honour her graduating class of girls by introducing them to men at a graduation dance. She called a nearby army base and spoke to the Colonel in charge and asked him to send a hundred of his finest man. He agreed. As an afterthought she said, "And please, no Jews." That Saturday night the army truck arrived at the dance and a hundred handsome black soldiers disembarked. Mother Superior, terribly upset said to the Sergeant, "There must be some mistake," and the Sergeant responded, "Colonel Sam Goldenberg never makes a mistake."

Creative hostility can be interactive.

A man calls room service one morning to order his breakfast and says, "Would you please send up some bacon and eggs, but make sure the bacon is barely cooked and almost raw. Have the eggs turned over, hard and dry. I'd like the toast burned to a crisp and the coffee full of coffee grinds." They reply, "Sir, I'm sorry, we can't serve a meal like that," and the man responds, "Why not, yesterday morning you sent me the exact same meal?"

Creativity pays off.

Three priests are discussing the way they manage church collections. One says, "I draw a vertical line on my table and throw the money into the air. What lands on the right side goes for God's work. What lands on the left I keep for personal expenses." The second priest says, "I do the same thing except I draw a horizontal line and what falls in the upper part goes to the church and what falls below is mine." The third priest responds, "That's interesting. I use a table as well. I throw the money into the air and God keeps what he wants."

Many jokes mimic life. Hypothetically, if I went to the Federal Drug Administration and said, "I have discovered a new antidepressant, it grows naturally, it's cheap, can be taken orally and makes you feel good even if you're not depressed. Unfortunately it has some side effects. One, it's addictive, once you start, you must take it for life. After many years it will cause serious lung and heart disease and premature death. Will you give me FDA approval?" The answer would be a definite, "No," and my response might be, "Why not? You allow cigarettes to be sold over the counter, without even a prescription."

The finest piece of creative assertiveness I have ever heard was the story of a young surgical resident. He was about to begin a new service with a surgeon who had a reputation as a raging bully, extremely critical of everyone, especially the new resident assisting him. The surgeon ranted and raved, attacking this young man continuously during their first operation. It was the most explosive, condescending, destructive verbal violence the operating room staff had ever witnessed. The young resident continued his duties in silence. At the end of the operation, the surgeon's parting insult was, "Try and sew him up without doing any harm, and if you're in trouble, ask the nurse, she'll do it for you." The nurses and the anesthetist were silent. They'd never heard a more degrading, humiliating attack. The young doctor began suturing the skin. Slowly, he lifted his head and looked at each of the people in the room. The silence grew louder. Finally, a smile broke across the young doctor's face and he said, "I think he likes me." The operating room staff burst into laughter. Over the next few months, whenever the surgeon expelled his venom, the young doctor would simply look around the room and with a twinkle in his eye, smile. Everyone could hear, "I think he likes me," and they could barely hold back their laugher. This was outstanding conflict management in an almost impossible situation. Direct complaints to the resident's supervisor always fell on deaf ears since the principle of mediation between a senior surgeon and a young resident is *"shit rolls down the hill."* The young doctor's creative humor was a survival technique, avoiding humiliation, feelings of inadequacy and possible depression.

When executives or organizations in power attack people below them it's destructive. The tormented underdog has difficulty coping, for his livelihood depends upon his job. Some of the most heartwrenching stories I've heard have been of employees or executives who are slowly demoted and stripped of their powers, as the company tries to make them quit without just compensation. This is often accomplished by sending them into a smaller office with assignments of trivial work. Should these employees manage to hang on for long periods of time because of financial pressures, they often suffer the devastating symptoms of severe depression.

A luxury Cadillac speeding along the highway was pulled over by a motorcycle policeman. He found a farmer driving and a pig sitting in the back seat. The policeman remarked, as he was writing out the ticket, "How come you're driving a pig in this expensive car." The farmer said,

"This is a special pig. One day on the farm he was digging in the field and suddenly discovered an oil well. I became a wealthy man." The policeman said, "Wow, that's quite a pig." "You don't know the half of it," said the farmer, "A few months later he was digging on the side of a hill and discovered a vein of gold making me doubly rich." The policeman said, "My goodness, that certainly is a windfall. Now I can understand why you are treating this pig so well, driving him around in the back seat of a Cadillac. But why has this pig only three legs?" The farmer answers, "A pig as good as this shouldn't be eaten all at once."

Anger for Positive Reframing

In my book *Cry Anger* I wrote about my ten year old son who was confronted by the neighbor, *"Your dog is eating my garbage."* My son responded, *"I know, he won't eat ours. He doesn't like my mother's cooking."*

At his son's wedding a father recounts the trials and tribulations of his son's youth and sums it up by saying, "When he was a baby his mother said he was so precious she could eat him, and as he grew older I wish she had."

The art of positive reframing a negative experience with humor can be rewarding, relieving, and at times, a matter of survival. It can also be a creative form of protest called *intelligent neglect*. It's not a cowardly approach to conflict nor a withdrawal, but a self assertive expression in a difficult situation. *A woman sitting in a restaurant is complaining to the waiter. She says, "It's too cold. Would you mind turning the air conditioning off." Politely, he says, "Yes, Madam." A few minutes later she calls him back and says, "Now it's too hot. Would you mind putting the air conditioning on." "Of course, Madam," and he walks away. The complaints continue throughout the meal. A couple at the next table, observing this irritating exchange remarked to the waiter sympathetically, "This woman must be driving you crazy." The waiter responds, "No, I think I'm driving her crazy. We don't have air conditioning."*

In upsetting, inflexible family relationships, withdrawal from a boundary of over-attachment, over-involvement and over-reaction, can be very effective self-assertion. For building a new fence is an absolutely independent move that does not depend on the other persons participation at all. You alone can decide if you want it to be an open or solid fence, how high or how low, and whether a gate with a lock is desirable.

Pro-Active Anger versus Reactive Anger

Many of us react to someone's criticisms with righteous indignation. However, if we protest with questions, like "what did I do wrong?" we lose our position of equality and power. To rise above it all and reclaim our personal strength, we need to be pro-active. Take action that you deem necessary. Start with the "I" and state what you believe, feel, want or don't want. Respect your assertion as self caring, not selfishness. Protect your individual boundary and don't trespass into the dramatic triangle of rescuer, persecutor or victim. Now you've achieved two goals, self respect and acknowledgment of others as separate individuals. Too often our arguments become repetitive and circular in our determination to impose our views. We often persevere with the hidden agenda of wanting agreement. Being pro-active accepts the right to differ and remain as equals.

Prejudice

Some popular humor is ethnically based and may be racist, with the most flagrant jokes bordering on hate. Why are they so popular? They represent a universally felt xenophobia, a fear of strangers. Strangers may be dangerous. To be safe, recognize and avoid.   On another psychological level there it is distortion, a generalization used to describe all.   One black man commits a crime, all blacks are criminals.   One Jew may have turned Jesus over to the Romans, so all Jews betrayed Christ and must be punished.   The Nazis took this to its ultimate extreme in the Holocaust. We have an underlying need to disown our anger and evil. Often, this is done by projecting it onto others. Ethnic jokes can be a personal release of hostility, without physically aggressive behavior.   The range of jokes can be mild and playful, from recognizing cultural differences to stereotypes.

Mr. Cohen is lying on the road, hit by a car. The policeman comes over, takes off his jacket and places it under Mr. Cohen's head. He then asks him, "Are you comfortable?" Mr. Cohen moans, "I make a living."

That's probably as mild as they get. Is the following in the mid-range zone?

A genie gives one special wish to a Jew, a Mexican, a Black, an Italian and a Wasp. The Jew's wish is to live in Israel, at peace with its neighbors. It is instantly accomplished. The Mexican wishes to go back to Mexico and have all poverty erased. It's done. The Black man says he wants to go back to Africa and take all the blacks and let them live in harmony and comfort. It's done. The Italian man wants to go back to Italy with his family and have a great majestic home in the city of Rome. It's done. The Wasp is the only remaining person and he asks the genie, "Let me clear this up. The Jew has gone back to Israel, the Mexican back to Mexico, the Black to Africa and the Italian to Italy. Is that true?" The genie says, "Yes." The man says, "Okay, I'll have a diet coke."

Does this cross the line? *A Jewish man accompanies his Catholic friend to church one day. They are sitting in the front pew. The priest walks by placing a holy wafer in each of the parishioners mouths. The Jewish man inadvertently opens his mouth and the priest puts a wafer inside. After the service he asks his friend the significance of the wafer. "Well it's a reconfirmation of your faith as a Catholic," and the Jew responds, "You mean I'm a Catholic now?" The friend says, "That's true." The Jewish man races home and calls for his wife, "Sadie, Sadie, you won't believe what has happened." His wife, obviously in a hurry, says, "I'm sorry, I'm late for the hairdresser, tell me later," and runs out of the house. He goes upstairs to speak to his son who's playing with his guitar and says, "You'll never believe what's happened to me." The son says, "Hold off, Dad, I need to finish composing this song." He runs next door to his daughter's room and she's in the midst of drying her hair and she responds, "Dad, I must finish drying my hair or it will be in tangles." He walks out in anger and says to himself, "I've been a Catholic less than an hour and already I hate three Jews."*

Racial jokes illustrate cultural differences. Jackie Mason says, *"Coming out of the theatre, you can tell the difference between the Wasps and the Jews. The Wasps are saying, "Let's go for a drink," and the Jews are saying, "Let's go for a piece of cake."*

The next joke expands cultural values. *A Jewish racketeer, shot in a gang fight in Manhattan, is badly wounded and limps around the block to his mother's apartment. Covered in blood, barely able to stand, he knocks at the door. His mother answers and he says, "Mom, I'm hurt." She responds, "First we'll eat, then we'll talk."*

Racism can be creatively and positively reframed through humor.

An expensive, elegant department store refused to hire ethnics, fearing a loss of image. Under social pressure they hired a token Jew, Mr. Liebowitz, to work in the warehouse. One day the manager saw him talking to a customer and discreetly listened in on the conversation. Mr.

Liebowitz was talking, "This fishing rod is our best." The customer said, "I'll take it." "You'll need wading boots as well," said Mr. Liebowitz. "Fine," nodded the customer. "And of course a motor boat to travel down the river." "You're right," agreed the customer. "Do you have a trailer to carry all this." "No," answered the customer and purchased one. Finally Mr. Liebowitz asks, "What kind of car do you drive?" "A Mini Minor," replied the customer. "That's too small to pull this boat," and he sold him a Land Rover. The sale was over $200,000. The manager, pleasantly shocked, said to Mr. Liebowitz, "I've never seen such a great salesman. This man came in asking for a fishing rod, and you sold him everything." "No," corrected Mr. Liebowitz, "he came in for a box of tampons for his wife and I suggested that if he was free for the weekend, why didn't he go fishing."

Not all ethnic humor is ridicule, some can recognize cultural differences as valuable assets.

Got Cha

Here's an interactive joke you might want to try on one of your friends.

The Pope gave out medals to everyone who did not perform oral sex.
Do you know the inscription on the medals?
The friend says no.
And the response is, "Didn't you get one?"

That's a "got cha" joke, a mixture of wit and hostility in a subtle form of attack. It is also a subtle form of revenge. *Like the elderly woman who was having her portrait painted. When she looked at the completed picture she asked the artist to paint some very expensive jewelry on her, a diamond necklace and a diamond ring. When one of her girlfriends saw the picture she remarked, "It's great, but you don't have that kind of jewelry." "I know," said the elderly woman, "But when I die and my husband remarries I want his new wife to go crazy looking for the jewelry."*

One of my patients, a bright independent woman, successful in her own business, was having love relationship trouble. It was the same in all her love relationships. They never felt right, and she always felt trapped. She disliked her critical nature, continually finding fault with her boyfriends. Ruminating, brooding, reviewing and analyzing were desperate attempts to find the answers to her troubled love life. Her whole left brain was cognitively dedicated to understand. In therapy she realized that these thoughts were mainly self critical and judgmental, like "why did you do this," "what's wrong with you," "you know better," "you should be smarter," "you never learn." She stopped the critical judge and began to shift towards realistic adult awareness. She then opened up inner anger, an anger at all the men in the past who had abused her, either emotionally or physically. An alcoholic father and then as a teenager the men who sexually abused her. She knew she was scapegoating her boyfriend with all the anger from the past. She tried to find lyrics to her music of rage and the words were "got cha." She lit up with excitement and relief. With this music as a theme we did mental imagery and fantasy resolution. In her mind's eye she made a movie and with her imagination she "got" each one of the men in her past in very special ways. A release of frustration followed, and with a burst of laughter and a sense of liberation she said goodbye to the past. Revenge freed her from past trauma and past regrets and she began to live in the here and now. The present love relationship became fulfilling and continued to grow.

Revenge is simply anger at someone who did you harm. It's blaming someone for what happened. While it may be emotionally satisfying or even exciting, it's basically a waste of energy. As one patient shared her best fantasy of "I got cha," she saw herself succeeding in a major ambition or quest of life and "those people who did her in" could "eat their heart out." A dramatic shift, from blaming to self assertive anger, it is at once more mature, rewarding and adaptive. Revenge can end past traumas or disappointments and be the last chapter of a book or the last scene in a movie. Accepting the concept of revenge as normal does not necessarily lead to violence or destruction. You can use humor or fantasy in a delicious way for closing the past. As one French professor said, *"Revenge is a meal you can eat cold."* One of my Italian patients reaffirmed this by saying, *"You Jews forget, we Italians get revenge."*

Personal Power

I was a member of a Psychiatric Association called P.A.P.A., Psychiatrists Against Psychiatric Abuse. We protested the misuse of psychiatry for political purposes, primarily in the Soviet Union. The Russians dealt with political dissidents by falsely diagnosing mental illness, claiming they were suffering from sluggish schizophrenia. They confined them to mental hospitals where they were drugged. Our organization, and others concerned with human rights, protested with occasional results. A prominent human rights activist in the Soviet Union, a psychiatrist, Anatolly Koriagen, protested against the abuse of psychiatry. He was jailed and tortured in Cristapole Prison in Moscow. In the 1980s, after a visit to Russia as a tourist, I wrote a letter to Premier Gorbachev under the P.A.P.A. letterhead. A Russian doctor who owned a Russian typewriter translated my letter. In the letter, I shared the pleasure of my trip and acknowledged the beauty and majesty of the country, contrasting it with the brutal and unjust treatment of Anatolly Koriagen. I never heard from Premier Gorbachev directly but a few months later Anatolly Koriagen was freed. Was it grandiose thinking to believe that one letter freed Dr. Koriagen? *Probably no more grandiose than the man who woke up after surgery to find a ribbon tied around his penis. He smiled with pride thinking the perfect specimen had finally won recognition by the medical profession, only to find that one of his surgical friends had slipped into the recovery room and tied the ribbon around it.* Of course, I don't really believe my letter freed Dr. Koriagen, but there was satisfaction and a sense of personal power. Incidentally, governments receiving protest letters from members of Amnesty International have released 50% of their prisoners of conscience within two years.

When I was reassuring one of my friends before a simple hernia repair I over dramatized the shaving of the genital area. I described the straight razor procedure in detail. I suggested he stay quiet, subservient and respectful, not to upset the orderly's concentration. While said with tongue in cheek my friend took it seriously. When the orderly pulled down the sheet he said, "See, I shaved myself." However, the orderly, reasserting his position of dominance replied, "Sorry sir, I have to do it a little better," and much to my friend's dismay repeated the whole procedure exactly as I described.

The Fight For Power

The power struggle in human relationships is universal, sometimes subtle and subconscious. Often the dominant person becomes domineering as he or she switches to the rescue role, treating the other person as a victim of life's experiences. When the great advice fails, the rescuer becomes the persecutor, attacking the victim for not heeding his suggestions. Of course, the circle goes around and around and the victim finally attacks the rescuer/persecutor for doing such a lousy job. Or the quiet passive person shifts to passive/aggressive behavior. While they ask for help or direction, they subtly reject the advice by "yes butting" everything. Does this sound like you and your teenage children? The relationship for power degenerates into *NIGYSOB* (Now I Got You You Son-of-a-Bitch) where each party continually attacks the other with righteous indignation in a game of one-upmanship to retain power. The game can go on and on indefinitely, for the goal is not resolution of conflict, but control and domination.

An overbearing husband suspicious of his wife, checks her purse after a day's outing. He finds $200.10 in her purse. With angry condescension he says, "I checked your purse last night before you left. There was no money and now you have $200.10. I know how you got it. You've been whoring around. You've become a bloody prostitute. But who gave you the ten cents?" The wife responds with one-upmanship, "Everybody."

I suggest we are all looking for our moment in the sun, our place of power. *Like the two Mexicans discussing the great Rodrigues, the infamous bandit. One asks the other, "Have you ever met the famous Rodrigues?" The other man answers, "One day I was walking along the road and a horse comes galloping up and the rider was the great Rodrigues. He pulls out a gun at me. Then the horse makes something on the road. The great Rodrigues says, "Eat it." Now, I don't want to eat this but the great Rodrigues, he's got his gun, so I eat. Then the horse rears up in the air and the great Rodrigues falls to the ground. His drops his gun and I pick up the gun. Now I have the gun. I point the gun at the great Rodrigues and I say, 'See what the horse make? Now you eat.' Now the great Rodrigues, he don't want to eat it either, but now I have the gun, so he eats. So, you ask, do I know the great Rodrigues? Of course, we had lunch together."* If you can't be powerful in your own right, at least associate with important people.

If you watch young children playing you'll often see overt power plays as they compete for each other's toys. Sibling rivalry, competition and combativeness, are parts of the natural aggressive drive for survival. These qualities begin at the "terrible two's."

There's a Catholic boy and a Jewish boy arguing. The Catholic boy says, "Our Priest knows more than your Rabbi," and the Jewish boy answers, "Of course, you tell him everything."

The next few anecdotes illustrate the subtlety of the power play.

A university professor was having trouble with raccoons getting into his garbage. At first he bought a special garbage can with a special top. The raccoons quickly mastered that. Then he put blocks on top of the can. The raccoons threw it over. Then he began getting up early in the morning trying to scare the raccoons away from his garbage. All this trouble to stop the raccoons from getting at something that he was trying to get rid of in the first place.

On a cold winter evening as I was driving down a busy street I saw an elderly gentleman waiting for a bus. With my quick analytical mind, I concluded that he was an unlikely mugger with a hidden gun. I stopped and offered him a lift. His spontaneous acceptance, motivated by the pain of hypothermia, overrode his risk of accepting a ride from a stranger. He immediately began to bless me for my act of kindness. I was pleased to accept the recognition of my good deed, characteristic of my benevolent grandiosity. When the blessings extended to my children and my children's children, I became embarrassed at the excess. Fortunately, it was a short ride for his destination was the synagogue a few miles down the road. When I suggested that I let him off at the corner, he quickly replied, "The blessings don't hold unless you deliver me to the front door." As a man of science, my religious beliefs have decreased as my medical knowledge developed. Now as a secular Jew, basically an Agnostic who prays to "whom it may concern" (Woody Allen), I was put to the ultimate spiritual test. Instantly I veered into the outside lane and made a quick left turn, delivering my religious companion to the front steps of the synagogue. Leaving the car with a smile and a twinkle in his eye, he said "God bless you." At this moment there was a dramatic shift in the power play, I felt like a small boy learning from a wise old master.

The best way to come to terms with the fight for power in a close relationship is compromise. *An example is a man about to be married discussing the wedding invitations. He says he wants 300 at the wedding. His wife-to-be says she only wants 200. A compromise is made, 200 people are invited.*

A sneakier search for power and dominance appears while driving. The nicest people explode with totally irrational behavior. Have you ever had somebody cut you off while you're driving? What do you do? You race ahead at breakneck speed and try to cut him off. Risking life and limb, not only to get even but to be one up. Or did you ever make a mistake while driving, like moving into somebody else's lane to make a left hand turn? There's no doubt you've made a mistake, but the viciousness of the attack, being cursed as a lousy driver, is the self righteous indignation of "Now I've Got You, You Son-of-a-Bitch."

Think of it. How many times in a relationship do you use one small mistake as an excuse to get the bastard.

Abuse of Power

Increasing reports of past sexual abuse of boys are surfacing. The predators are respected individuals within honorable institutions. The clergy in religious schools, the doctor in his office, the coach with his players, the devoted father with his child. While sexual abuse is the presentation, the underlying problem is abuse of power. The mentor, in a position of trust, dedicated to protect and guide, is often the abuser. The child or teenager is manipulated and seduced by the powerful authority. Torn by ambivalent feelings of admiration and fear, the victim withdraws and dissociates, trying to forget, for confronting your abuser often threatens your only security. The ratio of sexual abuse has been five females to one male. However, with the recent exposure of institutional abuse, a higher incidence of sexual abuse of males is emerging. With courage to overcome shame, and risk humiliation, the victims are coming forward, sometimes many years later, to demand justice, long overdue.

I wonder how many car accidents are actually "road rage" caused by a desire for revenge and a search for power. I wonder if the game called chicken is more common than we admit. When you're driving, drive defensively. *A man was driving a visitor around his city and kept driving through red lights. The puzzled passenger said, "You keep going through red lights. What's wrong?" The man responds, "Oh, it's okay. My brother does it all the time." A little later they approach a green light and the driver slams on his brakes. The visitor questions, "Now you've stopped at a green light?" The driver responds, "Yes, my brother might be coming the other way."*

The ultimate absurdity of the search for power is revealed by this anecdote from the Middle Ages. *It was quite common for the religious leader of the community to call in the head of the much smaller Jewish community and challenge him to a debate, essentially a debate for survival. This particular anecdote goes back to Mediaeval times when the Pope tells the Jews they are going to be expelled from Rome unless one of their wise men beats him in a debate. However, if the man loses he also loses his head. The Jewish community, frightened, foreseeing the outcome, has no volunteers, except the idiot of the community who is subsequently coaxed into facing the Pope. After all, there's really nothing to lose. At their meeting the Pope holds up his cross and the idiot puts up his finger. The Pope bows his head knowing he's lost round one. Then the Pope eats a grape. The idiot opens a bag, takes out an apple and eats the apple. The Pope bows his head, knowing he has lost round two. Then the Pope cries out with the name "Jesus Christ" and the man responds with "Yahodi." The Pope bows his head, again knowing he has lost round three. The Jews are thrilled, but puzzled. The Pope's advisor congratulates the Jewish community on sending their wisest man, who won the debate. He explains that when the Pope put up the cross, the symbol of Catholicism the Jew put up his finger saying God was one. When the Pope ate the grape, the fruit of benediction, the Jew ate the apple, the fruit of the Garden of Eden and the symbol of God's creation of human life. Third, when the Pope cried out "Jesus Christ" the name of the son of God, your wise man came up with "Jehovah", the personal name of God as revealed to Moses on the mountain. The Jews asked the idiot what happened and he said, "Well, when he stuck the cross in front of me, I put my finger up to say, 'Don't put that thing in front of my face.' When the Pope ate the grape I thought he was having lunch so I opened my lunch bag and ate my apple. And when the Pope shouted a name I thought he was introducing himself so I told him my name, "Yahodi."*

The need to be right is a drive for dominance. Many times the search for power is absurd. At the opposite end of the scale, heads of state use devastating words and the abhorrent suppression of human rights for personal power.

The need for personal power is a natural, human drive and competition is one of the ways to achieve it. This visual anecdote illustrates the point. *There's a father rabbit and his son at the top of the hill looking at a group of female rabbits playing in the valley. The father rabbit is going to introduce his son to sex. After giving him some preliminary instructions on mating the father says, "Son, you start at one end of the line and I'll start at the other." The young rabbit, filled with excitement and overflowing with sexual energy, rushes down and begins the act of copulation. After each encounter he says, "Bon Jour, Madame, Merci Beaucoup." He goes to the next one, "Bon Jour, Madame, Merci Beaucoup, Bon Jour, Madame, Merci Beaucoup, Bon Jour, Madame, Merci Beaucoup, Pardon, Papa, Bon Jour, Madame, Merci Beaucoup."*

Without healthy competition, life is boring, with it there is excitement. Envy, the wish to have what someone else has can encourage and stimulate motivation. Jealousy, the wish to have what others have and the wish that they lose it, can be neurotic and destructive, indicative of the jealous person's low self esteem.

The narcissist can be a pompous self centered braggart. He talks endlessly about his own achievements because he is envious of yours. You are never heard, you only exists as a mirror reflecting his omnipotence. Through grandiosity he exaggerates his conquests, and degrades yours by comparison. Always competitive, fighting for dominance, he needs to win to avoid underlying feelings of inadequacy. If the top cracks he tumbles down the mountain into deep depression. A typical remark might be *"I never made a mistake until this morning. I thought I was wrong, but I wasn't."*

Beyond conflict resolution, the unexpected bonus of expressing your anger is personal power. Self-empowerment is completeness, freedom and maturity, and the confidence to stand alone. The genuinely powerful person does not need to dominate for you enjoy the competition and stimulation of other powerful people. Motivated by the pride of achievement you take chances, and risk the anxiety of exploration. You know that if you try and fail you many be disappointed but if you fail to try you may miss an opportunity. Is power addictive? An interviewer asked a wealthy man, *"How much money is enough?" The man responded, "Just a little bit more."*

Fear of Loss of Control

A middle aged woman, a recent grandmother, emerging from her depression, finally protested effectively. Her children had been using her as a constant babysitter. Despite the draining experience she did not say no. Her daughter asked her if she would babysit the three children while she and her husband went away for a holiday. They would arrange for extra help if needed. She suggested another idea. Why didn't they all go together? Then the three of them could look after the babies. She enjoyed both the power of her assertion and a well-deserved holiday. A simple easy shift from compliance and repression to assertion.

Why did it take so long to speak up? The usual risks of anger expressed by my patients range from, "I want to be nice," "I'm terrified of rejection," "I can't stand being alone," to "I may hurt their feelings." They're all excuses, for the universal fear of anger is loss of control, the fear of "going crazy" and opening killer rage. Most of us have strong adult egos in charge, plus an overbearing conscience that reduces risks of violence. It's like keeping an angry child locked up in an adult maximum security prison, patrolled by twenty-four hour guards and under constant video surveillance. You are more likely to have rage attacks if you suppress your anger. Like pressure building in a boiler without safety valves, one small incident explodes into inappropriate rage. And you confirmed your false belief system that you need more control.

The other fear of loss of control is "going crazy," running wild, ranting, raving, raging and losing your mind.

A quiet professional woman suffered recurrent depressions from childhood. She always suppressed her anger. Her chronically ill mother taught her that if she became angry, she would make her mother sick and possibly kill her. In group therapy, she observed other members expressing their aggression and realized her anger would not kill or hurt. Through mental imagery, she sensed her anger as a picture of a Whirling Dervish and became acutely anxious, fearing loss of control. Another patient responded with a similar image of a Whirling Dervish and saw herself dancing around obstacles with total control. Paradoxically, she could be out of control and in control at the same time. This leads to excitement and joy, while the fear of loss of control leads to repression, dissociation and depression. *Take a risk, cry anger louder.*

Absurd Life Humor

A joke often has a core of truth. Reality exaggerated to absurdity can make a point, subtly, diplomatically and resolutely.

A woman asks the butcher the price of his ground beef. He responds, a dollar eighty-nine cents. "The butcher across the road sells it for a dollar sixty-nine cents a pound" she complains. "Then why don't you buy it from him?" "Well, he is sold out" answers the woman. "Well, when I am sold out, the price is a dollar fifty-nine cents a pound" replies the butcher.

A patient with chronic ear infections had become addicted to cleaning his ears with Q-tips. The doctor's wise advice for prevention is *"don't put anything in your ear smaller than your elbow."* As in so many problems, especially the emotional, the tempted solution is the problem. For effective treatment do the opposite. *Try "harder not to try so hard"* or the next step in helping a friend or lover may be *"one step back"*.

Absurd life humor is a form of self-assertion that clears the air with minimal risk in a delicate situation. It is a direct communication that breaks through destructive interpersonal games of manipulation.

A patient described his relationship with an overbearing brother. Frightened to confront him, less his anger hurt him, he withdrew with a knot in his stomach and endless ruminations. "I feel like he's a Sumo wrestler sitting on my chest." My psychiatric question was, "can you see your words hurting him?" He smiled, as the absurdity in the visual image overrode his left brain inhibitions.

Sarcastic humor can lead to creative assertion. A patient is frustrated with a friend who has not paid back a large loan of money, claiming he's broke because he has no work. My patient put an ad in the local paper asking people to please offer his friend a job so that he can pay back his personal debt. The creative advertising brought instant results. The next day the friend came to his doorstep and paid his long overdue debt.

Don't despair if you can't remember jokes or you're uncomfortable telling them, for the greatest humor is repartee, the interactive playfulness with words that is spontaneous and natural. It's a talent we all have and is one of the most creative forms of effective assertion. Stop editing your thoughts, fire the censor in your head. Stop future worries for it's only bad fortune telling. Don't read other people's minds. Be open, spontaneous and free, and let your fun kid play. Stand back and look. Let your right brain see through the absurd without the inhibition of logic or reason, and express itself through the human gift of left hemispheric speech. It's not risk free, but the bad predictions rarely happen and the satisfaction is worth it. Remember Oscar Wilde's statement, *"I never know what I'm thinking until I say it."*

CHAPTER SIX

Getting older is getting better!!??

Two aging war veterans were recently overheard in the shower of a health club. One said to the other, "Do you recall back in the war they gave us that stuff to get rid of our sex drive?" The other one responded, "Of course," and the first veteran said, "You know, I think it's starting to work."

As one gets older the sexual drive decreases. Looking positively, aging does cure premature ejaculation, although increased use would do the same. It's not easy to live with the deterioration of one's masculinity or femininity but there are creative and humorous ways to think about it.

An elderly man walks into the doctor's office and says, "You know, Doctor, when I was eighteen I had such a powerful erection that with all my strength, using both hands I couldn't bend it. When I was thirty-five I could just barely bend it with one hand. Now I am sixty-five. I can bend it with my little finger. Doctor, does this mean I'm getting stronger?"

What a great example of positive reframing through humor.

It is not insincere, euphemistic or patronizing to convert a negative thought to a positive one. It is the reflection of a mature mind looking at reality creatively. Humor incorporates these capacities extremely well and naturally.

An elderly man walks by a nudist colony. Filled with curiosity he asks the manager for information. The manager offers him a complimentary pass and advises him of the club's routine, "You walk around nude in a casual way and enjoy the activities." As he's walking around looking at the gorgeous nude women he gets an erection. To his surprise an attractive woman comes over and performs oral sex. Excited, he runs back to the manager, exclaiming, "This is a great club! I want to join!" The next day as he's walking through the club, totally nude, he drops his cigar. As he bends down to pick it up he's penetrated from the rear by another man. Raging with anger, he rushes to complain to the manager that he's been sexually assaulted. The manager responds, "Yesterday you had oral sex and you were thrilled. Today you have anal sex and you're terribly upset. Why are you reacting with such extremes?" The elderly man responds, "It has to be put into perspective. I am eighty-five years old. If I get one or two erections a year I'm lucky. But I drop my cigar about ten times a day."

The above joke began with the right brain imagery but the humor is wit, the surprise switch to left brain reality.

Curing Alzheimer's Disease?

We may be living longer but not necessarily better. Alzheimer's disease is a living death, with the early signs of recent memory loss extending into confusion, disorientation and eventually total mental and behavior deterioration. The initial humiliation for the affected person disappears as they don't remember who or where they are. They are a terrible burden on middle aged children, who watch helplessly as a loved and admired parent changes into someone they don't know or like. It's important to realize that this is an organic, biological change due to brain atrophy, not willful behavior. A reversal of roles occurs as the children now parent their parents. The middle generation is in a difficult position as they are also coping with the prolonged adolescence of their own children. There may be a precious moment or two in all the suffering. I know there have been some for me personally. My father-in-law, totally forgetful, confined to a wheelchair after breaking a hip, formed a deep emotional bond in the nursing home with a woman he hardly knew. They would be found together smiling, unable to exchange a sentence, not even knowing each other's names. Yet there was a joy of togetherness, as they smiled and touched each other. On periodic visits with my family we would sit down with the couple and have a cup of tea. They would beam with joy as she would say, "Isn't it nice that the children have come to visit us." One day I came to take my father-in-law home for a holiday supper. As we were walking away the woman screamed at me, "How can you break up our family!" Stunned, I asked the head nurse if I could get permission to take her to my home as well. Fortunately, her own family was on the way to take her home for their traditional holiday celebration.

My mother, after years of Alzheimer's disease was transferred to a palliative care unit in a hospital to die peacefully and comfortably. Paradoxically, while it was one of the saddest moments it was one of our best, for my sister and my mother and myself were laughing and enjoying each other's company. My sister had been typing some of my notes for this book. "I couldn't stop laughing," she said. "Where did you get your sense of humor?" At this moment I turned to my mother and made some joking remark. She replied with a big smile and a little quip. We all burst out laughing and my sister said, "I never knew Mom was so funny." A precious moment, the joy of togetherness, as we were waiting for my mother to die.

My mother, as she deteriorated over the years, never ceased to surprise me. She always played the piano but during her latter years someone would have to sing the tune first before she could play it. It was usually a song she had played in the past. If we didn't change the song she would continue playing the same tune over and over again, laughing vigorously. I was thrilled that despite her severe left brain deterioration, her right brain was active. One evening I sang a song and my mother began to play. I suddenly realized that she had never heard that song before. Again, another surprise, she could still learn. The music center of her right brain was alive and well.

Paradoxically, there is a cure for senile deterioration. It's the treatment of depression. Many elderly people suffering losses of loved ones and personal health have retreated from life into an atypical depression. They're not crying or expressing their plight, they retreat into a wall of silence. Anhedonia is primary with lack of joy in living. Their interests are gone and personal hygiene is neglected. Appetite drops and there is loss of weight. They suffer psychomotor retardation, their mental processes are slow and sluggish, they have decreased concentration, a constriction of ideas and poverty of speech. They divert the physician's attention from emotional concerns to physical illness. Loss of memory and decrease in intelligence is not brain deterioration, but a symptom of treatable depression.

An old man is sitting on a bench crying. A passerby stops and asks, "Can I help you?" The old man says, "Yes, I'm married to a beautiful young woman. She's a marvelous cook, takes care of me and we have wonderful sex." "So," the passerby says, "Why are you crying?" He says, "I can't remember where I live."

A devoted Jewish son visiting his senile father is trying to stimulate recognition. He brings the whole family to visit. "Look, Dad, I brought your brother, Joe," he says. Dad responds, "I have no brother Joe." "Hey, here's your sister, Sophie." Dad replies, "I have no sister." "Look, I brought your grandchildren." "I have no grandchildren," says Dad. Undaunted the son continues, "and here's my beautiful wife to see you." "What, you brought the Shiksa?"

Perhaps memory is more selective than we know. We all have slips of memory, so don't get upset when you can't remember your best friend's name. Many years ago, while writing my book, *Cry Anger*, I was so involved with some idea that when my answering service called with an emergency I mechanically dialed the number as I returned the call. Quite frustrated to find a continuous busy line, I called the operator saying it was an emergency. As I repeated the number my daughter entered the room and quietly said, "Dad, that's your phone number." In all fairness to me, it was the answering service that had inadvertently given me my own number. Preoccupied with my book, I didn't think.

There used to be nude men's swimming at noon at the local heath club. When they made it coed many of us continued to walk in without a bathing suit, only to be embarrassed and run out. One member walked around for a few minutes ignoring all signs and gestures that he was nude. When he finally caught my eye he looked down and recognized that he was stark naked. He put the towel over his head and ran out. I heard some women laughing as he ran by. *One said, "That's not my husband." The other one said, "That's not my husband," and the other one said, "He's not even a member of this club."*

As you get older keep looking for the bright side and remember not only that Prozac but aging as well can cure premature ejaculation. Accentuate the positive. One of the finest examples of positive reframing of memory loss was a meeting I had with a Professor of Psychiatry at the health club. We had a very pleasant chat before we went about our own activities. After my shower I came back to the lockers and found him wandering around confused. I asked him what was wrong and he said, "I can't find my locker." I burst out laughing and said, "And you're the Professor of Psychiatry? You can't even remember your own locker." He responded astutely, "I have the privilege of being an absent minded professor."

While recent memory goes first, past memory stays intact for a long time and older people revel in telling some delightful stories of their past. Hopefully, in the near future, we'll have some treatment or chemical replacement for recent memory loss, just as we have insulin for diabetes. Do remember this: if you're losing your memory you meet a lot of new people and hear a lot of new jokes. Like the jokes in this book which I'm sure you've heard and forgotten. Check your memory. See which one of the following jokes I've told before.

The elderly gentleman informs his doctor of his upcoming marriage to a younger woman. The doctor says, "Sex at you age can kill," and the man responds, "If she dies, she dies."

The elderly man, proud of his masculinity, goes to a fertility clinic to donate his sperm. The nurse in charge hides her laughter as she gives him a specimen bottle. He goes to the back room to produce a sample. After a long time he finally emerges and says, "I'm sorry. It didn't work. I tried very hard with my right hand, then I tried very hard with my left hand. I even tried with both hands. But I couldn't get the top off the bottle."

An elderly gentleman reading the obituary column sees his name in it. He quickly calls his best friend and says, "You won't believe it. Look in the morning paper. My name is in the death notices." The friend reads it and says, "You're right. It's there. So, where are you calling from?"

A Priest, Minister and a Rabbi are told by their doctor that they have a fatal illness and each given one final wish. The Priest wishes, "I want to spend my final days in the Vatican." The Minister states he would like to visit all the members of his parish who've moved all over the world. The Rabbi, astutely responds, "I want another opinion."

(Answer: None. They're all new old jokes.)

It is interesting that all of these "elderly jokes" are about men, not women. Is it because a woman getting older in our society is not very funny?

Good Grief!

As with any human tragedy humor lessens the pain. Sometimes it's the laughter of denial, an attempt to avoid the pain and grief that must eventually be faced for life to continue. For "Good Grief Work" is the way to say goodbye to our losses, and leave us free to go on living.

We all recognize and accept grieving over the death of a loved one, but few of us accept the sadness and grief of personal losses, the separation of love relationships, disappointments in life and loss of personal health. Close friends and families, in times of life crisis, usually encourage you to forget, to "carry on," "count your blessings," "don't cry over spilled milk," "he isn't worth it." That's unfortunate, for they fail to understand that personal losses need a time to mourn. Going through grief is a way to put the past to rest, to heal so you can go on living in the present. How long do you grieve? For the death of a loved one, it's at least one to two years. Surprisingly, for separation or loss of a love relationship the average time of mourning is two to four years. How long do you grieve the slow dying of a parent with Alzheimer's Disease? Much longer, for the ravage is a living death.

Grief arrives in giant waves, where each crest falls into a trough of tranquillity, followed by smaller waves of sadness, bringing you closer to shore. Just when you think you're over it something happens to trigger an anniversary reaction with another wave of sadness. Mourning is more than a private personal experience, and sharing offers relief. Good grief work takes time, but it is important to end mourning, to say good-bye to your loved ones, to your losses and disappointments, to carry on with life in a productive way. End your grief with a closing ritual, add a final scene to your sad movie.

I treated a group of cancer patients with mental imagery therapy to stimulate their immune systems and help resolve the internal conflicts that may have contributed to their illness. Many suffered a deep depression, a failure to mourn effectively. A few exceptional people made dramatic changes and found greater richness in their life. One woman with cancer of the breast stands out. She refused surgery and began to travel around the world learning about macrobiotic diets as a possible cure for cancer. Her mental state of exploratory excitement gave her immense satisfaction and probably contained her disease by boosting her immune system. Fifteen years later she fell and injured her breast, requiring surgery. Surprisingly, the pathology report revealed normal lymph nodes, cancer had not spread beyond the breast.

Some of us do not believe that death is final. Perhaps there is an afterlife and this life is merely a stepping stone.

A young man at the funeral of his favorite aunt, a rough and tough vibrant woman, watches her casket lowered into the grave. Suddenly the casket is stuck. It won't go down. He turns to his father and says, "See, Auntie is still fighting."

There were a number of couples lined up at the Pearly Gates to be interviewed by St. Peter. He said to the first couple, "I have reviewed your life and I find you have been totally preoccupied with money. That's proven by the fact you married a woman called Penny. Therefore the doors of heaven are closed to you." The second man and his wife are interviewed and St. Peter responds, "Your whole life has been geared to material gains and that's proven by the fact you're married to a woman named Jewel. So, to hell with you." At the back of the line, overhearing these rejections, a man turns to his wife and says, "Come on, Fanny, let's get out of here."

There is a social irony about aging in our society. The Supreme Court of Canada passed a ruling that mandatory retirement at age sixty-five was an infringement of human rights but "not an unreasonable one". A terrible act of discrimination! Now aging people who may still have a valuable contribution to society are labeled useless. Paradoxically, they can now become politicians or president, or even a judge of the supreme court, whose average age is well over sixty-five.

If you're going to wish someone a long life you might say, as one man suggested, *"May the Lord's will be that you live for a hundred and twenty years, plus three months." "Why three months?" "So you won't die suddenly."* I missed a recent medical class reunion where the president announced my death. When he discovered his mistake, he sent me a letter of apology. I answered him with a Milton Erickson line that I had been saving for a long time. "John," I said, "You don't have to apologize. You don't even have to worry because, *dying is the last thing I'm going to do."* Again, remember Dylan Thomas's poem - *"do not go gentle into that good night, old age should rage and burn at close of day. Rage, rage, rage at the dying of the light."* Since death is inevitable, make each day count. *Carpe Diem - Seize the Day.*

I asked a geriatric psychiatrist, "What's the etiology of sleep disorders of the elderly?" He answered, "I don't know. What do you think?" I said, "If I had an answer I wouldn't have asked you the question in the first place." He responded, "Behind every question is usually some opinion. Don't you have any ideas yourself?" I then asked, "Why do you always answer a question with a question?" He replied, "How should I know?"

Insomnia, frequent trips to the bathroom in the middle of the night, or commonly, early morning rising, are all the price of longevity. Early one morning I went to the health club to play racquetball. When I arrived at the court about 6:00 a.m. I found two elderly handball players finishing their game. "Don't you guys ever quit?" I said. In unison they responded, *"Old handball players never quit. They just lose their balls."* The opposite holds true as well. *"If you don't use it, you lose it."*

George Burns (born Nathan Birnbaum) worked successfully up to a few weeks before his death at 100. In our home, we often joked about being related to George Burns. My son, as a young teenager touring Beverly Hills, stopped at George Burn's house. George Burns came to the door in his bathrobe. After introducing himself, my son said "My Grandfather Leo says you're his cousin." George Burns, without missing a beat, replied "How is Leo" and invited my son into his home. Unfortunately, my son's friends were waiting and he had to leave. As they said goodbye, George Burns said "Give this cigar to Leo."

George Burns lived according to the song he sang "If you are the very young at heart." He said *"you can't help getting older, but you don't have to get old!"*

CHAPTER SEVEN

Communications

Be Precise

The commonest cause of miscommunication is the failure to listen and the lack of basic information exchange.

A woman greets the postman with "Merry Christmas" and invites him into the house for a piece of cake. She takes him to the bedroom, makes love to him and gives him $2.00. Overwhelmed and pleasantly surprised, he says, "It's a beautiful Christmas present, but why the $2.00?" "Oh," she said, that was my husband's idea. I asked him what should I give the postman for Christmas and he said, "ah, fuck him, give him two bucks." The piece of cake was my idea."

Sometimes we listen but don't hear. *The captain sees an elderly woman, somewhat confused, looking for her cabin. Graciously he asks, "May I escort you to your cabin?" Obviously appreciating his offer, she places her arm in his as they walk down the long hallway. She suddenly calls out, "You're passionate." Somewhat embarrassed, he thanks her as they continue walking back and forth. She calls out again, "You're passionate." He thanks her, but courteously asks, "But madam, where is your cabin?" She answers, "I keep telling you, you're passing it."*

This scene is from one of the Pink Panther movies. Inspector Clouseau is checking into a Swiss hotel. Beside the desk is a sleeping dog. Inspector Clouseau says to the clerk, *"Does your dog bite?"* The clerk replies, *"No, my dog does not bite."* Inspector Clouseau pets the dog and the dog bites him. In his strait-laced drawl he says, *"I thought you said your dog did not bite."* The clerk responds, *"That's not my dog."*

At times it pays to be obsessive/compulsive and expand the information until you have all the nitty-gritty details.

A man moves into a subdivision where all the houses are the same. He is invited into his neighbor's home and admires the kitchen wallpaper. He wonders if the neighbor would mind if he put the same wallpaper in his house. The neighbor replies, "Of course not," and tells him where he bought the paper and the name of the paper. "How many rolls did you buy?" asks the new neighbor. "Eighteen," the neighbor responds. When the papering job is completed the new neighbor says, "I think something went wrong. I did exactly what you said. I bought 18 rolls and now I have four left over." The neighbor responds, "There's nothing wrong. I had four left over as well."

Mind Reading

Don't mind read, you can never figure out what somebody else thinks or feels. "If in doubt, check it out." Many patients think psychiatrists are mind readers. I assure you they are no more gifted at mind reading than anyone else. In the following anecdote the telephone caller was not a psychiatrist.

The phone rings. A woman answers and says, "Hello." The voice at the other end says, "I know you want me to make passionate love to you. You want me to rip off your clothes, and have sex with you." She responds, "You know all this from one hello?"

Social Intercourse

Repartee, playful, spontaneous verbal interaction with people, is great social intercourse. I suffered from sciatica for many years. When it finally interfered with my racket sports, I had back surgery. After the operation I woke up in the Intensive Care Unit, and the pain down my leg was gone. I was thrilled and began to joke with the nurse. I asked, "In which leg did I have the pain?" She responded, "Your left leg." I said, "That's great, because if the operation failed, I would still have my right leg left." She answered, "I think the lights are on but nobody's home," a brief but delightful encounter.

Clever repartee, blended with the ability to positively reframe a negative, has great potential for resolving interpersonal conflicts.

A young man had recently began to work in a supermarket. His first customer, an elderly woman, had an unusual request. She asked for half a head of lettuce. Puzzled, he replied, "Excuse me, I'll ask the manager." He said to the manager, "Some old bag wants half a head of lettuce." As he was finishing his statement he looked over his shoulder and there she was standing beside him. Without hesitation he continued, "And this lovely lady will take the other half." The manager was so impressed with this man's creative response that he said, "How would you like to run my store in Kalamazoo?" The young man responded, "Kalamazoo? That's the place for whores and hockey players." The manager angrily answered, "My wife comes from Kalamazoo." The young man responded, "And what position did she play?"

My young nephew, in the presence of his grandfather, yelled out "shit." The grandfather, a prim and proper man, chased him around the room yelling, "What did you say?" His grandson replied, "Grandfather, I said ship, ship, ship."

You can even interact with God.

A man says, "God, what does a million years feel like to you?" God replies, "Like a minute." He then asks, "God, what does a million dollars mean to you." God answers, "A dollar." The man says, "God, could I have a dollar." God's reply is "Wait a minute."

A young man went to confession saying, "Father, forgive me for I have sinned." The priest responded, "What sin have you committed, my son?" The young man said, "I'm too ashamed to tell you", and hung his head down. The priest, with worldly wisdom and knowledge said, "Was it a sexual indiscretion?" The young man nodded and the priest went on to ask, "And who was it with?" The young man responded, "I'm so ashamed, Father, I cannot tell you." The priest then said, "Was it with Mary Jane?" The young man responded, "I am so ashamed, Father, I cannot tell you." The priest continued, "Was it with Lucy Brown" and there was the same response from the young man as the priest continued with yet another name. Finally the priest gave the usual atonement instructions then dismissed him. Outside the church the young man was greeted by his friend who said, "How did it go?" The response, "Well, not bad. I got four new names."

Embarrassment and Humiliation

The risks of open spontaneous humor are embarrassment or humiliation. Not everyone knows the difference. Embarrassment is the uncomfortable sensations of blushing, sweating and anxiety, when someone compliments you, says you have a beautiful body or a brilliant mind. Strangely enough, the recognition you've always wanted registers as pain and discomfort, a reflection of a pleasure block dating back to early childhood conditioning. Repeated exposure to the blush of embarrassment shifts to the glow of excitement and the pleasure of recognition. Humiliation is the same physiological response to an experience interpreted as shameful or bad. *A shy man with pain on urination approaches the doctor's nurse in a crowded waiting room. Speaking loudly, she asks for the usual patient data, the last question being "what is the nature of your problem?" Flushed with humiliation, he circumvents her question with "my ear hurts." "And, when doesn't it hurt?" she asks. He blurts out "When I pee."* You can survive humiliation with the help of this poem by Piet Hein:

> Some people cower, wince and shrink
> Owing to fear of what people might think
> There is but one answer to questions like these
> People may think what the devil they please.

A surgical resident assisting a surgeon at a colon/rectal operation is suddenly filled with the urge to expel gas. He tightens up every muscle in his body to avoid the eruption. The operation progresses for hours and just as the surgeon is about to close the skin the resident loses control but fortunately has a silent emission. He is relieved until the odour fills the room. The surgeon cries out, "There's a leak in the bowel. We've got to go back in." The young surgeon confesses with humiliation that the eruption was his! [1]

Is Seeing Believing?

Misinterpretation can be a visual distortion for not everything is as it appears.

A man was marooned on a desert island for years. He had a daily routine of climbing a tree, and looking out into the ocean for a ship to rescue him. One day he watched as a ship passed by and sank. There were two survivors, a man and his wife whom he greets with excitement and hope as he explains the daily vigil of watching for a rescue ship. "Each one will take a turn as lookout at the top of the tree." He goes first while the young exhausted couple sit at the base of the tree. Up in the tree, looking around, he yells down, "Stop that fucking. Stop that fucking." The couple are confused and bewildered by his words. A few hours pass and the husband climbs up the tree for his watch. As he is looking out over the ocean his eyes gaze to the bottom of the tree and he says, "My goodness, from up here it does look like they are fucking."

A woman gets stuck on the toilet seat and calls for her husband. He can't dislodge her and says, "I'll have to call for the plumber." While waiting he puts a small Hebrew black cap (Kepa) over her genitals. When the plumber arrives and looks at her predicament, he says to her husband, "We can free your wife, but I don't think we can save the Rabbi."

Is seeing believing? In the story of the emperor's clothes there was certainly a false visual system until the child pointed out that the emperor was completely nude, for which the child was duly punished. Anyone who questions a traditional belief system whether it's in politics, science or social living is seen as a misfit, a rebel, and perhaps dangerous. Even eye witness memory is far from foolproof. In memory tests, immediate recall of detailed pictures of a car crash were surprisingly inaccurate by a majority of respondents. In a conflict, when all reason fails, *"step back and take another look."* This functions as a double bonus, a cooling off period, as well as the possibility of opening new options through the right brain.

How would you pull a stubborn donkey into a barn? Milton Erickson, as a young boy on the farm, simply turned the donkey around and pulled it away while the donkey, resisting, backed itself into the barn. "See what I mean!?"

Punning

Punning, a play on words is a simple form of humor that rarely produces big laughs, only great groans. People who respond with a groan have an important role in the joke. Here's a good example of a bad pun:

A man has a problem with his leg requiring amputation. The surgeon mistakenly cuts off the wrong leg. The next day he re-operates to cut off the right leg. The patient sues the doctor but loses the case. Why? He doesn't have a leg to stand on.

Oh, I hear the groans coming. Rodney Dangerfield is a master of the pun. *I got a dog for my wife, a great trade.* Children love to play with puns. Here's one for five year olds. *It's a story about momma tomato and poppa tomato walking down the street and little baby tomato lags behind. Poppa tomato stamps his foot and says, "Catch up!"* (Ketchup). Another simple punning game with an older child might be pointing to your back and saying "back off", sticking out your bum and saying "butt out", pointing to your knees and saying "I need you" and if your legs aren't very strong perhaps you don't have good "understanding", or when you point to your knees, you may be "weak kneed".

Jackie Mason's response in court when the judge asked him, "Have you ever been up before me?" Jackie Mason replied, "I don't know. What time do you get up?"

What do you call a psychic dwarf who has escaped from prison? A small medium at large.

"Pain in the neck" or *"my heart aches for you,"* takes the pun into metaphor, where one thing stands for three or four.

Let's elevate the pun from the bottom of the pile and give it respect. For truly it is the exquisite combination in one word of the right brain image and the left brain thought, mixing the concrete and the abstract with conciseness and simplicity. *"If brevity be the food of thought, play on, play on." (Jack Shakespeare).*

If the pun can do it so can you, for your Corpus Callosum, the connection between your right and left cerebral hemisphere have not been cut by a surgeon's knife. The right and left brain were functionally disconnected by past conflicts and traumas for survival. Today they can work together.

- Join your feelings and your thoughts
- Play the lyrics with your music
- Harmonize, integrate
- Synthesize and celebrate

You can become "Whole." (A paradoxical pun for a hole is empty.)

Sexual Conquest

If you're thinking of sexual conquest here's an inventive interactive joke.

A man is sitting in a bar talking to an attractive woman. She asks, "What do you do?" "I'm a fork lift operator," he answers. Immediately she loses interest and walks away. He asks a friend, "What did I do wrong?" The friend says, "Well, let's face it, women are attracted to men with prestige, like a doctor or a lawyer." A few moments later he talks to another woman. She says, "What do you do" and he says, "I'm a lawyer," and within an hour they're in bed making love. In the middle of lovemaking he bursts out laughing and the woman asks, "What's so funny?" He says, "I've been a lawyer for barely an hour and already I'm fucking somebody."

Many miscommunications are on ethnic or cultural levels or perhaps language difficulties, where English is a second language.

In the height of passion our hearing may be impaired. *An elderly man and woman in a senior citizen's home become friends. One evening the*

woman invites him to her room to see her family pictures. Flirtation begins
and they kiss. The man explodes into sexual excitement and rips off her
blouse and her brassiere. She calls out, "Remember, I have acute angina."
"I hope so," he responds, "because your breasts are not so hot."

Games People Play [3]

Games people play are the most serious communication
distortions. The "poor me" of helplessness desperately whines and
cries in search of a rescuer. The "ain't it awful" player focused on
negative thinking and with an outpouring of complaints creates a
suffering personality which eventually succeeds in the self fulfilling
prophecy of life's tragedy. The misery persists with the unconscious
"waiting for Santa Claus." The histrionic personality, constantly
vigilant, accurately perceptive, seeing all problems at the same time is
flooded with anxiety. He or she reacts with dramatic flair exaggerating
disaster to catastrophe, draining the attachment to the significant
other, mother, father, lover, child. The "kick me" perfectionist, always
self critical, raging with self attack has 24-hour access to an internal
hanging judge, disguised as a realistic, reasonable adult. Constantly
critical and judgmental, the continuous put downs cause self-blaming
depression. The authoritarian judge reacts externally to loved ones
with the same devastating put downs causing painful, disruptive
relationships. The passive aggressive game is sneaky and seductive.
The weaker partner asks for help and instantly rejects the answer with
"yes, but" or "I can't" leaving the relationship blocked in constant
frustration. In the interactional game of "now I've got you, you son-
of-a-bitch," each party attacks the other relentlessly, simply to get the
bastard. It's a deadly relationship with couples on the verge of
breaking a love relationship or maintaining a loveless one.

Creativity in communication is the ultimate, ranging from literary
writing to humor. It incorporates the complex skills of paradoxical

thinking, positive reframing of negatives and transformational resolutions. The integration and balancing of left brain cognition and right brain metaphor interacting in an harmonious way leads to creativity. The final result may be simple but different and unique.

A middle aged woman takes a long arduous trip to visit a famous guru in Tibet to find an answer to her life's conflicts. She travels day and night with native guides, climbing over mountains. Finally, at the entrance to his retreat she is told that she will be able to see the Master tomorrow morning and given permission to ask him any question, with only three words. Shocked that she's made this horrendous trip for three words, she needs to call on all her creative powers to put this complex important message into three small words. The next day in her audience with the guru she faces him and slowly, deliberately enunciating clearly, says "Come, home, Sam."

Paradox, Metaphor and Positive Reframing

In the creative communication absurd life humor begins with paradox. Mae West might have said, *"I'm clean all over. The only thing dirty is my mind."* Buddy Hackett grew up in a Kosher home eating high fat foods which caused a continual burning sensation in the pit of his stomach, an experience he accepted as normal. When he was drafted into the army his diet changed. He woke up one morning and the pain was gone. In a panic he rushed to the doctor shouting, *"Doctor, I think I'm dying. The fire has gone out."*

An elderly woman said to her son, "The day drags but the years fly by!"

A punning paradox: If Milton Erickson and I were in the same room it would be a very interesting pair of docs.

Not all paradoxes are funny. Children growing up in homes where parents are giving double or opposite messages at the same time are under constant stress. A mother tells the child she loves him while her facial grimace shows contempt and dislike. The child, continually dealing with opposites, is torn by anxiety and confusion. Psychiatrists previously believed this was one of the psychological causes of schizophrenia, that double binding parents left you no where to go but crazy. It has been disproved since the predisposition to schizophrenic illness is mainly neurochemical. Nevertheless, growing up in a home like this has terrible consequences, from neuroses to personality disorders.

Positive reframing is making lemonade out of lemons. *A patient called his dentist and said, "Doctor, you left a cotton pad in my mouth." The dentist asked, "How long has it been there?" The patient said, "Two hours." The dentist replied, "Well, leave it in for another hour then take it out."*

Paradox can be used to positively reframe a negative. Oscar Wilde's remark, *"Sometimes the bonds of marriage are so heavy that it takes more than two to carry them"* becomes a euphemism for infidelity. In Winston Churchill's speech to the British people during the Nazi bombing of London, he said, *"This is not the end. This is not the beginning of the end. This is simply the end of the beginning."*

I met a work addicted lawyer who was, paradoxically, easy going. His appointments dragged on without concern. When I asked him the secret of his tranquillity, he replied, "I am a prisoner of the clock, so I ignore it."

One of my patients spoke with paradoxical wisdom when she said, "I don't know how to express anger at someone I'm not really mad at." Paradox can be useful for motivation or mental stimulation for it often creates anxiety and you have to move. Like the man said, "I don't know where I'm going, but I've got to go."

Communication is the fundamental of human connection. Neither giving advice, nor lecturing, nor rescuing, nor persecuting, but sharing with people you love leads to contentment. The human gift of speech is the vehicle of the message. *The Israeli rowing team came in last at the Olympic games. The coach sent one of his players to Cambridge to study the art of sculling. After the completion of the course, the coach asked the rower what he had learned. This was his response, "In England eight men row and only one man talks."*

Paradoxical intervention or double binding is a powerful psychotherapeutic technique. Picture your "self" made up of an infinite number of different parts called ego states. You probably have an angry, sad, sexy, needy, internal child, as the center of feelings and experience. A realistic adult hopefully manages the whole structure with logical and realistic thinking. We all have an internal parent ego state made up of at least a benevolent, caring self-loving part and a critical judgmental part to protect and comfort. Now the rebellious child needs to fight against its real external parents, simply to grow up. The need to separate from parents is crucial for survival, for in the natural course of life the child will outlive the parents and needs to be strong and independent to survive and become a parent in his own right. Now what has this explanation to do with therapeutic double binding? Simply, the rebellious internal child is always fighting, possibly subconsciously, all authority figures including the psychiatrist. Yes, another ongoing power struggle for the healthy purpose of self growth, maturation and emancipation. The therapist accepts this human drive and builds in a therapeutic double bind for continual growth. If a patient makes a positive change then I as a therapist acknowledge it, praise it, and condition it, giving it more attention than negative or painful symptoms. Then I respond with the opposite. *"I have good news and bad news. The good news is the personal growth; the bad news is the old habits, behaviors and feelings always come back first in the next crisis."* Then I quietly add, *"Briefly."* If there is any resistance from the patients hopefully it will be to prove me wrong by continuing their success. If the change is towards assertiveness I warn of the danger of not being liked. If it's a move to independence, I comment on the inevitability of standing alone. In the celebration of personality growth I may mention the anxiety of change which is inevitable for the unfamiliar may be more distressing than the secure but uncomfortable old neurosis. Occasionally, I prescribe the very symptoms they're complaining of. *"Your rage is a sign of delayed timing. Why don't you practice getting angry more quickly."* Often the real problem is their attempted solution and I encourage them to do the opposite of what they've been doing. One of my more subtle therapeutic double binds at the time of success is "That's a great beginning." Now, I ask you, is this therapy or manipulation? Perhaps it's mutually understood that the psychiatrist works in strange but wonderful ways.

Believe it or not words are not the major ways we communicate. Social intercourse depends on the tone of voice, the way we speak, the body movement and actions are all the medium that is the message. Take the word "fuck", one of the most commonly used words in the English language. The sound alone can cover the range of life experiences from pain to pleasure.

Dismay - *fuck it*
Anger - *fuck you*
Threats - *don't fuck with me*
Failure - *I'm a fuck up*
Trouble - *I'm fucked now*
Confusion - *What the fuck*
Disappointment - *fucked again*

Philosophical - *who gives a fuck*

On the positive side we have:
Agreement - *you're fucking right*
Of course, sexual - *let's fuck*
Erotic - *let's fuck*
Romantic - *let's fuck*

A psychiatrist brags, *"I'm a great sex therapist. I give the best fucking advice."*

Paradoxically, sometimes the fucking I'm getting isn't worth the fucking I'm getting or "I like to get kissed before I get fucked." If you're disgusted with the obscenity of the word FUCK let me remind you of the dirtiest work I've ever heard, CAN'T, a dead end word that traps you into helplessness, stagnation and dependency.

I love metaphor, where one thing stands for three or four, an abstraction, a picture or symbol of an idea. Look at the power of one little finger. Simply pointing it in many directions sends powerful and diverse messages. *Jackie Mason was banned as a comedian for twenty years after he gave the television host Ed Sullivan the "finger". He pointed the middle finger of his right hand, which was interpreted as a crude gesture of anger, a "fuck you." If he had raised the little finger and the index finger at the same time, it would have changed the message to "bullshit." He would have escaped the wrath of Ed Sullivan if he had explained, "I made a mistake, I meant to point my index finger forward, not up, to say listen to me."* Many patients believe they are in their realistic informational adult only to discover the critical internal parent by the pointing finger and the dirty "should" words.

It's amazing how many body parts are used to vent hostility. You little fart, prick or cunt. I don't give a shit, or don't give me that shit. The reverse is as perplexing, describing ecstasy, "I feel like a pig in shit" or a fine person as a "great shit." Why has our contempt focused on our most treasured body parts? I can understand hostility focusing on our anal excretory organs, whose function is to get rid of things we don't want, but why all this vitriolic anger at our most prized and sought after possessions, our sexual organs?

In psychotherapy metaphors are the bases of positive reframing. *"You're at the bottom of the barrel and there's no way to go but up."*

"There's always a light at the end of the tunnel."

One of my patients in group therapy showed marked despair and depression and when I suggested she go into right brain mental imagery and feel the despair she sensed it in her chest. Going into her chest she felt like she was in a deep cavern and there were three tunnels. She chose a dark narrow tunnel where she could move with difficulty in a crouching position, crawling a step at a time. She moved her arms, pushing the walls out and the tunnel expanded. As her pace quickened there was a burst of light surrounding her. Surprisingly, the image expanded and now she moved in many different ways, like the motion of a gyroscope, weaving through the skies and the clouds. She glowed with excitement.

Another group member identified with the tunnel experience but felt exhausted and hopeless that he would ever get through it. He realized he could rest and then take one small step at a time for there was always tomorrow. Hope was rekindled. Another patient going through her tunnel hit a white wall and found more sadness. She began to think about the difficulties in today's life with a learning disabled son and then kept saying over and over again, "I don't know", "I don't know". When it was interpreted that "I don't know" was a search for someone to tell her the answer, she burst out crying and went back to her own eleven year old childhood experience where her father, recovering from a major illness, never returned to the warm caring person he had been. She recognized she was still yearning for a father to help her and show her the way. Paradoxically, this discovery, while sadder, was relieving, with the insight she had found. It was not the pleasure or excitement of a positive experience but more the "Ah Ah" as Eric Berne said of self discovery, however painful.

When my patients say, "There I go again," I answer, *"You never step in the same river twice." (Because the water is always moving.)* The patient may respond with a mixed metaphor, *"The river feels like the same pile of shit to me."* Many patients say *"I've had enough, I want to get rid of this pain and suffering."* I then reply, *" The best way to get over it is to go through it."* Look how easy it is to discover your source of anxiety and burnout by seeing, *"Too many things on your plate,"* which opens up the door for change since it's easy to see the next small step. One patient thanked me by saying, *"You helped me deal with one tragedy at a time."* One patient told me a slogan on her "have to's," "got to's," "musts" and "shoulds." *"Don't should on yourself."*

If a patient responds with more than three "yes, buts" to any recommendation I answer with, "You've butted out," change the discussion or go on to another member of the group. "Yes, buts" are fascinating. Usually the patient starts with a question, asking for help or advice "I don't know where to go?" If the therapist responds with "try this" then the "yes, buts" begin. This is transference, asking the wise therapist, the parent figure, for help then rejecting it with continual "yes, buts". It is a passively angry response of a child to a parent, a fight that belongs to a much earlier era. The back and forth battle now persists as neurosis in the grown up. People who never got what they wanted as children are still searching for it as adults are *"Going back to an empty well."* As well, the passive resistance to change is a need to stay stuck in emotional pain where the familiar feels secure. For any positive change always produces realistic anxiety of the new and the risks of the unknown.

To avoid the trap of future worries and predictions of "never making it", I say, "never say never" and encourage future planning in the present. For future worries are only bad fortune telling. Taking action today for tomorrow is realistic and lowers the level of stress. When people attempt to change but bring in all their past failure I say, "No past regrets," as I acknowledge the differences from yesterday to today and warn them that the anxiety of the present is sufficient enough. *Yesterday's anxiety doubles today's and if you add tomorrow's predicted failures you triple the anxiety.* No one can function with a high level of anxiety and make a change.

"The Phoenix rising out of the ashes," is a marvelous metaphor from Greek mythology of a transformational resolution, when the very cure lies within the problem itself, for inside pain is the potential for relief and pleasure. "Yes, your rage attack may be like an atomic explosion, but you can convert it to electrical energy." Remember the Hans Christian Anderson fairly tale, where the ugly ducking becomes a beautiful swan.

The right brain, with its capacity for mental imagery working through the imagination, has a greater capacity for transformational resolution than the logical, rational, thinking left brain. A depressed patient saw herself in a black hole. As she focused on this experience the image shifted to a cave with a small light at the top. Her sadness shifted to tranquillity as she felt safe. The cave had become a safe place where she could periodically escape for rest and healing, away from the turmoil and ongoing problems of her daily life. The rays of sunlight at the top of the cave rekindled hope that there was always light at the end of a tunnel.

Milton Erickson offered the transformational solution of psychological rebirth to the depressed, suicidal nurse, through the metaphor of the dying flower that blooms again each spring. Transformational healing predates modern psychiatry. It existed in ancient times with the mystics of many primitive cultures. The ancient Jewish rituals of grieving are as psychologically sophisticated and effective today as they were in days of old. For only by going through the pain of the loss of a loved one we recapture the love of living.

Interpretation of Symbols

People fascinated with symbols in movies, art and theatre are always looking for deep intellectual meanings. Your ability to interpret becomes a social symbol of your brilliance, extensive educational background, knowledge and cultural sophistication.

In an ancient Egyptian tomb a hieroglyphic was found that confused the brightest Egyptian archeologists. There were pictures of a tomato, a donkey, a shovel, a fish and a cross. Reluctantly, they called in an Israeli archeologist who interpreted it with ease. "This is simple," he said, "you have to read it as we Israelis do, from right to left. It's not an ancient hieroglyphic, but recent graffiti. It says, 'Holy Mackerel, dig the ass on that tomato.'"

The symbolism is often lost in the limitations of language.

A flood hit a town and the waters rose swiftly. The Rabbi climbed onto the roof of his house. A canoe came by and offered him assistance. He refused, saying, "I'm in God's hands and He will save me." As the flood waters rose a motor boat came by and the driver said to the Rabbi, "Jump in." The Rabbi thanked him and said, "I will stay. God will save me." Finally the water rose so high that the Rabbi was hanging onto the chimney. Fortunately, a helicopter came by and the pilot said, "Rabbi, grab the ladder," and the Rabbi said, "No, I'm in God's hands." The water rose and the Rabbi drowned. When he arrived in heaven he was angry, "God, I've been a devout and honorable Jew and you let me down. Why?" God responded, "I tried my best. I sent you a canoe, a motorboat and even a helicopter."

Chief Complaint

The first words of the psychiatric consultation are called "chief complaints" as the psychiatrist asks "what is your problem?" Occasionally the patient responds "if I knew I wouldn't be here." Sarcastic humor is always appreciated but pleading ignorance and lack of any personal awareness is an expression of helplessness. The patient has immediately declared him or herself as dependent and the purpose of their therapy is to find a therapist who will rescue and protect. The search for Santa Claus was revealed in the opening statement.

If you want to give your psychiatrist nightmares use one of the following lines:

- I've seen ten psychiatrists and no one helped me.
- My wife said I should see a psychiatrist but I know there's nothing wrong with me.
- "I don't know," is the only response to questions and with improvement it goes to "can't" or "yes, but," follows.
- I rarely drink but last weekend I was charged with impaired driving.
- I want to get rid of all my shit.

- I've heard on Oprah that you suicide on Prozac.
- I want to find myself.
- With all my problems I must have been sexually abused as a child but I can't remember. I want you to hypnotize me to recall the memories.

Therapeutic Paradoxical Intention

I would like to share a composite anecdotal consultation interview. (I will describe my psychiatric insights and interventions.)

Patient: I lost my job. My wife left me and I've been drinking to get rid of my pain. I want to get to the bottom of this. (Diagnosis: Reactive depression with alcoholism. There's a subtle denial of the problem by rationalizing his drinking.)

Therapist: You're already at the bottom. (Sarcastic but realistic clarification to override denial.)

Patient: I mean I want to understand my problem, why I drink. (Dependency, plea, underlying search for help. Looking for magic. If I understand my problem it will go away.)

Therapist: Good. Stop drinking and we can find out.

Patient: Angry. If I could stop drinking I wouldn't be here. (Transference, for who could be angry at a nice guy like me.)

Therapist: You sound angry. (Mirroring the patient's emotional response.)

Patient: You piss me off. You're like my father, telling me what to do. (See, I'm right, it is transference.)

Therapist: Wanna talk about it? (Are you motivated to do some therapy?)

Patient: Sure, but I don't know what to do. I don't know what to say. (He's playing stupid. I told you he was dependent.)

Therapist: Well, you're mentally sluggish, your memory seems poor and you're not concentrating well.

Patient: How do you know that?

Therapist: It shows right here. That's what alcohol does. It depresses brain function and you can't learn. (Realistic information and education.)

Patient: That makes sense. I'll quit. (First positive step.)

Therapist: That's not easy. How will you socialize with your drinking buddies? (Setting up a therapeutic double bind by reverse psychology, the beginning of paradoxical interventions.)

Patient: I'll drink Virgin Marys. (Now his protest against the therapist is becoming a positive move.)

Therapist: It's not easy. Do you need help in getting off the alcohol?

Patient: No, I can do it myself.

Therapist: Great, but if you do there's a good addiction counselling center I can refer you to.

Patient: No, I'll do it myself.

Therapist: When?

Patient: I'll quit now.

Therapist: Perhaps you should stop slowly over the next two or three weeks. You could have withdrawal symptoms.

Patient: No, I've stopped before, no problem.

Therapist: Okay. Call me a month after your last drink. It takes one to two months for brain cells to recover.

Patient: I'll book the appointment now.

Therapist: Okay. But if you do drink will you cancel the appointment for a least a month?

Patient: I will.

The paradoxical intention is using the patient's resistance to change, the natural opposition to the authority/therapist/parent figure. After telling him to stop I switched my approach to the opposite, telling him it's too difficult, encouraging him to drink to avoid withdrawal. Now his anger towards me is positive, leading him towards sobriety. It's a win/win game. Manipulation? No, simply therapeutic intervention!

CHAPTER EIGHT

Looks like a penis to me

A young man with a severe personality disorder, in a group therapy session, exploded with rage at me, his therapist. When I asked him to focus on his body and feel the center of his rage, he experienced it over his heart. Through mental imagery, he imagined a serpent, tightly entwined around the heart. Torn by ambivalent feelings of disgust at this internal image and the sense of power it gave him, he was stuck, unable to move in the midst of his inferno of hate. A female patient listening to him in the group, burst out crying and felt like vomiting. As we explored her experience she went up to the board at the front of the room and drew a picture of a large snake around a heart, with the head of the snake pointing downwards towards the face of a fearful young girl who was gazing back at the head of the snake with outstretched hands. Her sobs increased and she cried profusely. The group was stunned, except for one young man in the corner who was trying to cover a smile with his hand. When I encouraged him to speak, he reluctantly said, "That snake looks like a penis to me." The rest of the group burst out laughing and the patient at the board began to smile as she said, "A penis can love you too." At the next meeting she told us of a remarkable shift. Her husband, a long-term alcoholic, had quit drinking many years ago. Damaged and angry at the past experience, she never forgave him. They lived together in a cold and rejecting marriage. After the last meeting she felt warmth and caring for her husband and they rekindled their lost love. Much to her surprise she also began to feel a closeness to her only daughter. She was not even aware that she had shut her out of her life, as well as her husband. It was difficult to logically explain and understand what happened. It wasn't even necessary.

Interestingly, by opening a new dimension of one's self through mental imagery, the visual, experiential side of the brain, this woman was able to take an unexpected and rewarding journey re-opening her love for her husband and her daughter. The paradoxical humor of the situation transformed her fear and negativity back to closeness with her family.

Depression is a common, almost universal illness. It's difficult to find the fine line between overwhelming sadness, disappointment and depression with hopelessness, loss of pleasure and self confidence. The good news is that depressions are self-limiting, lifting even without treatment. However, there is a class of resistant depressions that go on for prolonged periods, despite all the innovations of psychotherapy and the newest antidepressants. Some years ago I saw a successful executive suffering from a deep chronic depression. Motivation was there. He sought out the finest therapists all over the world and was as well-versed in the understanding of depression as any expert in the field. Despite all his work, readings and therapy, his depression continued. In one of our sessions I told him a joke and he burst out laughing. Now, usually in serious psychotherapy when a patient laughs the therapist quietly waits till the laugher subsides before continuing with the serious work of treating the depression. However when he responded with laughter I continued telling jokes. We spent the rest of the session telling jokes to each other and laughing. On the next visit he returned with an enlarged picture of a young, happy, smiling little boy about two or three. He presented me with this picture as a gift. "This was my child when I was young. I was playful, happy and full of fun. Since I've become an adult I have become serious, driven by ambition, money and success. I've lost this kid. I want him back. We touched him last week in therapy and I went home and looked through my pictures and found him. When he is with me I laugh and I'm happy." The next few sessions focused on integration of this happy little boy into the adult today. He made many changes quickly, gave up his executive position with the company and became a nature photographer, integrating his fun kid into the adult pursuit of living. He left me with this picture which I often show to my patients to help them find their natural, fun, free kid that was there somewhere in the past.

A middle aged woman left an alcoholic husband some years ago. While the decision was right it left her alone, without children and riddled with physical illness and a sense of deep, deep, deep sadness. The depression was the futility of living with an overwhelming suicidal wish. Despite good psychotherapy and the best of antidepressants the depression persisted. One day, doing mental imagery work, she went into the past and found herself as a little girl walking through the park with her older sister. Coming from a dysfunctional alcoholic family where she was unwanted by her mother, she realized that her depression had started in infancy. As we viewed the pictures of her childhood there were moments of joy. She recalled times with her older sister who took her everywhere, and loved her as a devoted mother. At this moment she was a happy, playful little girl and the older sister nicknamed her Daisy. Daisy was bright, witty, curious about life, enjoying every moment. How could we get Daisy back into the adult woman? With the discovery of Daisy, a sarcastic wit and humor began to emerge in the group therapy sessions. This was Daisy in her adult form. With a great smile she could pick up on the slips and mistakes of the therapist. She would gently rib and tease me with a perceptiveness that stimulated the laughter of the group. For there is no greater joy than putting the therapist down. As little Daisy became more and more integrated into the adult woman, her wit and humor expanded into her work and her depression lifted. Depressions did recur, for her life was not easy.

There have been terrible moments, but Daisy comes through with her brightness and her laughter.

Another patient, a mature woman returning to work in a new career as an adult teacher was terrified as her first day approached. "My hands are shaking so much I won't be able to write my name on the board." Another member of the group suggested she write "For a good time call Mary." She burst out laughing, switching her anxiety to excitement. Humor became her key to success at her new job.

A few years ago while crossing the Canada/USA border a surly Immigration Officer examined my passport. With his head down and in a monotonous voice he asked the usual questions, "Where are your going? How long are you going to be there? What's the purpose of your visit?" When he said, "What's your occupation?", I paused, reflecting on the Chicago Bulls recent win of their NBA basketball title, also I was wearing a Chicago Bulls cap. I responded, "Would you believe I'm a seven foot basketball player for the Chicago Bulls?" Slowly he lifted his head, gazed at me with an expressionless yet disdainful face and slowly uttered these words, "You may think what you said was funny." There was a long and painful pause. Frightening thoughts jumped through my head, Did I cross the line of criminal intent, giving false information to an American Customs Officer? He continued, "You may think that's funny, but do you know you have rights to American citizenship?" I was pleasantly surprised and was tempted to give a discourse on United States immigration law. Suddenly, discretion was the better part of valor, and I kept my mouth shut. He didn't say anymore. (His straight faced humor was better than mine.) I thanked him and passed through Immigration. My mind kept repeating his words, "You have rights to American citizenship."

I was born in New York City and as a child came to Canada with my parents. I've lived here except for post graduate training in the United States. When I graduated medical school I took out Canadian citizenship. Shortly after, I received a formal document from the United States government saying I was expatriated from the United States of America. I lost my rights to American citizenship because I had taken out citizenship of another country. Duality at that time was illegal according to American law. In the late 70s the law was reversed and I approached immigration lawyers to regain my lost status. But it was a costly, difficult process that could best be handled when I was ready to move to the United States. Since my practice and family were in Canada I dropped the issue. After the encounter with the Immigration Officer, I was haunted by the words "birth right." Returning to Canada I went to the American Embassy and filled out an application for citizenship. Answering the question that said, "On what basis are you applying for American citizenship?", I wrote, "My Birth Right." Eight months later I received my citizenship of the United States. I'm still amazed at the reward for risking a little humor.

Lighten Up and Laugh It Off

A compulsive, tight assed professional living by the Avis Rent-A-Car motto of "we try harder" sought psychiatric care. He wanted to understand his behavior of withdrawal, alternating with rage attacks. His left brain was overworked trying to figure it out and his right brain had been totally neglected in a life of anhedonia. In the first of session of mental imagery therapy I helped him through self-hypnosis, to cross from the left brain to the right. I asked him to recapture a happy past event. He went back to camp - happy, mischievous, playful images cascaded through his mind. Laughter as they raided the girl's cabin, pranks on the counselors, and plotting with his buddies the next devilish act. His goal today was obvious, to "lighten up" for his serious side had alienated his friends and family. His first homework assignment was to take the playful camper home. At the next visit he was smiling, his playfulness with his children had been easy and fun. He approached his wife with trepidation for their relationship had drifted apart. Sex was only a memory and he was very frustrated. Through playful repartee and sexual humor he described taking "matters into his own hand" and bragged of his sexual skill from practicing so long alone. She responded not with sex but with humor. They laughed together and intimacy was rekindled. He glowed with satisfaction, for he knew he had made a fresh start in a troubled marriage.

So often the serious individual sees humor as a cover up (and at times it may be). They discount its value as an entry into the lighter side. The right brain with its solace center for nurturing and its capacity for love and joy, may be an easier resolution for today's conflict than hammering away at the rigid, analytical left side of the brain filled with negative tapes. *Remember you have your right brain left.*

After many years a patient had finally conquered the ravages of alcoholism and depression. Recent therapeutic work had focused on previously unrecognizable physical and emotional childhood abuse from a "crazy mother." Now he felt in touch with life, rather than disconnected. He could feel more pain and more joy. Periodic bursts of irritability would be quickly recognized and when excessive connected to origins in the past. In his new marriage, the periodic flare ups were quickly resolved. Not by understanding or insight, not by confrontation or compromise, not by the need to be right or dominate, but the ability to simply *"Laugh it off."*

Most people came to psychotherapy driven by pain or serious conflicts, looking for resolution, a cure, a change. There are many roads to Rome. Humor, with its innovative, paradoxical thinking and imaginative way of looking at life, can positively reframe problems into absurd life living. Recognizing and reowning a playful part of yourself you've lost or forgotten, may be another way of healing. If you've never had a happy playful child, adopt one. Mirror an external happy child and through the power of mental imagery transform and program it into your right brain.

Now you have a free, playful child living in the adult that needs affection, protection, care, and guidance. Take him/her everywhere, to explore and adapt to your external world, to harmonize internally with all your ego states. Play all your music. Risk embarrassment and humiliation and let the blush in your cheeks become the glow of pleasure. Approach the new and unfamiliar, to switch the realistic anxiety of exploration to the excitement of discovery. Be patient, you might be bright but the learning curve is slow.

Remember:
How to get to Carnegie Hall? - Practice, Practice, Practice!

I leave you with two messages:

DON'T TAKE HUMOR LIGHTLY
and
IT IS GREAT TO BE IN YOUR RIGHT MIND.

PART TWO
THE PAST GETS IN MY EYES

CHAPTERS

The Past gets in My Eyes

Part Two

CHAPTER ONE

Who am I?

Jackie Mason said, "I went to see a psychiatrist and the psychiatrist said, *'The trouble is you don't know who you are. I answered him, 'If I don't know who I am, why am I coming to you? You never saw me before. I'll go to my friends. They know who I am."* The dialogue continues until the end of the session when the psychiatrist asks for his fee. Jackie Mason replies, *"Why should I pay you? You don't even know me. You should pay me. I know you."*

Is it trite or self centered to ask who we really are? How do you get in touch with your true self? When you find yourself, are you all there? How do your friends respond to the real you? Society is excessively preoccupied with outer achievement, and I fear the inner self is rarely seen. I was invited to the 85th birthday party of a friend's mother. She was a charming lady, but did not remember me. Walking arm and arm with both sons, she said, "I want you to meet my sons. This is Joe, my son, the doctor." Then she pointed to her son, a successful businessman and said, "This is my son, Marvin, the other one." Obviously, the performing self, the doctor, was more significant than her son the entrepreneur. Acknowledging only the performing self is more than sad, it's a waste. Each of us is unique, and failure to develop the inner self leaves a limited, unfulfilled person.

Personality Pie

I see individuals as a personality pie, each made up of an infinite number of pieces called ego states. Each ego state is simply one complete part of your personality, a "persona", with all the characteristics of being, sensation, knowledge, feelings, moods, expressions, tone of voice, words, actions. You have as many parts as you can imagine: sad, happy, angry, strong, weak, sexy, playful, wise, scared and on and on. An adult realistic ego, an authoritarian parent ego, a loving parent, an internal playful child and a needy child all interact within you and with the external world.

A woman felt pain in her leg and coldness in her upper arms. By focusing on the pain she felt a shift to warmth in her body and a glow in her face which felt like excitement. When she noticed that her fists were clenched she was able to make a powerful sound that fit her energy. In her mind's eye, she saw a picture of herself as a warrior. Laughing, she was able to share her emotional state of power. Her warrior ego state became a complete experience with feelings, sounds, words and images.

Between each ego state is a boundary, dividing each slice of the pie. If you're healthy the wall is thin and permeable, allowing you to flow from one ego state to another as you react to different life experiences. What problems can arise? Sometimes, the walls are so thick that one ego state is not aware of the other. Or an ego state may have been partially or totally disconnected, called dissociation, and the person functions with a limited number of ego states. From my experience most of us function with only ten to fifteen percent of our personality potential. But we can grow and expand any time in our life for all our basic ego states are present, if only in early or undeveloped forms. We cut off parts of ourselves to survive childhood or adult trauma and conflict. The journey to growth is simple but not easy. Through ego-state therapy, re-experience, reown, accept, resolve, develop, expand and integrate our many different ego states.

Polarities

I was talking to an extremely pleasant young man recently. He was polite, quiet spoken and gentle. In our discussion he rarely took initiative. He answered all questions briefly, cooperatively, but void of substance. He may have been reticent, perhaps shy, nevertheless he appeared as a nice person. Looking a little deeper into our interaction I saw him as basically passive/aggressive, never opening up, nor trusting, nor sharing, nor taking any initiative. The excesses of his niceness, called pseudomutuality or false friendliness, suggested its hidden opposite, his aggression or anger.

Imagine a figure eight and at each end opposite parts of your personality. If you cut off your anger because you don't like it you'll only have half of your potential. If you reown both parts the energy flows, along the figure eight, opening new responses to life events. It certainly expands your range of interpersonal activity. If you see an extreme in a person, you know there's an opposite deep down that's been rejected, suppressed or dissociated. The dependent person has an independent part. The domineering controller has a hidden needy child, and the sad or troubled person has a happy face.

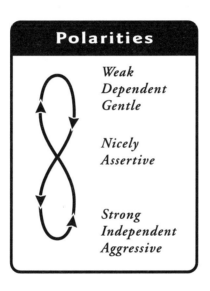

Draw a figure eight and examine your polarities. Look at your opposites. If you're independent at one end, describe the dependency at the other end. If you're too strong, can you accept your weakness? Are you too nice, then where's your anger? If you're self involved, where do others fit? If you're too serious, where is your fun part? If you accept your opposites, you've become complete, a much bigger, fuller human being. The bonus is movement. You can now flow from one to the other, reacting appropriately to life events.

Where the eight crosses and dependence and independence meet, interdependence occurs. Now you're able to love another in a healthy way. When a passive, quiet, much too nice person reowns their anger and protest, they usually stay in character, becoming nicely assertive. The acceptance of your polarities proves Mae West's line, *"When I'm good, I'm very good, but when I'm bad, I'm better."* Accepting your opposites allows polarity flow and you become "WELL BALANCED." Reowning, re-experiencing, and filling out, completes the personality pie and is the journey of reassociation.

At a recent group therapy session three of my patients were seriously depressed and suicidal. This touched the remaining members who shared their past depressions and recovery. In recognition of their achievement I suggested positive mental imagery and invited the depressed members to do some positive future planning imagery. During the exercise the depressed patients suddenly burst out laughing. When I focused on the laughter, each of the depressed patients became perplexed and embarrassed. When I explained that we found a cure for their depression, they were even more confused. "Look, you found the polarity, the opposite ego state of your melancholy, a happy part does still exist." The young woman rejected her laughter as silly. She'd grown up in a home where pain and suffering received attention, but playful giggling was called crazy. Experiencing her laughter now caused a shift in her belief system toward acceptance of laughter as fun. A depressed man, totally involved in a massively self destructive lifestyle colored by gallows humor, experienced relief and recognized his special ability to shift self attacking humor into perceptive absurd life humor. The third, obviously threatened by his laughter, called out with his resistant child, fighting the therapist as an authoritarian, critical parent, "Am I supposed to laugh all the time, even when I'm depressed?" A mature, successful business woman, locked into her rigid performing lifestyle, recognized her disconnection from her opposite playful ego state. I pointed out her extensive wit, which she came to see as an embryonic form of flexibility, freedom and playfulness. At this time I shared my personal experience. As a serious doctor completing the last year of psychiatric training I attended a Transactional Analysis group workshop in Philadelphia. Working in a group, like my patients had done, the group leader helped me discover my funny child ego state, which I've treasured, nurtured and matured to take everywhere, even into my psychiatric practice.

The traditional dynamic treatment of reactive depression is to discover its hidden roots, and deal with the crisis. It is effective psychotherapy. However, looking through the eyes of dissociation, and the polarity of ego states, you discover and reown your opposite, the happy playful kid. Now you have another resource to conquer depression.

Polarity Shift

A young woman survived a terrible childhood with a drug addicted mother, and a sexually abusive criminal father who abandoned the family when she was a child. After the parents' separation, she spent two years in an orphanage before returning home to be cared for by an older sister. At thirteen she became promiscuous, craving the affection of men, and accepting sex as its price. An older man became her protector. When she became pregnant they married. By forcing her to have sex with other men while he watched, he revealed his latent homosexual tendency. She left the marriage after a failed suicide attempt. She sought therapy only when her next relationship disintegrated.

In the psychotherapy session she sat quietly waiting for direction, pleading helplessness with, "I don't know." Examining the therapeutic interaction, she became aware of her dependency needs. Anger erupted at her childhood neglect and abuse and she felt strong and confident. Shifting to her polarity of independence she left the relationship. Now insightful, she recognized that fear and anxiety triggered her dependent side, while anger pushed her to her independent side. But she lacked control and her dependency prevailed. Paradoxically, when anxiety and insecurity became overwhelming, rage burst through with strength and assertive action. (When you hit the bottom of the barrel there is nowhere to go but up.) Her anger was the key to control and personal power.

The Past Gets In My Eyes

Each ego state of the present encapsulates all the experiences of the past. Unresolved childhood trauma or conflicts that have been repressed or dissociated emerge in a disguised form. Therapy explores the past when it interferes with the present. Review the Peanuts cartoon by Charles Schulz which expresses this psychology with majesty and humor.

PEANUTS reprinted by permission of United Feature Syndicate, Inc.

Whenever you react to something excessively, unrealistically or inappropriately, the past is intruding in the present.

Ego State Evolution

When I demonstrate the personality pie with each slice a personal ego state, we often explore its origin and development. The traumatic times are drawn visually, demonstrating their connection to the present, making a time line.

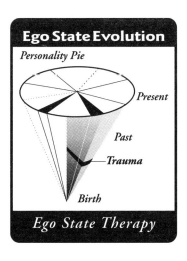

A nurse, the head of an intensive care unit in a large metropolitan hospital had an acute psychotic episode. No one knew why, perhaps the stress of work? After a period of hospitalization she made a full recovery and returned to her previous job. She entered psychoanalysis and for the next five years progressed well. There was one lingering, disturbing symptom. Out of the blue, she would explode into panic and an almost uncontrollable suicidal impulse. If she was driving her car she would have to fight the urge to crash into another car or go over a bridge. It was only with the utmost willpower that she controlled these impulses. These spontaneous, unremitting panic attacks brought her to see me. After a few individual sessions I remained puzzled, not having a clue to their cause. I discussed her case with her former psychoanalyst but got no answers. After five years of intensive therapy this one symptom still persisted.

She began group therapy while I was still in the early stages of developing mental imagery therapy. One morning she entered the group in a state of panic, she was also suicidal. I asked her to describe her pain. She pointed to her stomach. I asked her to focus on the anxiety in her stomach without thinking about it. "Don't let your thoughts intrude. Don't judge what's happening in any way. Simply feel and experience the anxiety in your stomach and let the feelings expand, imagine yourself in the middle of your own stomach." As I said these words, she rushed into the corner of the room, screaming like a terrified child, "Don't touch me. Don't touch me." She had regressed and was reliving an early childhood experience of sexual abuse by her father's best friend, a neighbor who had the keys to the house and kept an eye on the children when the parents were away at work. He was their protector. As her therapist I was concerned and frightened. Was she having another psychotic episode? She had lost all contact with the reality of the present, as she relived this forgotten childhood experience. After an hour or more of intense reality oriented therapy she slowly began to return to the present. She was mentally intact, but totally exhausted. The group was exhausted. I was exhausted. This was a moment of dramatic discovery. In 30 seconds, using a new and powerful therapeutic technique, we had discovered an early memory of childhood sexual abuse. A mystery traditional psychoanalysis had failed to solve in five years. We had found the origin of her panic attacks.

Many questions rushed through my mind. This patient not only remembered the incident, she relived it. It was as if it was happening all over again. Was this experience therapeutic? Was she retraumatized? Could we trust the memory of a young child from the distance of a grown woman? We have a new category today called false memory syndrome. Therapists are accused of inducing memories of early childhood sexual or physical abuse into susceptible patients, especially under the suggestibility of hypnosis. The childhood abuser is usually someone close, a parent, a friend or relative. If falsely accused the consequences could be devastating. On the positive side, she discovered the cause of her recurrent bouts of suicidal anxiety. Perhaps we could help resolve the trauma of the past and help prevent it from exploding in the present.

This had been more than a recall of a memory, it was a flashback, an actual reliving of an earlier traumatic experience. Flashbacks are one of the major symptoms of Post Traumatic Stress Disorder. In one case, a Vietnam veteran was baby-sitting his infant son for the first time. When the child began to cry he relived an episode of men dying in Vietnam. The past trauma had not been resolved or grieved. The intrusive past was in the present. The past does get in your eyes.

The use of mental imagery provided a dramatic and powerful entry into the right brain. Could it also be used as therapy? Could the moving pictures, the fantasies, the daydreams and feelings be used to develop a right brain psychotherapy. Can it help you to discover who you really are?

CHAPTER TWO

The Faces of Dissociation

Brainwashing

The first descriptions of brainwashing came out of the Korean war in the 1950's. One of the most puzzling incidents occurred when American prisoners of war converted to communism and denounced the United States for its "aggressive policy." After the war, when prisoners returned to the United States, a group of psychiatrists investigated the source of this most disturbing condemnation of democracy. The prisoners had not been tortured. In fact they were treated humanely. If they participated in regular lectures on the history of Korea and Communism they were rewarded with good food, recreation and social activities. If they refused they were isolated in their cell with minimal survival needs. Sensory deprivation, isolation and hunger for long periods became unbearable and many agreed to the simple act of attending these "innocuous" lectures. Insidiously, the brainwashing occurred through the simple conditioning of rewards for "good" behavior. The real question was how those who refused to participate in the Communist educational program survived intact. One case I know of survived through right brain imagery. Every day he fantasized he was living at home in America. Every day in his imagination he would live through the daily activities of family, work and friends. Living in his right brain, he remained mentally stable throughout his confinement.

Mental imagery, with pictures, feelings, sounds or smells is the building block of the natural phenomena of self-hypnosis. Self-hypnosis can also be used as the mechanism of dissociation.

Many American prisoners of the Korean war, through creative dissociation with mental imagery, preserved their sanity and prevented brainwashing. At the opposite end of the scale of dissociation is the pathology of Multiple Personality Disorder. Now called Dissociative Identity Disorder, it occurs in 1%-2% of the psychiatric population - the whole range of Dissociative Disorders present themselves in 20%-30% of the psychiatric population.

Dissociation, when used as a noun, describes an altered state of consciousness ranging from normal to psychiatric disorders. As a verb, it expresses the process of disconnection from the outside world or the inside self. As a normal process it's a useful and universal method of coping with massive conflict, death or loss. At times of overwhelming pain, catastrophic experience, or death of a loved one, we would disintegrate if we couldn't partially numb out, or dissociate. We put away our painful feelings and bring in our adult to function, to survive, and do the things we have to in a time of crisis. The abused child dissociates under childhood trauma for basic survival. The definition of childhood abuse encompasses repeated episodes of physical, sexual or emotional abuse, usually by a trusted adult the child either loves or believes is there to protect him. The subsequent state of confusion and helplessness is as painful as the trauma itself. The terror of powerlessness, aloneness, and abandonment is intolerable. Dissociation is one of the many routes for survival. The pathology of dissociation is its persistence. It can continue to block the flow of conscious reality leaving the adult emotionally flat, dazed, out of contact with self and the world. When disconnected, fragmented, and without full capacity to judge, the child becomes an easy victim again.

Depression

Depression, the commonest of all psychiatric illnesses, is rarely considered a dissociative reaction. Traditionally, it is conceptualized as an emotional disorder, precipitated by biochemical changes or a reaction to life events. Though depressed patients may complain of feelings of sadness or irritability, the primary symptom is emotional flatness. Deadness, with a loss of interest in usual activities, a lack of motivation and withdrawal, are signs and symptoms of dissociation. They are anhedonic (without pleasure), and cut off from feelings. Alternating with overwhelming anxiety, the patient spills over into depression. From a perspective of dissociation, secondary depression is much easier to tolerate than the tension of panic and terror. In effective psychotherapy, the feelings of blocked grief, repressed anger, or disappointment, burst through with the relief of the depression. Paradoxically, the sadness of mourning, or shaking rage, is more painful than the depression itself. The walls of depression have basically become a defense to protect the individual from underlying pain. The principle of therapy is true here as it is in all Dissociative Disorders. Facing and experiencing the realistic emotions of distress are necessary for the process of recovery. As my patients often say, "How do you ever get over the pain?" And I reply, "By going through it."

The obsessive/compulsive personality, driven by perfectionism, constantly anxious, and constantly reviewing under the guise of analyzing, is only in his left brain. The dissociation is a functional commissurotomy, splitting the cerebral hemispheres and leaving the right brain experience disconnected. An intellectual professional was fully aware of the events surrounding his parents' death, but his reactive depression persisted for months. Through hypnotic abreaction he was able to bypass his thinking and finally cry and grieve the loss of his parents. Recovering from his depression, he found his right brain left, and continued in therapy to find the music for his words.

Hysterical personalities, the opposite to compulsives, live primarily in their right brain. They're ruled by emotional child ego states, and misinterpreted as a realistic adult. A young child has taken charge of the personality. When these patients, usually highly visual, image their life scenario, their style of functioning gradually crosses the corpus collosum to the left brain. As insights develop the rational adult reemerges, hopefully free of the critical internal parent. Initially, they hear the self blaming voice of the internal judge. As therapy continues, and clear boundaries develop, the adult emerges distinct and primed to eventually assume executive power. Who wants a young kid running the corporation?

The psychopath or sociopath, bonded to painful parental relationships, has dissociated his childhood trauma and acts out his repressed rage on society. Doing to others what has been done to him is the exciting power game of assault, reaping revenge on innocent scapegoats.

"Why Do Honest People Shoplift?" is the title of a book by Dr. Will Cupchik, a forensic psychologist and colleague of mine. Dr. Cupchik has researched the syndrome of the atypical theft offender. The few cases I've seen are honest but depressed patients whose underlying hostile feelings are acted out by petty theft. One case stands out from a dissociation perspective. A lawyer sent me a young mother for psychiatric assessment. She was a recent immigrant, who had been charged with theft. She had been under psychiatric treatment for depression, dealing with present day issues. As I listened with my third eye, I heard the details of the episode. She remembered walking in a shopping center with her child. The next recollection

was being tapped on the shoulder by a security guard inside the supermarket, and being charged with theft. Dazed, confused, and feeling unreal, she was shown a few strange items that she would never have purchased, but had obviously placed in her shopping cart. Amnesia over a limited time period had occurred. Wandering into an unknown place, a sense of identity confusion and emotional disconnection, were the symptoms of a fugue state. Exploring her past history, she revealed a traumatic period around age ten when she and her sister were sent to a religious school in another town. When her parents stopped making the payments she and her sister where treated as maids and frequently beaten. Protest to her family fell on deaf ears, for they would not question the benevolence of their religious order. She came to terms with the past by reowning her sadness and anger. She returned to fuller consciousness in the present. Fortunately the Crown prosecutor accepted my assessment of a temporary Dissociative state with automatic behavior rendering her not responsible for the theft, and dismissed the charge. The family rejoiced, for application for citizenship in a new country could have been jeopardized by such a trivial theft.

SOMNAMBULISM, is the deepest state of hypnosis, and is commonly know as sleep walking. A young man, a known sleep walker, awoke one night, drove 30-40 miles to a distant town, axed both of his in-laws to death and drove home. He had no memory of the event and was found not guilty by reason of the automatic behavior of somnambulism. This was a controversial legal decision for it acknowledges dissociation while excusing responsibility for a complex act of killing.

Where is the fine line between sanity and insanity, between levels of consciousness with awareness and responsibility for action and being totally dissociated without any self awareness or personal control? Can you do crazy things for a few minutes or hours and then return to full conscious awareness and normalcy? A policeman, under the stress of investigating a robbery, killed an innocent teenager in a dark alley. The plea was "automatism" due to the high level of stress. There had been a momentary dissociation and he fired his gun automatically. He was found not guilty by reason of temporary insanity, even though the period only lasted a few minutes. Where is the fine line between mental illness and responsibility? If you are aware of your actions and know the difference between right and wrong, are you legally responsible? And what if you suffer from some psychiatric illness, or have survived some traumatic background? The ethical dilemma rages on between "sick" or "bad", between "full awareness" and "dissociation." And, what of "impaired judgment" because of socially acceptable drugs or alcohol. Fortunately, the "Hostess Twinkie" defense attributing violent behavior to sugar intake was dismissed!

The Continuum of Awareness

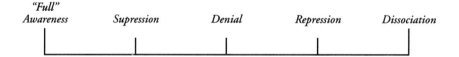

It is unlikely that anyone ever attains full awareness of himself or the external world. Nevertheless, we're always trying to be "more" or "in touch." The truth is that we are constantly trying to disconnect from life's painful experiences. When trauma or conflict happens we want to forget. Even memory causes pain and anxiety. Defense mechanisms against anxiety cover a wide range of avoidance techniques.

FULL AWARENESS is limited because of human brain capacity. We are never fully aware of everything. SUPPRESSION is the decision to consciously forget what we know, and the beginning of dissociation. DENIAL is the mind's defense mechanism to block awareness of an internal or external reality. You may have the information intellectually but emotionally you ignore its significance. "Sure I drink more than my friends, but I can hold my liquor. It doesn't affect my driving." Denial is truly a rejection of the truth. REPRESSION is an involuntary way of relegating to the unconscious mind unacceptable feelings or impulses. It is the putting away of unpleasant experiences as times goes on. DISSOCIATION is the disconnection from awareness of part of the self; an ego state with all its experience of behavior, emotions, body sensations, knowledge and memories.

As we look at the big picture of levels of consciousness where are we in control and responsible for our behavior?

The Continuum of Dissociation

Normal	Dissociative Episode	Atypical Dissociative Disorder	Post-Traumatic Stress Disorder	Somatoform Disorders	Dissociative Disorders	Dissociative Identity Disorder
- Hypnosis - Automatism - Daydreams	- Repression - Highway Hypnosis - Mystical Experience - Psychic Numbing - Sleep Disturbance	- Automatism (Sleep Walking) - Conduct Disorders - Depression - Anhedonia - Personality Disorders • Compulsive • Histrionic	- Shell Shock - Battle fatigue - Post Vietnam War Syndrome - Holocaust Survivor	- Conversion - Hypo-chondriasis - Somatization - Psycho-somatic Disease	- Psychogenic Amnesia - Fugue States - Depersonal-ization	- Multiple Personality Disorder

On the diagram of the Continuum of Dissociation, the traditional Dissociative Disorders include Somatoform Disorder, Dissociative

Disorders and the most pathological, Multiple Personality Disorder, now known as Dissociative Identity Disorder.

All healthy individuals dissociate. We all daydream and fantasize about pleasure, success and sexual encounters. This is the road to altered levels of consciousness, accessible through mental imagery and a natural state of self-hypnosis.

Post Traumatic Stress Disorder is a diagnostic category that emerged mainly from the Vietnam war. It is an evolutionary term growing from the "shell shocked" of World War I and the battle fatigued of World War II. Post Traumatic Stress Disorder is comprehensive and psychologically sophisticated. The essential feature was the development of characteristic symptoms following a major traumatic event, one beyond usual emotional experiences, ranging from rape or assault to man-made disasters of war, torture and death camps, to nature's wrath of flooding, earthquakes and fire. The major symptoms of Post Traumatic Stress Disorder range from numbness, withdrawal from the external world, emotional constriction and detachment, to intense flashbacks with the reliving of the trauma.

Somatoform Disorders were previously classified as Hysterical Disorders. The name was probably changed because of the sexist depiction of women, for the term Hysteria is derived from the Greek word, "Hysteros" meaning wandering uterus. This group of disorders have physical symptoms of illness with no demonstrable organic findings. There is a strong assumption of underlying psychological conflicts. Conversion is the process of converting emotional conflict into physical symptoms, such as fits, paralysis, seizures, blindness, loss of speech or abnormal movements and sensations. Conversion symptoms, common several decades ago, have generally been replaced by more refined psychological neurosis, due to the greater sophistication of the general public.

Somatization Disorders are recurrent physical complaints presented in a vague but exaggerated way without any physical basis. The complaints vary from aches and pains to sexual discomfort, cardiac stress, palpitations and dizziness. Hypchondriasis is the excessive preoccupation with these pains, and an unrealistic interpretation of devastating illness, as a sign of impending death. Psychosomatic diseases include demonstrable organic diseases like Rheumatoid Arthritis, Peptic Ulcer, or physiological disturbances like Migraine, where psychological stimuli contribute, initiate or exacerbate the physical condition.

The standard Dissociative Disorders, recognized by the American Psychiatric Association are Dissociative Amnesia, Fugue States, Depersonalization and Multiple Personality Disorder. Psychogenic Amnesia is a sudden inability to recall important personal information too extensive to be explained by ordinary forgetfulness. Fugue states are sudden unexpected travel away from your home or work with the inability to recall your past, often including assumption of a new identity. Depersonalization is an alteration in the perception of the self so that the usual sense of ones own reality is temporarily lost or changed. Simply, you don't know who you are. Derealization is when you don't recognize a familiar person, thing or place. One patient recognized the dissociation between herself and her body, which had been a way of surviving childhood abuse. But the on-going split interfered with sexual feelings, for she wasn't fully "there."

The most extreme and serious is Multiple Personality Disorder, diagnosed by the existence of one or more distinct personalities within the individual, each of which is dominant at a particular time and determines the patient's behavior. Today it is called Dissociative Identity Disorder since the individual is not many individuals but one fragmented single personality.

The Continuum of Dissociation covers a wide range from normal to abnormal and most of us during our life time will experience some degree of alteration of consciousness, amnesia, identity or behavior.

You go through the normal range of dissociation every day of your life. Waking up in the morning "still half asleep" or "out of it", a numb feeling that quickly disappears after that first cup of coffee. At times you carry on through the day with "psychic numbness", functioning like a robot without emotion and without pleasure. Simply doing your job.

How about daydreams? A great way to cope with boredom, a dull lecture or a tedious corporate meeting. You can have some fun without leaving your chair, and no one even knows you're "not there".

Automatic behaviors are part of daily living. Walking, eating and dressing are repetitive behaviors you do by rote. Driving a car, shifting gears, moving one foot back and forth from the gas to the brake is done without conscious thought. Hopefully, your alert mind is focusing on the road. You can even be in a mild state of hypnosis while driving, surprised at how quickly you've arrived at our destination, and hardly remember the trip or passing your favorite landmarks. Mystical experiences, religious enlightenment or out-of-body experiences, and contact with UFO's (unidentified flying objects), are dissociative experiences that periodically gain world attention. They are believed true by the observer but are based on a semi dream-like experience. My favorite is the "power nap." A few minutes in the ultradian zone refreshes me for the next activity. It is not really sleep as the level of awareness of outside reality is only decreased. Vague dream-like images and sensations quickly pass through my head leaving my body and mind refreshed and relaxed.

Where does normal dissociation cross over to impairment? When the periods of dissociation, either brief or prolonged, interfere with daily living and emotional relatedness. You cannot learn from life experience if you are not there.

The trigger of severe dissociation is major stress, childhood trauma or adult disaster. When trapped in overwhelming pain the only way out is to mentally detach, it is a fundamental defense for survival. Moving in and out of the dissociative states may be automatic and without personal control. To make it healthy, build in an off/on switch. Be in charge of yourself. Decide when to make dissociation adaptive and useful for stress management. In times of death and life crisis, it is crucial to cut off emotions to get things done. Sometimes it's necessary to cut off right brain feelings for left brain realistic and logical control.

Mapping

Draw a map of your inner parts. Imagine your very own personality pie with all your ego states, or draw all the personas within your total self. Do it spontaneously using color. Now look at each figure. Do they have eyes, mouth, fingers and toes? Are they incomplete or fully formed? Small or large? Where is their place in the picture? Whom do they associate with? Are they separate or attached? Do they seem to be on the right teams? Do you accept them all? Which ones do you want to get rid of? Now relax for a few minutes, meditate, gaze away, focus on your breathing or see a pretty color in your mind's eye. After a few moments come back and complete the drawing and be surprised at what you will discover.

CHAPTER THREE

Hypnotherapy

The mental imagery capabilities of the right brain with its marvelous pictures and deep emotions are the building blocks of hypnosis. The hypnotic state is a natural, altered state of consciousness with alertness. It brings you expanded sensory abilities, with visual and emotional access to the past. Like a zoom lens on a camera it can focus in on the details and avoid the distractions of the wide angle view of life. With increased concentration it can access the power of your imagination for creative and innovative solutions for your problems. This is the artful science of hypnotherapy.

My journey into hypnosis began in the days when I was a "real doctor." As a family physician, I made daily rounds at the hospital. One morning I met a surgeon leaving the hospital, carrying a bottle of intravenous fluid. He was taking it home to feed his wife who was five months pregnant and vomiting continuously. All medications had failed and intravenous glucose was the only way she could maintain nourishment. I asked if he had ever tried hypnosis. He said he hadn't and asked me if I knew anyone who could do it. Revealing my novice hypnotic abilities I agreed to help. His wife was an excellent hypnotic subject and went into a deep trance quickly. With a simple, direct suggestion that she stop vomiting, she did. I returned weekly to reinforce the hypnotic suggestion. She progressed and had an uneventful pregnancy, delivering a healthy child. We all celebrated the birth with a family dinner.

I used hypnosis in my obstetrical practice but had only moderate success in controlling labor pain. But there were some life saving experiences. I was on vacation and my medical colleagues were to cover my practice. When I returned I had a frantic call from a pregnant woman who had been vomiting continuously despite all the medications my colleagues had prescribed. I made an emergency house call and found her jaundiced and with an enlarged liver, a serious illness called Hyperemesis Gravidarum, the pernicious vomiting of pregnancy. In a stage of early liver failure, about 25% will die. I hypnotized her immediately and she stopped vomiting. For the first time in many weeks she took fluids. I admitted her to the hospital and replaced fluids intravenously. Fortunately her liver pathology subsided and she continued with an uneventful pregnancy and delivery. I was amazed by the success of hypnosis.

At that time I was also treating a young woman dying of secondary cancer of the breast, with excruciating back pain from metastases into her spinal vertebra. The medication was not controlling her pain and I suggested hospitalizing her for intravenous pain management. She wanted to die at home, surrounded by family. I hypnotized her and gave her pain management suggestions that helped enormously. She was now more responsive to the medication and died comfortably at home. My early naiveté came out during one of our reinforcement sessions. I left the post hypnotic suggestion that she felt so good she felt like walking. She tried and fell to the floor. The advanced disease had damaged the nerve to her legs. She rejected my apology, but thanked me for relieving her pain through hypnosis.

Previously I had used hypnosis only for relaxation and symptom control. When I became a psychiatrist it was difficult to blend hypnosis with my new role as a psychotherapist. My infrequent attempts were somewhat clumsy. I treated an obese woman by giving her a future mental picture of thinness. She never lost a pound, but thanked me, for she now saw herself as a much slimmer person, no longer preoccupied with obesity.

Periodically I explored hypnotherapy and Milton Erickson, the famous hypnotherapist was my teacher. Reading his books or looking at his movies only confused me. This strange man who spoke in a funny voice, with rambling words and scattered illogical thinking only put me to sleep. Later I realized that he had put me into a deep hypnotic trance. After reading the books of other professionals who had studied Milton Erickson, like Bandler and Grinder, I developed psychological insights into Dr. Erickson's hypnotherapy. With that knowledge I attended the first Milton Erickson conference in Phoenix, Arizona in 1980. Unfortunately Dr. Erickson had died the previous winter, at the age of 79. He was a brave man who had developed polio as a teenager and had been paralyzed and confined to bed for over a year. He learned to walk again by watching his younger sister take one step at a time. He recovered except for weakness in one leg. Tragically, later in life, he was again struck with a recurrence of Poliomyelitis and ended up in a wheelchair. We now know it was Post Poliomyelitis Syndrome. Many years after the initial damage from the polio virus, the nerves wear out. This didn't slow him down. Milton Erickson continued treating patients and teaching students. He gave his time freely and openly to anyone who came to his home in Phoenix, Arizona.

My days at the Milton Erickson conference were unforgettable. For two days I watched video tapes of his work and was enchanted, finally understanding Ericksonian hypnotherapy. This was my initiation and I decided to convert hypnosis into hypnotherapy. At the conference I heard his marvelous stories about his life and practice. Milton didn't talk for his first four years and people would ask, "What's wrong with your son? He's not speaking." His mother would answer, "Milton will talk, when he's ready." Shortly thereafter he began talking and never stopped, till the day he died.

There was always a twinkle in his eye and humor in his soul. It was impossible to tell if he was serious or playful. Through a combination of left brain brilliance and right brain imagination, he developed an extremely creative therapy. In one of his most creative moments he assigned a specific task to his patients. Go to the botany gardens, or climb Sqaw Mountain and look for some rare plant. He gave them the idea that in their journey they would discover the solution to their problem. Often, the patient came back with an exciting personal discovery. Everyone, including other therapists, thought Milton had deep insight and knew the answers they would find. Milton had no idea; he simply sent them on a journey to distract their rational, conscious mind and allow their unconscious to emerge and give directions.

Dr. Erickson's basic principle of therapy was to bypass the conscious mind. Through indirect hypnosis he talked directly to the unconscious mind. I have adapted his work in my right brain/left brain model. Firstly I listen to the left brain analysis, leading to an understanding of the problem. Then through mental imagery and hypnosis, I enter the right brain experiences and see what insights prevail.

A young man I had treated in the past returned for therapy to deal with the loss of a recent love relationship. He was exploding inside with rage at his former girlfriend for rejecting him and at times felt he could kill her. He became obsessed with the internal thoughts and began to see himself as a bad person because he wanted to harm her. His rational left brain knew that even though his internal raging child was potentially violent, he had never lost control. Through right brain mental imagery and self hypnosis he went back to a recent experience of anger. He then regressed to a seven year old child yelling at his father for beating him and his younger brother. He raged at his mother as well for not protecting him. The raging child of the past came into the present and was searching for resolution.

My work is a combination of Ericksonian hypnotherapy, the theory of Dissociation of Pierre Janet, Ego-State Therapy from Helen and Jack Watkins, Transformational Fantasy of Dr. John Schaffer, the Gestalt therapy of Fritz Perls, Eric Berne's Transactional Analysis and Cognitive Therapy developed by Dr. Aaron T. Beck. I've had a fascinating journey which I will share through my case studies.

We all dissociate to some extent. The normal range of cutting off is from anhedonic clicking out, or numbing out, to drifting off into fantasy and daydreams. This is a natural human condition, pathological only in extremes. In one of my professional workshops a therapist described her "numbing out" experience. It was beyond the normal, waking up in the morning feeling as if she got up on the wrong side of the bed, drugged and out of it. This "numbing out" occurred after visiting her parents' home. Her alcoholic father had been drinking for most of her life, but in the past few years had stopped. Now he was a good man. She liked him and felt that the past was over. Yet this clicking out occurred with each visit home and she was very uncomfortable, unable to understand the symptom. Paradoxically, her dissociation, protection against anxiety, occurring automatically in times of stress, was now an infringement on her joy of living.

During hypnotherapy I asked her to imagine herself going down a flight of stairs or up a flight of stairs or across a hallway to a room called the "Dissociative Work Room." When she entered this special room she found a table with chairs around it. "Sit in one of the chairs and look around the room and see whoever is there connected with your numbness." In her imagination she saw herself as a young child growing up in her parents' home. Dialoguing through the adult self, she reacquainted herself with her child. She re-experienced the fear of growing up in a home with an erratic, irrational, screaming, intoxicated father. Waiting for him to come home and never knowing his state of mind caused pervasive anxiety. He never beat her but filled her childhood with the psychological terror of a raging alcoholic. Paradoxically, when he was sober he was charming, pleasant and loving. As the adult woman revisited her seven or eight year old frightened child, they talked and acknowledged her horrible childhood. Now that dad was different, why couldn't they forget and forgive? At this very moment she numbed out. The mother was sitting around the table, and pleaded helplessness against this violent, raging husband. Her job was to keep the peace. The patient again numbed out. Surprisingly, the grandmother was sitting at the table, the father's mother. Grandmother shared the terrible ravages of the drinking tantrums and wild behavior as she too acknowledged this young girl's frightened childhood. Again the patient numbed out. A moment later the woman said to me, "There's something I don't want to tell you." "What?" I asked and she said, "My father's in the room. He's standing around the table." "Why didn't you want to tell me?" She answered, "Because I don't want him there." As a therapeutic coach I had my first entry into her process of resolution, possible change and recovery. "Well, let's get him out," I said. She said, "Great." At first she called out loud to her father, "Get out. Get out," but he didn't move. As she expressed her anger the numbness disappeared. I, as the coach, went along with this experience to help her do it more effectively, checking each time to see if her move was in harmony with her feelings. Finally she said, "He isn't leaving." I asked, "Well, what are you going to do?" Then she broke into a smile and said, "I just threw him out of the house." At this moment there was a shift in facial expression, from pasty gray to glowing red, filled with the radiant energy of excitement. Emerging from hypnosis she related how good she felt, never realizing how angry she had been at her father all these years. Of course, there were moments of anger, but she was too frightened to express these feelings less she be like her raging father. For her the childhood picture of anger was horrible, disgusting and terrifying. Paradoxically, by reowning her anger today she felt powerful. It was a gift she would never give up. There was a long slow journey ahead to accept her anger and adapt it into the effective, assertive ways she had never seen as a child.

Dissociative Table Technique [3]

The dissociative table is an exciting and valuable hypnotherapy technique designed by Dr. George Fraser, head of a stress disorder clinic. Dr. Fraser's creativity and innovation are matched only by his expertise in Scottish bagpipes. The dissociative table has the advantage of not only sensing different parts of you internally, but actually experiencing and seeing them as well. Dialoguing between each ego state, doing internal group therapy, can lead to resolution of conflict or trauma. Is it risk free? No, nothing is. Occasionally, the ego states emerge as separate and distinct, often appearing as multiple personality. A warning to any therapist: under the highly suggestible, imaginative state of hypnosis, the diagnosis of multiple personality is NOT valid. The diagnosis of Dissociative Identity Disorder can only be made by observing alters (alternate personalities) in a state of full consciousness, and not those states which were engaged merely through ego-state therapies.

A little more compulsive than Dr. Fraser, I added the word, work, and call it the Dissociative Work Table Technique, for it's crucial that patients work towards a goal to stay on track. A competent, professional man, with a compulsive personality style, conscientious, hardworking, analytical and insightful, was battling a lifetime of recurrent depression. With a flair up of depression, he came for brief intensive imagery therapy. Knowledgeable and sophisticated, he shared his left brain analysis of his recent depression, a family conflict highlighted by the recent estrangement of a son, a realistic major life crisis. All his understanding was futile for there was no shifting, no movement, no relief of his depression. After the induction into the hypnotic state he went down a flight of stairs to the dissociative work room to see who was connected with his terrible depression. His mother, sister and father were there. He talked to each member of his family, asking what they knew about his depression. The father spoke first, blaming a crazy mother. The mother then protested, claiming her son's depression was caused by living with a raving maniac of a father. The sister seemed distant, a non participant. As he listened to the family discussion he felt an excruciating headache like a cylinder ready to explode. I asked him to put a sound to his pain. I explained that by trial and error he could find a sound that would feel right and perhaps shift the experience in some way. He made an excruciatingly painful moan and began to cry. An image flashed by and he saw himself as a little boy sleeping in his mother's bedroom. His mother and father slept in different rooms. It was in the middle of the night, he was frightened, his mother's behavior was agitated, frenzied and he was confused. Later he discovered that she was mentally ill. Periodically she would run down the hall raging and screaming at her husband's bedroom door in a bizarre way that terrified him, but that didn't connect with the moaning sound. He continued moaning until another scene flashed by. He was awake in the middle of the night watching his mother. In her sleep she was crying out with the strange loud groans he was making in my office today. The little boy, hearing his mother's cry of agony, exploded into his own cry of sadness as he recognized her unhappiness. The burst of crying cleared his head and the headache disappeared.

Through the next week he continued with waves of sadness, a grieving that he had never done for his mother's sad life. As the mourning progressed his depression lifted. His mother had died that year. This was the underlying event that triggered an anniversary grieving of a long repressed and dissociated child's sadness for his mother's pain. In a follow up consultation a year later he remained free of depression, the first time ever.

Traumatic Abreaction

The intense emotional reaction that occurs under hypnotherapy is called abreaction. More than a memory, it's a reliving of a forgotten experience or a partially remembered experience. There is considerable controversy over this technique since the excruciating pain of reliving can be almost as painful as the original trauma itself. Is the abreaction therapeutic? I was giving a workshop on imagery and hypnotherapy at a convention on Multiple Personality and Dissociative Disorders in Chicago and attended some of the other lectures. At one lecture a fine speaker strongly criticized abreaction as a dramatic retraumatizing event with no therapeutic value. He presented his case so well that I walked out thinking he was right. In the next lecture I heard another experienced clinician present the opposite case, that abreaction of the trauma was essential to the process of healing. I walked out of that lecture thinking he was right. Puzzled, I knew that two opposite approaches to the same problem could not be right. I then remembered the rabbi's wise words while adjudicating a conflict. He replied, "You're right," to each of the arguments. An observing student protested, "Rabbi, it's impossible that two plaintiffs with opposite arguments can both be right. And the rabbi replied, "You're right too." Then I realized that I too was right.

But I remained troubled. In the first case of the nurse with suicidal anxiety the regression to childhood sexual abuse definitely retraumatized her. Another patient doing Gestalt work imagined her sexually abusive father in an empty chair. Previously she had discussed the sexual abuse by her father, but this was the first experience using mental imagery where she confronted him. Her rage and pain exploded with such intensity that she began to hyperventilate, develop tetany, with spasm and paralysis of the hands and fingers and twitching of the face. This terrifying physical reaction triggered an asthmatic attack, compounding her distress. After considerable time re-breathing through a paper bag she calmed down, reintegrating into the present. Was this effective healing psychotherapy? No, for the abreaction was out of control. Paradoxically, hypnosis came to my rescue. I had previously thought that adding hypnosis to mental imagery could open deeper access to the unconscious mind. Strangely, I discovered that mental imagery alone was as effective, but through hypnosis I could build in automatic protection to control the abreaction. With a safe induction I and the patient could stop an abreaction as if it were a movie or video, edit it, add a scene, change the dialogue, correct distorted thinking, replace false belief systems; and then start the movie again. With this discovery the abreaction became therapeutic and rewarding, giving the patient the opportunity to do trauma and conflict resolution without re-tramatization.

Hypnotic State

Another therapeutic paradox: I ask patients not to let their thoughts intrude, to give up control by putting aside their left brain logical adult ego and their judgmental controlling parent ego state. Let the child run free. Bizarre, yet I'm promising them more control than they had. No more paradoxical than Fritz Perl's remark, *"Lose your mind and come to your senses."* If you give up control could you go crazy? Again, the answer is no. Let me explain. First, the hypnotic state is a natural but different state of consciousness, an alert state with an increased capacity to concentrate and focus attention, like a zoom lens on a camera. In the hypnotic state senses are sharper, with increased ability to concentrate on the images of the right brain, the unconscious mind. No therapist or hypnotist produces the hypnosis. This is a natural meditative state omnipresent in some more intensely than others. Think personally. While driving a car, how often do you drift off into other thoughts or fantasy and shortly you've arrived at your destination surprised how fast the time went? Well, you've been in an hypnotic state. How many times do you doze off, but you're not asleep, with all kinds of images and fantasies going through your mind? That's daydreaming, another example of the mild hypnotic state. Of course we've all had the experience of being at a lecture and drifting off to some other place. But we feel as if we're there, in a suspended state of relaxed, tranquil disconnection. There is scientific evidence for the hypnotic state. In the day/night circadian rhythm there is an ultradian rhythm occurring every 90 minutes of drowsiness and tranquillity, opening up the hypnotic state. How many of us in the middle of the afternoon feel sleepy and crave a caffeine lift? That's the ultradian rhythm kicking in. Give yourself a few minute's "power nap," you'll feel refreshed and relaxed. That's self hypnosis, a natural human state. You create the trance, the hypnotist, like a coach, helps you enter it.

Safe Hypnotic Induction

I will describe a safe induction to access the auto-hypnotic state. Sit back, relax and gaze upwards at your forehead and gradually close your eyes. With a positive eye roll, judged by the degree of the eye roll upwards and eyes converging, I evaluate hypnotic ability. The more sclera or white showing, the greater the hypnotic ability. By focusing on regular abdominal breathing you will gently relax and begin the process of self hypnosis. Ask your thoughts not to intrude and even imagine your adult thinking ego and judge ego sitting back and watching. Your rational adult and internal judge can come in at any time if they sense any difficulty whatsoever. Now, I recommend you find a safe place in your mind's eye where you can go at any time for relaxation, security, protection or rejuvenation. You can speak at any time under hypnosis. Nevertheless, let's build in a second set of communications with hand signals called ideomotor responses. Ideomotor signaling (ideo = idea; motor = movement) is believed to tap a deeper level of consciousness with recognition of disturbing events. Which finger will move with a yes response to questions or a no response to questions? Make a stop sign, on the same hand, which you can use any time you wish to end this journey into self hypnosis and return fully integrated to the present. Now build an emotional switch in your mind's eye, a dimmer switch that you can turn up or down, degree by degree, to modify the intensity of any experience.

Containment is essential. Psychiatrists and patients alike look for intense emotional experiences as a quick recovery. Spontaneous abreactions, or instant reliving of past trauma, may be overwhelming and impair the opportunity for therapeutic intervention. A containment devise is needed to store painful experiences until you're ready to work with them. It's important to have things under control. Imagine a personal storage container or special place where you can prevent overflow or too much on your plate. See yourself putting things away until you're ready to deal with them, one thing at a time. Now create a high tech interactive television in your mind's eye, and check that you have all the TV controls available. On the screen you can watch any life experience you've ever had and you, the survivor of all your past, can interact with any past experience and change it in any way that fits or feels right.

As you're relaxing you can hear everything; in fact, all your senses are very alert. However, you will notice the hypnotic state by a change in body sensation. You may feel a little lighter or a little heavier. If there's a sense of lightness in one hand, it may feel like rising without any effort on your part. If there's a sense of heaviness, you can sense it in your body or your eyelids. You are now in an hypnotic trance, able to focus attention and explore conflicts using mental imagery. More than visualization, imagery includes feelings and all the sensations of touch, smell, taste and sound. The laws of imagination, different from the laws of logic, are based on emotions that fit or feel right. The imaginative movie, fantasy, day dream or video stops when you're stuck. If the images move or shift, then you're on track, a psychological journey of exploration, discovery and healing has begun.

Ego strengthening is the first hypnotic journey to discover your past experience of happiness, success or joy. Recapturing your positive experience develops a resource for strength and hope that you can use in conflict resolution. Many traumatized patients find the search for past pleasure futile, quickly recalling an experience of childhood pain. The psychotherapy has begun with a racing start; fortunately, all the controls are in place and the power brakes working well.

The hypnotic induction for safety and protection can manage any abreaction, or reliving a painful experience, and protect you from re-traumatization. If you've taken the induction, you probably feel peaceful and tranquil. Some of my patients find this state so pleasant they are reluctant to come out of it. No concern, for the natural rhythm of the hypnotic state ends spontaneously. Due to the time restrictions of a therapeutic session, the therapist cannot leave the patient in a trance for prolonged periods. If they refuse my suggestion to return to the here and now I may remind them of their distended bladder, or bowel pressure that may require conscious intervention, or simply suggest that they sit in the waiting room until they are fully alert.

Affect and Somatic Bridge

Before I use hypnotherapy we examine the problem in detail. Most patients have partial recollection of an early childhood trauma. Through conscious left brain analyses we discuss the conflict. When we've gone as far as we can go, we're ready to use hypnotic or guided imagery techniques. Guided imagery is another term for self hypnosis, but it's the patient that does the guiding, or the writing of the script. The therapist is simply a director, or a coach helping them do it better. The next stage is controlled abreaction, going back to re-experience the event. There are three entries. One is regression, having the patient go back to an earlier time or age when the event occurred. Another, which I've shared, is the dissociative work table with its internalized form of group therapy, and the third, and the most fascinating, is called, "Affect or Somatic bridge." This is a technique that John and Helen Watkins perfected over many years of hypnotherapy. Wonderful teachers, they mix charm and expertise in a humanistic and therapeutic way. A beautiful blend of fine people and academic brilliance. The affect (meaning feeling), and somatic (meaning body sensation), is a simple technique. If at any time during our work there is a painful or disturbing body experience, or an emotion that seems inappropriate or excessive, I help the patient move into a light hypnotic state. I would say, "Use your body sensation, or emotion, as a bridge to the past. Gently, go backwards in time, across an imaginary time line to the earliest experience of the present pain. Respect any image or experience in your mind's eye without censoring, or trying to figure it out. As the journey goes back in time different layers may be uncovered. Accept and work through each level until the original source is discovered."

An academic in psychotherapy had finally resolved significant turmoil and was now experiencing a year of pleasure and success. Paradoxically, he was disturbed by the feeling of anxiety that accompanied his new found joy, as if he was waiting for the axe to drop or "waiting until they find out" that he's a phony. When I complimented him on his achievement he blushed with embarrassment, which quickly turned to sadness as he cried. The automatic thought was, "I'm grieving my mother's loss of a son," namely himself, for in the last year he had completely detached from his parents for personal survival. In his mind's eye he heard his mother saying, "I'm sorry," and he replied with forgiveness. At the next session as he grieved the loss of the relationship with his mother, different scenes of mother recurred and his mood shifted from sadness to anger. Suddenly he felt nauseated and I began a somatic bridge focusing on his nausea, taking him backwards in time. He went back and re-experienced a recent migraine attack. Using the headache as another somatic bridge we went to a deeper layer, back to age five or six, when he would force himself to vomit to avoid going to school. He was a terrified, frightened little boy. He suddenly knew why. He had been emotionally neglected by his mother, who was too busy with his younger brother, and treated him as a bad child. His father, an alcoholic, repeatedly beat him. A loving grandmother, aware of his neglect, complained bitterly to his mother. Back in the present he consciously processed his imagery journey. For the first time he understood his terrified and abandoned child, an inner child that he had forgotten, repressed and dissociated in the grown up man through migraine headaches and a left brain, analytical personality that left his emotions behind.

A woman, searching for a comfortable, safe place found herself floating in a boat in the Greek islands. In the middle of this magnificent experience her lower lip began to quiver, an uncomfortable feeling beyond her control. Through a somatic bridge experience, she returned to the scene in the Greek islands and the trembling of her lip recurred. "Focus on your emotions, increase the intensity," I suggested. She did and her arms began to shake. "Now cross a bridge in time back to an earlier period where this first began." Within a few moments she imagined herself in an early childhood scene, in her parents' bedroom with her father lying face down on the bed, nude to his waist. She was massaging his upper back, evidently helping Daddy relieve some pain. When she re-experienced this childhood scene she shook even more, feeling something was wrong. Her adult ego state was aware of sexual overtones that she couldn't understand as a small child. Her body began to shake more and more, turning into a full blown anxiety reaction. I suggested she let her imagination do a healing image and within a few seconds a big smile crossed her face. She said, "I now see myself at the beach with my Mom and Dad. My Dad is in the water playing whale, and I'm on his back, we're having a great time. It's great family fun." The scene was over. She ended the hypnotic experience and returned to the alertness of the here and now, beaming and glowing with pleasure. With her insight that the playfulness was not sexual in any way, but simply a daughter having a lot of fun with her father, and symbolic of the close and loving relationship they had until he died.

Resolution and self discovery often comes with a bonus. She felt better than she ever had, and had a sense of wholeness. It was as if these repressed memories caused unconscious sexual conflict, invading and intruding in every contact with her Dad and other men. Now they were resolved. She could accept the wonderful relationship she had with her father, the pleasure of being her Dad's daughter, as well as her sexuality.

A woman, a drama instructor for a children's group, was preparing them for a skit at a Remembrance Day ceremony. She began to notice an unusual irritability toward the young children, something that had not been present before. Seeing this as excessive and inappropriate, she began to explore it in therapy, doing an affect bridge. Initially, she went back to the irritability at the children, and then let her emotions take her into the past. She went back to a seven year old sleeping in her parent's bedroom. She is awakened by a loud noise. Her father appears to be hurting her mother. She is aware that he is forcing her to have sex. She wants to scream out, but doesn't. After realizing how angry she is, she begins to cry with the deep, deep sadness of a little girl. She then recalled the story of her Dad. He had come home from the war a year or two earlier, released as a hero. Strangely, he didn't fit in and became irritable and withdrawn. (Probably unrecognized Post Traumatic Stress Disorder.) She didn't have her Dad. She understood this now. She lived the experience of what it was like to be him, coming home and finding he was a misfit. While she was empathetic for him, there was a new dimension of sadness for herself, for she never did recover the Daddy she lost. As she grieved for herself, for her childhood's loss of the father she wanted, she ended her therapeutic experience and came back to the present. She then connected it to today's activity. Her irritability toward the children during the preparation of their Remembrance Day skit brought back memories. On an unconscious level the event symbolized the return of her father from the war. The joy of playful children triggered her sadness which she covered up with irritability. Grieving the loss, she felt an energy to return to teaching drama to the children. The past was removed from her eyes. Now, in the present, she was free to move on.

Anger is a protest to deprivation, lack of basic needs, abandonment and aloneness, to losses of self and others, and, especially, to dreams. Surprisingly, its easier to feel the anger than tolerate the underlying sadness of loss.

Regression

Simple hypnotic regression to re-experience an early childhood experience can be therapeutic. A woman recalled the incestuous relationship she'd had with her father. There was no memory loss nor amnesia for she could clearly recall most of the incidents. She felt ashamed and depressed, blaming herself for letting it go on until puberty. She felt ashamed and called herself bad because she didn't stop it. Her left brain had most of the facts, but her inner child had created a distorted belief system. Under hypnotic regression she re-experienced one of the incestuous acts. She could feel her father upon her, smell his sweaty body and bad breath. She suddenly felt the oppressive weight of his body and recognized how big he was and how small she was. When the abreaction was complete she returned to left brain consciousness and processed new insights. "It was not my fault. I was only a little girl. For the first time I realize how much bigger he was than me, I couldn't have stopped him."

When a patient recalls a childhood period of distress we discuss it in detail, attempting to understand its significance today. After comprehensive analysis I recommend an imagery journey to the past. Under hypnosis the patient regresses to an earlier age and relives a specific experience which may or may not have happened, an experience that may be purely symbolic. New emotional, visual, sensory, or intellectual revelations are experienced that often take surprising directions. Therapeutic interventions may be done within an episode, especially corrections of cognitive distortions or false belief systems. New imagery may be added to express suppressed emotions or complete the Gestalt. When a patient returns to the here and now we begin conscious processing, or analysis, of the experience, often adding new memories to previously incomplete ones. New insights are formed, leading to different directions for potential change.

A middle-aged man recalled childhood trauma of being beaten, threatened and ridiculed by an older sister. Under hypnosis he went back to age twelve and relived a creative, artistic experience. He was sitting in his room drawing a train. He was looking out the window at the station across from his home. At this point his sister came into the room and criticized his drawing. He threw the drawing away. Recognizing that he hadn't drawn since age twelve he went back into the mental imagery and re-edited the scene. He took the drawing, hung it up on the fridge, and felt a glow of pride.

An ambitious, successful business woman complained of boredom. "When I was a child, I was creative and excited. Now I am wealthy and empty." "Let's go back to this child," I suggested and she quickly re-experienced her artistic little girl, excitedly painting and drawing. This quickly turned to sadness. In a flashback, she heard her raging alcoholic mother. She saw herself run into her room and paint feverishly to escape the anguish of the moment. She now realized that the present dissociation of her artistic self was an attempt to avoid this childhood pain. The ego state had all the anxiety and sadness of her traumatic childhood.

A very competent, successful businessman was separating from his wife. He had found genuine and realistic relief, but paradoxically, he was overcome by a fear of aloneness. In imagery flashbacks he went back to a childhood experience. He was twelve and was hiding behind a furnace with a flashlight. He caught his father having sex with his younger sister. He had suspected by the way his father treated his sister when he was intoxicated. This night he had taken a flashlight and hid behind the furnace. His father came down, undressed and took out his penis. He had his young daughter fondle him while he touched her. The patient jumped out and began to scream. His father chased him around the basement. The boy ran outside. Later, the father, in a pathetic way, apologized to the son. The young man never recovered from the discovery and emotionally detached from his family. He found himself all alone.   At this point he began to cry, recognizing the tremendous personal abandonment that had followed this horrifying incident. His sister had thanked him, when she was an adult, for saving her life. He never recovered from growing up emotionally alone and today felt this sadness again.   Initially, wanting to get rid of it, he finally accepted it as realistic, and acknowledged his twelve year old courageous young boy. Obviously, the twelve year old still existed there in the grown man about to leave his marriage.

While working with regressed experiences therapy is more involved with the narrative nature of the memories, rather than historical accuracy. I remind patients that without collaboration they cannot be sure that their recollections are a hundred percent accurate. Without undo emphasis on validation, the imagery processing of the past trauma to resolution, has been therapeutic and rewarding.

CHAPTER FOUR

Trauma & Conflict Resolution

Hanna's Story

Hanna is in her early thirties, married with two children. Sex was never exciting, but three years ago she suddenly became anxious during lovemaking. Puzzled, reflecting on her past, she remembered a sexual assault at age ten. A friend's father, during a stay over, had sex with her. She was ashamed to tell anybody, especially since she had liked it. There were other minor incidents. There was an uncle who always touched her in the wrong places, but everyone knew to stay away from Uncle Joe. There had been an attempted rape at age seventeen. She had screamed and the man ran away. A year before, a friend's father, while putting sun tan lotion on her, had fingered her vagina. While she had never forgotten the past she began reviewing it again, searching for the cause of the recent anxiety during sex. When her husband touched her, the memories increased. There were periodic flashbacks of herself as a young child, and an incident where her grandfather touched her genitals. As time went on these scenes became clearer and sex more distasteful. As far as she could recollect she was two or three when her grandfather began this sexual touching. It had continued until his death when she was four. More scenes returned. Once her grandmother walked in while the grandfather was touching her and yelled, "You're a dirty child," then walked out. Recently, on her way to a company Christmas party, there was the return of an old social anxiety, with self consciousness and feelings of inadequacy. Explanations failed, the symptoms persisted, and she felt socially out of place at the celebration. During hypnotherapy in a group session, she went back to the experience of a few days earlier and re-experienced her poor self worth and social distress. She then took an affect bridge to the past and the imagery took her back to childhood. Her grandfather had forced her to perform oral sex and she was vomiting. The grandmother came in at this moment and looked at her with disdain. The grandfather spoke up, "She's sick to her stomach. I'll look after her." The grandmother silently turned and walked away. The patient burst out crying with these words, "I didn't count." Her grandmother had failed to protect her. The past had leaked into the Christmas party of today and the old script, "I don't count" had resurfaced. I suggested she test out a healing image. The adult survivor imagined comforting the child, but the "don't count" belief prevailed. While not particularly religious the image of God appeared before her and she said, "I didn't even count with God because he didn't protect me. He didn't protect me because I was bad." She then recalled a spiritual poem where a good man was asking God why he had been abandoned on the seas of turmoil and God replied, "There was only one set of foot prints in the sand because I was carrying you." The patient smiled and said, "God was there, for her grandfather died suddenly and prematurely when she was four, saving her from ongoing sexual abuse. Reassured and calm, she accepted the new script that she did "count."

As the memories came back, sex with her husband had become disgusting and revolting. After months of giving in she finally said no and stopped intercourse, explaining the need to heal herself. During therapy, the full story gradually emerged. She questioned the memory of such a young child. Was this a false memory? Her father corroborated her story of the grandfather's sexual abuse. Her mother had told him of her own sexual abuse and her daughter's abuse by the grandfather. He also confirmed that the grandfather had abused others. Mother knew but didn't take action. How could she have exposed her own child to this monster of a man? How could she leave her at the grandparents' home? Her mother died a few years before the memories returned.

Each psychotherapy session began with left brain recollections, discussion and understanding, followed by right brain imagery, experiences and hypnotherapy. Each time we explored her trauma the anxiety became overwhelming and her body shook uncontrollably, convulsing like a seizure. Through hypnosis we were able to control the intensity of the upset, by turning down the dimmer switch. We did healing work. The first piece of work revolved around talking to her deceased mother in a way she'd never done before. Imagining her mother in an empty chair, she expressed all the anger at her neglect. Down in her workroom, at the dissociative table, she frequently spoke to her mother, asking, "Why did you take us to his home when you knew the terrible things he had done to you and your sister?" All mom could say was, "I was afraid and I'm sorry." She sensed her mother's sadness and cried for her pain. After venting her rage she then understood her mother's insecurity and forgave her. She wrote her a passionate, detailed letter and shared all her anger. She came to forgiveness and expressed her undying love to her mother who had been a beautiful woman. Grieving for a mother who died much too young and feeling the rage of childhood neglect was a horrendous experience. It was a process that took months to complete. Waves of sadness returned for a long time afterwards. Now our job was to complete the movie by resolving the past abuse.

It was a monumental task. She was a gentle, soft-spoken woman. Facing her rage at her grandfather, and at other men who had sexually abused her was exhausting. After each confrontation her shaking subsided. She had vented her killer rage and opened aggressive energy for resolution, torn between the urge of killing her attempted rapist, and being reasonable. She had the police jail him for a long time. After many Gestalt confrontations with her grandfather, imagining him in the present, she killed him, cut off his penis, and stuck it in his mouth. The rage boiled at her father, who had left the family when she was seven years old. She also raged at her girlfriend's father, who had seduced her at age ten, and at the over sexed uncle who fondled the children. The reowning of her rage was certainly the opposite of her basic character trait of excessive niceness. All the fantasies paid off. Now she could put the past behind her. She reowned her anger in day to day living, especially in her stressful executive job. Now she was able to stand up and speak when she was overloaded with feelings. She became confident and secure, pleased with her affective assertion.

Was she cured? No. There was still a major sexual block. The movie was incomplete. The final piece of work focused on coming to terms with herself. She had to acknowledge her pain, and grieve the sadness of her childhood. Then she needed to accept this child, for the initial reaction was to get rid of her, to disown her, because she felt that this was a "bad" child. Rationally, she knew she wasn't responsible for the sexual assaults, nonetheless, she blamed herself. Shame was the last obstacle, for when she was touched by her grandfather and some of the other men, she had liked it. How could she have enjoyed such disgusting acts? Intellectually she understood that it was normal physiology for the body to respond to pleasurable touch. As a young child hungry for affection, any attention at all would be welcome. After her father left, she became vulnerable to any caring man. This was the most difficult piece of therapeutic work. Finally, she accepted that as a little girl she couldn't be expected to understand. She forgave the inner child and reowned her. Not easily soothed, this child wanted a guarantee that it would never be abandoned or left open to assault again. The adult who had survived the trauma promised to protect her, but the inner child would not believe her. They both came up with a fantasy solution that worked. This woman needed a loving, caring parent. Her mother was never effective and her father had abandoned her. There were no good parent models to look after this inner child. Watching TV reruns of Dr. Kildare, she chose him as the interject (or was it Dr. Birnbaum?) to became the benevolent parent who would protect this frightened child from harms way.

This woman blossomed and grew, free of anxieties and depression, and happy with herself despite continuous problems. Her sexual feeling returned. But she had outgrown her husband. She left him, with minimal separation anxiety, intensely confident and excited about her newfound self. In the last scene of her life movie all the different parts of her, the three year old baby, the ten year old who was sexually abused by a friend's father, a fat teenager, the adult, came together in a big hug. They were overjoyed at the integration of self and resolution of the childhood trauma. Now she was emotionally free to live in the present. But she would never forget the past. "The good news, bad news scenario." I warned her that the past will always come back, usually under stress, but only briefly, for the new self is too exciting ever to be lost.

The therapeutic purpose of my work with mental imagery and hypnotherapy is to make a movie in the mind's eye of the conflicts or traumas of the patient's life. Scenes from life's experiences must be completed in a way that is more emotional than intellectual, more imaginative than rational, more experiential than simply words. The scenes are essentially symbolic and flow easily when the patient is on the right track. The goal is a dramatic resolution of the conflicts, not the search for the absolute truth of past memories. Distorted thinking is edited of self blame, personal devaluations, and false belief systems that were developed by the child at the time of abuse are worked through and corrected. The movie offers effective, imaginative healing that works. Once the movie has been played it's important to end it, and put it away. The patient writes the script and plays all the parts. The psychiatrist is only the director, helping the patient do the work effectively. The ending is crucial, for only then can you say goodbye to the past.

The Last Scene

A man in his late fifties had suffered a lifetime of chronic depressions with many hospitalizations. His story was tragic, one that had continued throughout his childhood. His father rejected him because he was a bastard son. He had been conceived during an affair his mother had while married to his father. Her husband stayed in the marriage, but scapegoated the son. He physically, mentally and sexually assaulted him. This man had reviewed every detail of the sexual abuse during many hospitalizations and long-term psychotherapy. Nevertheless, his depressions continued. I was the last therapist to see him and I felt he had experienced all the sadness and anger, and clarified the puzzle of his terrible childhood. The movie was over. But the ending was missing. How could he put to rest such a horrible childhood? We focused on his strong sense of survival. In spite of recurrent depressions he had worked, married, and fathered a son. His childhood trauma was his motivation to be a devoted father. His relationship with his own son was filled with love and pride. He chose this as the final scene. The movie was over, the childhood pain was now behind him and he looked forward to a depression free life, a life he created.

Dissociation of early life experiences is a survival technique to avoid pain. A small child is helpless against assault by a big person. Cutting off is the only way to cope. If you continue dissociation as an adult, you're functioning with less than your full capacity. If you dissociate completely you become a fragmented personality. The incidence of Dissociative Identity Disorder is five times more common in women than men. Sexual, physical or emotional abuse is the underlying cause in over 95% of cases, a terrible and surprising reflection of modern society. Does all childhood trauma produce Dissociative Disorders? It varies, depending on the capacity of the child to dissociate, the nature of the abuse and frequency of repetition. The more frequent the more severe the illness. Who is the perpetrator? A close friend or parent causes confusion and ambivalent feelings. Self blame is safer than protest, as protest may threaten a needed relationship. Lack of protection, loss of trust, and absence of a caring parental figure, leaves the child vulnerable, powerless and terrified. To keep the past from getting in your eyes, go back, rediscover and heal the injured child.

I was surprised when patients re-experienced the traumatized part of themselves. Distorted thinking and false belief systems made them see their inner child as bad, or weak and they rejected it. If your leg is hurt do you heal it or cut it off?

Healing the damaged inner self is a formidable task. A divorced woman went back to nursing after her family had grown up. She slipped into a deep depression despite good stress management techniques. She thought the depression was a reaction to the pressure of her new career. We went into the dissociative workroom and looked for someone to help with her depression. There was only one person, her sad little girl. When I asked what chair she was sitting in she said, "She's sitting in all the chairs." As we explored the sadness of this little girl she discovered a lonely inner child. "What do you want to do with her?", I asked. "Get rid of her. She's interfering with my life. She stops me from getting on with my career. I don't want her." True to my Ericksonian strategies, I helped her get rid of the little girl. In mental fantasies or under hypnosis, the right brain follows the laws of the imagination. Any action or feeling has to feel right. If it does the image moves like a waking dream or a movie. If you're off track the movie stops and you're stuck. We tried to get rid of this little girl, give her away for adoption, push her out of the room. It didn't work. Finally the patient unfolded her arms and reached out to embrace all the lonely children. They jumped into her arms and she smiled. Everybody felt happy. As she emerged from the hypnotic work she consciously processed her experience. Left brain interpretation follows spontaneously upon the completion of a successful mental imagery journey. She said, "I'm very lonely. I was devoting my whole life to school. It's not very rewarding. I'll have to expand my relationships. I can't just study day and night." The insight and inner acceptance lifted her depression. A single parent, who had successfully raised her family, she still had personal gaps to fill. The children were grown up and gone and she was scared, but free to explore.

A patient in intensive therapy protested, with tongue in cheek, "I know I'm getting better, but why do I hurt more than I ever have?" Reowning his physically abused and neglected inner child was a twenty-four hour a day ordeal. "I feel exhausted, caring for this stubborn, angry, mistrustful part of me. I need relief." Through mental imagery he found a fine, caring day school to help share his burden. A woman, sharing a similar dilemma, found a playroom in her house where all her internal children could play. Sometimes, she would sit and watch, or leave them alone as she got on with the necessary activities of life. We all need rest from stress of any kind, and an imaginative respite is in order.

Back From The Present

It is not enough to reown dissociated ego states, feel repressed emotion, relive and grieve the losses of childhood. We need someone to nurture and protect this abused child. If we are lucky, there's a benevolent grandparent, a caring teacher, or some substitute as an effective, loving, caring internal parent ego state. Paradoxically, healing is most often done by the grown up who survived the childhood trauma. The adult goes back in time in imaginative ways to comfort and protect this inner child. In the fantasy, the adult has to stop the abuse, for the child must no longer be traumatized. Through internal negotiation between the surviving adult and the abused child, trust must be rebuilt. Too often the adult blamed the helpless child. Ashamed of the assault it rejects the victim. Through realistic understanding the child's pain is acknowledged. Respecting and honouring its experiences initiates the process of reowing and lifting dissociation. Back to the present these integrated ego states can now work as a effective team. Strangely enough, the fantasy works! It allows resolution, completion and an ending of a past that keeps haunting the present. Now you are free to live here and now, not there and then.

A woman was sharing the excitement of her daughter's first pregnancy. Her daughter was only sixteen and single. Nevertheless, this woman talked about how happy she was for her daughter. She accepted the pregnancy and was looking forward to helping raise the child. I said that this was an unusual response, as the young girl had just lost her boyfriend. This took her back to an early experience when she too, at sixteen, was pregnant. She lost the baby at six months. Subsequently, she married her boyfriend. As we went back and looked at the video of her first pregnancy, she reviewed a few scenes, mainly of the rejection and condemnation of her mother, who criticized her in a very cruel way, labeling her as "bad." She felt ashamed as she did in the scene with her minister where his solution was, "They should get married." She was very sad as she saw no support, only condemnation. Strangely enough, as she emerged from the visual imagery, she talked about how no one was there for her during her pregnancy. She said she was pleased to be there for her daughter. At this point, in full consciousness, she had a major abreaction of happy/sad. Symbolically, she realized that being there for her daughter was also being there for herself twenty years before. This was a very satisfying moment, for after twenty years she finally put an end to her first pregnancy and resolved the experience. Now, all she needed was an ending ritual or ceremony that acknowledged the end of an experience she had carried with shame for twenty years.

Quid Pro Quo

Quid Pro Quo means something for something, or let's make a deal. A patient, successfully completing years of psychotherapy, was finally integrating her last piece of work, the reowning of her neglected, physically battered, inner child, and developing a caring parent. Now she was on her way, feeling free of depression and enjoying life. In the final step of saying goodbye to her past, and her therapy, she suddenly felt she was going crazy. A roller coaster of emotions exploded and she raced from anxiety to depression, over reacting with paranoia to the external world. Small issues were exaggerated to catastrophe. An observing adult was aware of the excessive and inappropriate reactions. Listening to her thoughts, she heard a yelling critical parent, ranting and raving all over the place, "You can't do it." "You're bad." "You're going crazy." All the old tapes were playing again, and she recognized that she had projected this critical judge onto friends, colleagues and her boss. Internally dialoguing, the critical judge protested that he had protected her all these years from going crazy and now she would certainly lose control without him. She recognized that the original terrorizor was now terrified. She tried to get rid of him, with a deal. "You've been working twenty-four hours a day for all these years, why don't you retire to the farm you've always wanted? I'll visit you, and certainly call for help when I need it." The judge accepted the deal. Calmly and at peace, she now visualized him on a pig farm, happy in all that manure.

When different parts of your personality clash, when all the "shoulds" conflict with the "don't want tos", when the mean part and the nice one disagree, when the desire for action is overcome by the fear, it is time to invite all these parts to your mediation table, and do internal group therapy. Let them talk to each other, listen to all the opinions, and make a deal. You can do external Gestalt therapy by imagining all your ego states in empty chairs around you. Play each part until you work out the problem. Perhaps a new idea or feeling emerges, or an election is held and the new chairperson of the board, hopefully the adult, is elected to manage your corporation. One young man hated work, but needed the money. He made a deal with his internal child who wanted to play, ski and have fun. "Look, I need the money to feed us," he said, "and then I'll be able to buy you even more of the things you like." The kid picked a new bike, and a deal was made. Now he goes to work without complaint, riding his bicycle both ways.

Any deal involves compromise and trade offs. But the payoff is a final cessation of the internal bickering, procrastination and waffling. Ambivalence, indecision and stuckness shift to action.

Fairy Tales Can Come True

An accomplished professional woman, raising her family as a single parent, complained of rage attacks and a roller coaster of emotions from anxiety to depression, interspersed with strange periods of emotional detachment. Bright and insightful, she attributed her symptoms to the high stress of being a working mother. Her hair trigger of irritability, occasionally verging on the physical assault of her children, set off a danger signal which she recognized as behavior that was excessive and inappropriate. Her past history revealed ongoing childhood physical abuse by her father and repeated emotional and physical abuse by controlling men, especially her ex-husband. In the first phase of therapy we discussed her past and present, synthesizing her life story. Then we began mental imagery and hypnotherapy, highlighted by vivid, dramatic fairy tales, blended with her past experiences. The Trial of Her Father, The Dance, and The Magical Self spontaneously emerged, blending with each other in a fascinating journey of discovery.

In the first session at the dissociative work table an organizing, observing adult sat at the head of the table. Around the table were a small terrorized child, an older scrapper and a playful child. I spoke to each part separately and asked who they were and what part they played in the adult's life. As each part spoke, it took on a personality of its own. The terrorized child curled up in a ball, appearing to be four or five, and cried out in fear about her Daddy hitting her. She shook uncontrollably with anxiety. When I asked her to watch herself on the interactive television screen the pain decreased to tolerable levels. As she calmed down, she asked why her father was always hitting her. The seven year old scrapper, in an angry loud voice, called out, "I don't know why she's crying. I was the one who took all the blows." This was a tough and defiant ego state. A playful, happy, smiling, bubbly child didn't get involved in this argument. She said she was the forest child, "I play outside. I never go in that house." Periodically, the mature, confident adult observer expanded the historical information, or talked for some of the child ego states. I was struck by the completeness of each child part, each with its own voice, body gestures and beliefs. I felt as if I was watching a play full of distinct characters, except they were all one. I thought I found my first case of Multiple Personality Disorder, only to discover that when conscious she had total recollection of each part and could flow back and forth between them. I realized that through the freedom of hypnosis, and with her exceptional imaginative ability, she had given each part a total personality, but in full consciousness she was totally integrated.

The trial began with a flashback from anxiety to the recall and reliving of episodes of repeated physical abuse by her 'hell and damnation, 'fire and brimstone' fundamentalist father. Scenes flashed by quickly. A young child doing her homework, and her father yelling when she couldn't get an answer. The more he yelled the less she remembered, and the more frightened she became, and the less able to think. Finally, banging her head on the table he would yell, "Stupid!" With this flashback, she went to the dissociative work room. At the table were the observing adult and two fourteen year old teenage selves, one the shadow of the other. Father was at the end of the table calling her "whore and slut." One fourteen year old hated him while the other smiled, stating she never came in the house. She was having too much fun outside. This was the adolescent forest child. In conscious processing of the session she filled in the picture of repeated childhood physical and mental abuse.

Between sessions she faced high anxiety and was terrified of going crazy. She had flashbacks from childhood, from the scared child to the worn out forest child. Recognition, acceptance and understanding led to calmness. She realized the emotional abandonment of her mother who did nothing to stop the beatings. The observing self spoke with detachment and understood that the mother's rejection was jealously. Her father was always angry at her mother for favoring her older brother. A fairy tale of dancing appeared in a dream. A handsome father danced with his beautiful daughter, he dressed in gold and she in a colorful flowing Spanish dress. Father was smiling, proud of his blooming daughter who respected and trusted him. She too smiled with delight. This dream triggered the anxiety of sexual fears and she questioned possible incest. Back at the work table the trial progressed. All the child ego states were giving evidence, not of sexual abuse, but intense physical and emotional abuse that went on day after day. Two women sat at either side of the adult: Queen Victoria and an Old Lady. The Old Lady was the keeper of the family's generational story. She told a sad tale of family shame. The adult observer burst out with rage at the father's assaults and vowed to protect all the children. When she promised to comfort them and heal their pain she sensed an icicle in her body turn into a warm heart. She had a sense of pulling her day to day life together and developing closer and warmer relationships with her women friends. Her rage attacks continued, but were interspersed with effective assertiveness. The appropriate words now flowed with ease, good timing, and a sarcastic wit.

Insomnia increased as she sensed the turmoil of the fourteen year old teenager over sexual feelings. In the hypnotic work room the scrapper raged at the sexual teenager, and the forest child hid. The sexual part shared her shame of the "whore complex" created by her father and older men she had met. This was contrasted with the enjoyment of sex with boy/men. She realized that she had married her husband purely for the joy of sex, even though she understood the relationship was bad. In conscious processing she understood her catastrophic marriage to an alcoholic, deceptive con man had been caused by splitting off parts of her personality. The forest child had been acting independently, without the good judgment of the others. During the grieving process she had a flashback to her first teenage romance. It had been a beautiful fun relationship which included her boyfriend's loving family. Happiness and sadness exploded as she thanked them for their loving care and said, "I'm so glad I knew them."

A passion for dancing emerged. She began to attend dance classes, and began to explore men, not romantically, but as dance partners. As this excited stage developed she began to examine her past love relationships. She concluded that they were good boy/men, much like her teenage lover, or adult controlling men like her father. A happy/sad developed as she now saw dancing partners who respected her and recognized her as a special person. She moved from excitement to grieving over her father's loss of joy for his children. There was another goodbye scene with father. She flashed back and recalled some earlier scenes where he had been very caring, especially when she was ill. She actually remembered his comforting when she was vomiting. This was the good father part and she rejoiced. But soon the scary feelings returned as she lost him again as a teenager when he abandoned her with sexual accusations. Her emancipation into womanhood was a definite threat to her father. His fundamentalist sexual repressiveness exploded with vile contempt. Her anxiety of abandonment exploded with a flashback to the physical abuses of the past, and sad scenes of self comfort in her room with her teddy bear. Over the next period there were real life meetings with men through her work and dancing, with a reawakening of her playfulness and sexual feelings. At times an underlying distrust of men returned. With emerging sexuality she began to explore her dance partners romantically. When one did not call her back she panicked and again returned to early scenes of missing her father and the terror of abandonment. She was now able to deal with the transference, the relationship between her and me, her therapist. I was the good father and the anxiety of ending treatment brought back the childhood terror of abandonment.

Back to the dissociative table, she sat around her table with all her ego states present. She found the terrified child of about five or six. She was terrified of being alone and missed her father. The adult in charge agreed with the child and said, "If you get close to men, they all leave you." The child became more frightened. The old woman emerged from the background, came close to the child and said, "Of course you were hurt when your dad left you, but that was then and this is now." When she came back to conscious processing she laughed with an obvious insight. "I've grown so much over the last years, I feel so strong and capable. I know that if I fell in love and was abandoned I would be hurt, but I'd get over it."

In the next session she switched in quick succession from fairy tale to fairy tale. First, the baby scene appeared, with the adult embracing a baby. The Old Lady told her she had to do something to make this complete. Suddenly, the dancing scene appeared, with the father whirling around with his daughter. Then her anger exploded at her real father, yelling at him to respect her like the father in the dream. She burst out crying, grieving the loss of the dream of a real loving father. Released by her tears, an integrating scene followed with the four child ego states, the scared child, the scrapper, the forest child and the sexual child, swimming together in a river.

The trial of father finished and he was found guilty. Now for the punishment. A ten to twelve year old appeared yelling, "Kill him." This was the sneaky avenger. The others echoed her feelings. Surprisingly, the scared child began to cry and told more of her story. Yes, Dad beat her but he also cared. Her mother kept her hungry and gave her smelly food that made her sick. It was Dad who would clean her up and be nice to her. The others were moved by her tale and Dad was set free. Her ego states were more integrated but the sad little girl was kept separate, protected in a cocoon.

Throughout the therapy, her dependency needs for nurturing care and protection were the most difficult to acknowledge and accept. This young baby was neglected and abandoned by an inadequate mother. How could she ever trust again? A period of anorexia gradually improved as friendships with other woman became more rewarding, accepting that her loneliness left her vulnerable to men. In earlier love relationships she had found domineering men and became over-dependent. Betrayal and physical abuse in her marriage made her feel invaded. She felt the loss of a part of herself and often cried out, "I don't want a man in my life, ever!" One day dramatic resolution imagery occurred and she exploded with a happy/sad, as the old lady put the Queen's head on the teenager who then danced with the Father/King.

Final imagery scenes emerged erratically over the next few months, often returning to comfort the baby within, whom she loved, a baby the real mother was trying to destroy. This was interspersed with relationships with men, and always came back to her brutal marriage. She suffered more than physical abuse, she suffered lies and deceit that were confusing, for they almost drove her crazy, and caused her to lose confidence in her judgment. The recollections of her marriage that had ended many years ago were always distressing. The emotional ending was incomplete. An imagery trial was held for her husband. It took place in the same room as the trial for her father. All the children were there, giving their stories through the voice of her older brother who took charge. Each part confirmed the mental and physical torture she had suffered. The verdict was guilty. While awaiting sentencing a magical child ego state appeared and laid a secret curse on her husband. While she never revealed the curse, all the children rejoiced, for they trusted this magic part and knew this man would never hurt anyone again. The magic one was recognized as her creative part and began to play a major role in her career. The roller coaster of emotional distress had now ended, except for periodic outbursts. Most of the time she was calm, at peace, and filled with the quiet joy of living, mixed with the excitement of her work and her outdoor activities which she shared with her children.

With the marriage trial over she again went back into her imagery to look for the baby. She found it undamaged in the rubble of devastated buildings. She gave it to her mother to hold but mother was terrified saying the baby was not hers. The scene switched back to the castle and the King/Father was now holding the baby and performing a tender ritual ceremony of love. The grown woman now entered the ballroom and began to dance, alone, growing bigger and bigger, brighter and brighter, more and more confident and laughing. Happier than she ever imagined possible, she asked the magic child if this was true. The magic child confirmed the fantasy as real. In the discussion that followed she realized that she had fully understood the betrayal in her marriage and the havoc it wreaked, destroying her self confidence. She felt the healing of the inner needy child and reowned her creative magic self. Erratic scenes flashed by, of a screaming baby ignored by mother. She understood that Mother was jealous of father's affection to the older children, and did not want this baby. Mother's behavior throughout her childhood was full of double bind scenes, voicing concern while physical neglecting her at the same time. Seeing the child as different and strange but wanting to help her, calling the child bad and encouraging her husband to punish her to make her good. The basic script was, "you don't exist," and the new one became "I am." She forgave her mother simply by accepting her mother's limitations. Today their relationship is pleasant, but distant.

Final celebration rituals occurred within her inner group as she integrated the Queen and older woman as loving mother figures. Now the mature woman was confident, active, innovative and content. Most of the states were fully present, active and mature and she flowing harmoniously from one to the other, as they reacted to life experiences. The roller coaster is mostly quiet, but the old stuff comes back briefly. She feels integrated, grounded, free, and happy. While comfortable with men, even enjoying their company, she's not yet ready for a romantic relationship, for the embers of hate toward men still smolder and any trigger from the past fans the flames high.

The therapy is incomplete, but it's in the goodbye stage. The movie needs a final scene, the book a last chapter. What will it be? Will all the insights and understanding free her from the past? Will she be able to forgive and forget? Forgiveness, more than a religious concept, is a psychological process of completion. Will reclaiming and healing of all her inner states and integrating them into a mature woman, allow her to rekindle the curiosity of exploration? Will the excitement of looking forward overcome the pain of the past?

An unexpected but potential direction for closure was emerging. The recent death of her father opened a massive outpouring of sadness. She was puzzled by the intensity of grief for a man who had assaulted her. She had to look deeper inside. She found herself grieving for the loss of a dream of childhood happiness, a dream she imagined after observing her friends' loving fathers. The crying exploded with a massive abreaction of deep sorrow at her father's painful life. She had now reached one of the most mature levels of personality development - empathy. She could now feel and experience her father's pain, as different and distinct from her own.

The last major piece of work had been completed. She is mature, integrated, aware of most of her ego states which function together as a team. There is a clear sense of being whole and complete, capable of coping with problems, especially relationships with men. She has synthesized most of her life experiences, and put them together into a coherent story. The movie of her past is essentially over. Of course "the old stuff always comes back, briefly." There will be triggers in the future, events that will set her back, and rekindle old pain. The past will get in her eyes. But she'll quickly return to the mature, grown-up, capable woman and carry on with a creative exploration of life and new love relationships. She is now ready to leave therapy and face the realistic separation anxiety of saying goodbye to her therapist.

Ending Grief

Grieving is a necessary process for healing. It is coming to terms with losses whether through death, separation or disappointment. Prolonged or incomplete grieving is often the underlying dynamic of psychiatric illnesses, especially depression. How do you end mourning and finish the process, and finally say goodbye to the grieving itself? Mental imagery can offer some of the most unique and surprising options. A rigid, compulsive, very successful professional man was living a life of anhedonia. Nothing gave him pleasure. Living involved achieving, producing, and coping with the anxiety of his performance. There was rarely any satisfaction attached to achievement, only stress at the next goal. His Dad had suffered a severe and debilitating illness when the patient was a small boy. Even though he recovered physically, emotionally he had remained detached, distant, and probably depressed. Visiting his father now as an elderly man always brought back resentment at childhood abandonment. Recognizing his obsessions as unrealistic, he seemed powerless to stop them. Why couldn't he put the past to rest? Through hypnotherapy, he met his Dad at the dissociative table. Surprisingly, Dad was back in his army uniform, even more surprising was that the patient was now a grown man of about Dad's age, in an army uniform himself. He and his Dad were buddies. The next few scenes were fantasies of two army buddies having fun together. In the course of this imagery journey he actually burst out laughing and experienced a return of joy. He had created what he missed as a child. He was finally able to put the past away. The payoff was hedonia, a return to pleasure.

A macho, charming man was thrown out of his marriage by his wife for flagrant promiscuity. Reacting to the loss of his wife and children he became depressed. For many years he was actively yearning and grieving, all mixed with rage at his wife. Going back and forth over the same issues, day after day, month after month, only prolonged his depression. All the tried and true psycho-dynamic approaches were unsuccessful. One day he did a "Gestalt goodbye." I said, "Imagine your wife in the empty chair. As you see her say goodbye." Immediately, he burst out crying and the words that followed were, "Thank you. Thank you for the love you gave me. Even though I have a long way to go you helped me grow up as a man." His cry was now a happy/sad and he could say goodbye to his marriage. The final scene was in place, the movie was complete, and it could now be stored away. His depression lifted completely.

A woman who had just left a marriage some months ago was now in a new love relationship, where she was becoming over attached, over demanding, wanting complete attention. Even though she and her new lover had wonderful days together, there were pangs of jealousy that were overwhelming. In her psychological work, she heard two voices. One was a jealous part, saying, "I've lost him, it's over," and then the adult voice would give a realistic explanation for his behavior. Under hypnosis she went down to the dissociative work room. Sitting around her table was a fat, jealous woman, and an adult voice of reason. Surprisingly, she found her nine year old girl there too. Her Daddy had died that year. This little girl agreed with the jealous woman, "You're going to lose him, just like I lost Daddy." This little girl relived the burial of her father. At the graveside, she is screaming and crying hysterically and people grabbed her and took her away. In therapy she gave herself permission to stay and watch the burial and she cried and cried, saying over and over again, "I want my Daddy, he's gone." Crying, she fully experienced the death of her father and the unfinished grief of a nine year old child who desperately loved her dad and was left with an emotionally unloving mother. After the death of her dad there were times she would sit in his empty chair and hug it, yearning and wishing he was there. Now, thirty years later, she was completing the grief work that would free her from the pathological jealousy of today.

A man in his late fifties experienced depression and massive obesity. He worked through the depression, coming to terms with a critical rejecting mother, and a wife who many years before had left the marriage taking with her his only daughter. From a bitter, angry man hating all women, he's become empathetic, with renewed interest in relationships. Despite much effort over the years his weight had not changed. In the midst of a group session he became overwhelmed with feelings, and was on the verge of a spontaneous abreaction. I asked him to hold back and reinforced his hypnotic controls. As he calmed, with all his safety mechanisms in place, I went back to his discomfort. He felt an explosion in his stomach. "Using your imagination, be in your stomach," I said and he started to yell, "There's a snake in my stomach and it's crawling up." "Now the huge head is coming through my mouth," he screamed. He was agitated and began flailing his arms. At this point I asked him to turn down his emotions and he did. He was able to gain control. But he then screamed out, "What can I do?" I suggested he might pull the snake out. He did, screaming with pain, and threw the snake on the floor. "Should I kill it?", he shouted. With relief he said, "I'll let it live." As he came out of the trance the pain in his stomach and chest gradually subsided and he experienced relief. At the next session he shared his insight. The snake was his evil mother who had been inside him, literally eating him up. Since that experience he lost his appetite and eight pounds in one week. His aging mother was still alive and he experienced a major shift, and a change in attitude towards her. She was now simply an elderly woman who could not hurt him anymore.

Symbols of all kinds emerge from right brain imagery. Nature with all its glory, and animals with all their aggression, cover a range of emotions from calmness and security to rage and power. Interpretations by the psychiatrist are rarely necessary, for the patients' insights from the left brain flow spontaneously and synthesize the experience.

Never Ending Grief

An elderly woman, a survivor of the Holocaust, has spent most the last fifty years in and out of psychotherapy. She had been constantly depressed and suffers horrific flashbacks of the concentration camps, the death of her parents, her brothers, sisters and friends. In my brief intensive contact with her I diagnosed a Post Traumatic Stress Disorder of fifty years duration. It was characterized by depression and showed an incomplete grieving over the Holocaust and the death of her loved ones. My job was to help her end her grief. It was just before the High Holidays of Rosh Hashanah and Yom Kippur. She made her traditional visit to the cemetery and began to experience again an explosive anniversary reaction to the death of her relatives in Auschwitz. This allowed a point of therapeutic entry to help her grieve again and end it. As I made my interventions she exploded, "I'll grieve the rest of my life, and I'll never say goodbye." She then exploded with killer rage at the Germans and then at God for allowing six million Jews to die. She was a bright woman and understood it was not God's will, but in her heart she felt abandoned by God. Finally she accepted that God let some Jews live so that they might tell the story of the Holocaust. She went to the synagogue and forgave God.

The night horrors continued. She relived the death of her two year old cousin. She was nine at the time. He had fallen into a pot of boiling water and suffered burns to much of his body. As he screamed in pain a German doctor came and administered a lethal injection. She watched the little boy die, a child she had mothered, for his own mother had been killed. "He could have been saved," she said, "But the doctor killed him." Screaming with rage, she imagined killing the doctor, only to explode with sadness as she again heard the cries of the little boy. "I'll never say good-bye to him," she said again. She then imagined kissing him on his head as he lay dying, and stored the final picture in her heart where she would keep him forever. The following week she again cried and raged at the Germans. "I want to let it all go," she said, exhausted after fifty years of reliving this tragedy. "But I can't," she said. "God let me survive to bear witness to that horror." Her pain continued. Saying goodbye to the past meant giving up her duty as a survivor to remember. Her ongoing depression and flashbacks was her way of reminding the world of Nazi atrocities.

Unfortunately many survivors of the Holocaust continue on with the scars and transfer their pain to younger generations. Others have completed grief in healthy, adaptive and productive ways. Elie Weisel emerged from his depression through his writing on the Holocaust. Today, he fights for human rights, not only for Jews, but all oppressed groups. My patient's never ending grief is her only way to bear witness.

Saying goodbye is a simple, but not easy way of ending grief. While the painful feelings must be shared, the process must be completed for the person to carry on with living in a productive way. Paradoxically, even though the sadness fades, the memories of the loved ones are never forgotten.

The Jewish custom of unveiling the headstone at the gravesite occurs before the end of the first year after death. The rabbi's prayers and words, written long before the notion of modern psychiatry, have remarkable psychological sophistication and insight. As I've listened closely I've heard, "It's time to say goodbye to your loved one and shed your last tear. In honor and respect to his or her life you have the duty from this moment to get on with living in the most effective, rewarding way, with fulfillment and happiness." Grieving is complete. There will be anniversary reactions, triggered by the day of death, or other related events, that bring back the sorrow. They will subside naturally and spontaneously. Hopefully, you will never forget the joyful moments, but the sadness of loss is over. Whatever the painful past, whether an abusive childhood, a dream of what should have been, a separation or the death of a loved one, all need closure. You must find a final scene that fits, something that feels and looks like the end of the experience. Even tragic films have endings.

Waking Dreams

Fritz Perls approached dreams as if they were an unfinished movie in your head. Completing the movie through right brain visualization was his therapeutic goal.

A strong, dominant, controlling woman in the midst of a new love relationship crisis was anxious from the threatened loss. As she struggled with each day's turmoil she had a dream. She was floating underwater and couldn't move. As we explore the dream's mental imagery she imagines herself pulling at her right foot, again and again, unable to free herself. She's stuck. In between imagery scenes we discuss some of her issues. As she reflects on her anger, she looks back and sees a rope or vine tied around her foot. She can move it a little. As the group session goes on, she goes back and forth into the scenes of her dream. At the end of the group therapy session, she sees the final scene of her dream imagery. A number of boats are on the surface of the water and she realizes she's waiting to be rescued. This was a very powerful insight of her dependency search, a wishing to be cared for. The paradoxical polarity of a strong woman who spends most of her time rescuing other people.

In another group therapy session, a young woman who had been physically and psychologically abused by her mother dreamed that her mother was trapped in an egg. Her mother's head stuck out and she was throwing eggs at her. In the waking dream in the therapy session she continued throwing eggs at her mother with the joy of revenge. However, the dream remained stuck and scenes did not move. Dialoguing with her mother opened the message, "I'm going to throw eggs at you until you admit what you did was wrong." The mother repeatedly answered that she did what she thought was right. The patient was unable to find an ending for the dream. Other group patients, moved by the patient's work, were stimulated into their own waking dreams. A woman who had been psychically abused by her father and neglected by her mother saw her mother in an egg. But her mother appeared as a young, immature and incompetent child. The patient saw herself withdrawing from her mother without anger and shifting to friendships with women friends who loved and cared for her. There was an explosive cry of sadness and joy at the final scene. It was a peak human experience of a happy/sad as she resolved her relationship with her mother and brought her dream to an end. The Principle of Universality is a powerful group process. We all have problems in common. The very act of a group of people sharing in itself is therapeutic. Paradoxically, keeping secrets is at least 50% of the problem in emotional illness. The ripple effect of waking dreams touched others in the group and another woman saw her mother crying in the egg. Acknowledging her mother's miserable life and terrible marriage the patient cried with her. As the sadness intensified the patient saw herself moving away from her mother and saying goodbye to a mother she had always tried to protect and rescue. After completing the dream she burst into laugher, shouting, "I did it!" with a sense of relief and awareness of completing an emotional separation. At this time the first patient shared an insight. She hoped that if her mother had admitted her wrongdoing there would have been a chance for reconciliation. She was still searching for the mother's love that she'd never had.

Loss of a Dream

A single man in his late thirties had recurrent, similar dreams. He was in bed with a woman. It was time to get up and he couldn't. He tried, and fell out of bed. He then woke up, still in bed. The next night he had a similar dream. This time he found himself in the bathroom, trying to wake up. Then he woke up. He was still in bed. His left brain interpretation was the description of the dream, "I couldn't wake up." He went back to the dream through the safety induction of self hypnosis and found himself with a former lover who had left him ten years earlier. The next scene shifted to a beautiful home on the beach. She was now his wife, smiling and welcoming him home. There were two children, a boy and a girl, whose names he knew, and whose ages were appropriate to the length of the relationship had it continued. He imagined taking his son to play basketball. In the car they were talking and sharing. He smiled as he described the beautiful relationship, one he had never had with his own father. This was the last scene, and as he began to consciously process the dream, he said, with a joyful laugh, "That was a perfect dream," and then he burst out crying. This was the future dream he had planned with his girlfriend, a dream that never happened. While he had grieved the loss of the relationship many times, this was the first time he had to grieve what could have been, the future dream. He needed to complete the painful loss of the dream before he could free himself to explore new love relationships.

I'm always amazed at the spontaneous left brain interpretation that follows dream endings. If the patient is doing all the work, what is the therapist's role? It's true, the patient writes the script, acts all the parts and finds the ending. The therapist is the director of the movie, helping the patient to synthesize and integrate into a harmonious whole, completing the Gestalt.

Hypnogogic imagery are normal hallucinations that occur between wakefulness and sleep. Hypnopompic hallucinations occur just after sleeping, before full awakening.

My dog began waking in the night to go out and urinate. I began to wonder if she was developing diabetes. But soon she settled spontaneously and slept through the night. For a number of weeks afterwards I could hear her barking, woke up and got dressed, only to find her fast asleep in her bed. Physiologically, we do have waking dreams.

The imagery and hypnotherapy I do creates internal hallucinatory-like experiences. People appear in an empty chair, you look for parts of yourself around an imaginary table, in an imaginary room. Imaging yourself in another place, or another time, regressed to childhood or catapulted into the future. Perhaps even looking back from the future to give yourself advice. Or in the middle of a busy day, you suddenly take a holiday by going to a favourite place that exists only in your mind. Think about transformational imagery, a Jules Verne journey throughout your own body.

It may appear strange to encourage people to talk to aspects of themselves and visualize things that aren't there. It sounds like the symptoms of schizophrenia. Initially, I was concerned that imaginative therapies might produce psychosis, or that the patients would remain in their hypnotic reverie. They don't! In fact, most patients take to mental imagery techniques with enthusiasm, and are pleased with the experience when working with someone trained and competent in their therapeutic modality. The natural state of hypnosis is relaxing and tranquil. When personal insights and discoveries are made, anxiety switches to excitement. Again the wisdom of Fritz Perls holds true, "lose your mind and come to your senses."

During waking or sleeping dreams, or hypnotic reverie, the right brain is open while the left brain sleeps. Great discoveries, after years of industrious work, erupt with a vivid dream and a final, "Eureka, I found it." The imaginative visual imagery has finally connected to the years of research, culminating in the creative moment. A new concept, invention, or ego state, is born.

CHAPTER FIVE

Synthesis: Memory Processing

Memory plays a fascinating role in psychotherapy. [1] Recently the uncovering of early childhood physical, sexual or emotional abuse has swung from extremes. On one hand it's finally allowed the truth to emerge. The damaged adult can now be treated effectively by dealing with the intrusive past.

A large number of psychiatric studies have explored the relationship between childhood traumatic experience and adult psychopathology. The most striking finding is that childhood trauma is much more frequent than previously believed, and that individuals with such experiences are at greater risk for long term illness. It is suggested that trauma leads to the repression of memories. For this reason, the recovery of repressed childhood traumas is central to the practice of psychotherapy. Research on childhood sexual abuse shows that the more severe the trauma, the more likely long term consequences. In particular, the most painful sequalae are strongly related to father/daughter incest, abuse with penetration and abuse using physical force. A large body of research shows that a single negative experience during childhood does not cause adult psychopathology. Pathology is the cumulative effect of multiple risks, like repeated childhood sexual abuse and living in a dysfunctional family. Repetition of abuse over long periods of time by trusted family members is a major factor in dissociative disorders. [4]

In a retrospective study, children known to have been abused twenty years ago were interviewed as adults to determine the extent to which they were aware of these earlier events. The most significant finding was that 38% of women with documented sexual abuse during childhood failed to remember the incident. That is consistent with the concept of the repression of traumatic memories. [5]

In my practice most of my patients have partial memory recollection. This fits in with Pierre Janet's concept, *Partial Repression and Dissociation of Childhood Traumatic Experiences.* [6] The most effective therapy is the completion of the experience and discovering the belief systems that had developed at that time. Therapy becomes an imaginative and creative process of completing an unfinished childhood movie.

The opposite end of early childhood repressed traumatic memories opens popular hysteria. Patients seeking a magic answer, ask for hypnosis to discover childhood sexual abuse that they can't recall. They believe their emotional problems are caused by childhood abuse and recall of these memories will cure them. There are no typical adult psychological symptoms that point to childhood trauma, though many exhibit signs of Multiple Personality Disorders (Dissociative Identity Disorder). Patients vary in unique and personal ways. The pendulum of memories of childhood abuse, has swung to the extreme, with the False Memory Syndrome and recants of childhood abuse, overshadowing corroborative, genuine evidence of childhood trauma. Does it effect psychotherapy? Of course. On the positive side it cautions overzealous and poorly trained therapists to avoid memory implants while using the suggestible therapies in vulnerable patients. Traumatic memories cannot be validated by the therapist, only corroborated by eye witnesses from the past. On the negative side, legal entanglements have inhibited therapists from working with childhood trauma. A grave injustice, for those ill with Dissociative Identity Disorder can be healed by the appropriate process of recall, synthesis, abreaction and a resolution of past assaults.

False memories of childhood abuse have devastated families when parents were falsely accused. Preoccupation with False Memory Syndrome may be the excessive swing of the pendulum, persuading adult survivors of abuse to recant their childhood memories. How far back can memory go? I'm not sure. If it wasn't for her father's corroboration, Hanna's recall of sexual abuse by her grandfather at age two to four would remain questionable. Some patients recall only vague images and feelings from early childhood, experiences that occurred before the mind could truly comprehend or judge. A depressed physician doing affect bridge imagery regressed to an early childhood experience, and without a sound began to shake and shiver, complaining of freezing cold. This was a kinesetic abreaction without any visual or cognitive components. After return to here and now consciousness, he remembered his sibling's stories of how mother would leave them outside in the cold for long periods, or of being undressed in their cold bedroom.

Hypnotic events are like waking dreams. True or not, they are valid as screen memories, and a metaphor of life experiences. Working through these events in fantasy can be therapeutic without necessarily confirming the truth of the mental images. Evelyn Cotzer confirmed, in her book, *Eye Witness*, that even eye witness memory can be inaccurate. Certainly, early childhood recollections suffer the distortion of time. One researcher claimed that while memory may be false, "the body never lies." With the somatic or affect bridge, body pain, distress or feelings usually have a valid connection to childhood experiences, and are often corroborated by the recollection of the patient themselves or family members. Let caution prevail, for the body symptoms of anxiety could be caused by an imagined past trauma.

Recently research [8] has identified two main memory centers in the brain. The Amygdala and the Hyppocampus. Each share a special psychological memory function. The Amygdala is the alarm center, triggered by danger, and programmed by the characteristics of past dangers. For example, if a woman was walking down a street and saw a man with the characteristics of a previous attacker, her alarm center would be triggered. The Amygdala would produce an intense fear reaction. If she's come to terms with the past assault, the memory would be stored in the Hyppocampus, as a "completed story". When she sees the same man on the street she may only reflect on the past danger, but be aware of the differences between then and now. Concerned, but not flooded with anxiety, she carries on.

Effective psychotherapy uses the experiences processed with or without hypnosis, often in unison with left brain discussion and insights, to finish the book or complete the movie. This is called synthesis, or putting it all together in context. Often, the earlier traumas persisting in the present are incomplete experiences, or incomplete memories of the past that have been partially or totally dissociated. Psychotherapy fills in the blanks, not with every detail, but by reconstructing the experience and the memories. It's a process of reowning and healing damaged ego states. Abreaction of the trauma may be a necessary treatment in context. At a younger age, when the abuse occurred, the child had a specific personal experience and belief systems compatible with its age, like "I'm bad" or "it's my fault." During or after reliving the experience the observing adult can heal, repair or correct.

After we put the puzzle together emotionally and intellectually the childhood story or movie can be ended and stored in the Hyppocampus. Here it may serve as a reference book in a library rather than an alarm system. Once the past is healed it stops intruding in the present. The present opens and expands leaving the person free to grow, enjoy and create. Fusion, integration and reassociation of ego states can occur to produce a complete self.

Creativity

The fully expanded self is an odd contradiction, since the more you grow the greater the capacity and motivation to continue. Creativity is a bonus of maturity, leading to new directions, new roles, and innovative solutions. A sense of humor can be your special quality. The ability to see the absurdity of life, to use paradoxical resolution in conflict, to transform pain to pleasure, and above all, to relate with playful repartee for closeness and intimacy. An expanded consciousness with full awareness may open new opportunities for relationships or career changes. The new energy of creativity is the motivation to move beyond the complacency of present boredom. The rewards of positive future goals can override the pain of leaving security. The anxiety of exploration, facing the unknown and unfamiliar, can switch to the excitement of discovery.

CHAPTER SIX

Cognitive Retraining

Cognitive retraining is the psychological science of correcting distorted thinking and false belief systems. Despite my emphasis on right brain imagery and hypnotherapy we now cross the corpus callosium, the connecting fibers between the cerebral hemispheres to the dominant left side that thinks logically and speaks. For it is the integration of both sides that leads to personal wholeness.

False Beliefs

A depressed young man, whom I discussed in Part I, had spent ten years going from one menial job to another simply to survive. He described each failure with a gallows laugh and soon heard the lyrics to his smile, "I'm a fuck up." A false belief system that shifted upon analysis to anger at the whole world, a "fuck you" to bosses, society, and eventually to older brothers and a father who beat him as a child. This only increased his resistance, for work was the symbol of the authority he hated. Going down to the dissociative table to explore his attitude to work he found his mother, father and teenage self. There was a sudden shift and he became a six year old child playing in the basement of his home with his friends. Suddenly, he burst out crying as he shared the only good thing in his life, his buddies, a gang where he belonged and who protected him even from the beatings of his brothers. He was leaving the neighborhood. He was moving to a better area, but losing his best friends. In the waves of sadness he felt the loss of his friends. In conscious processing he filled in the gaps of this painful period and expressed shame for crying. Going back into the hypnotic state I asked if there was anybody he knew that could help this inner child.

Reluctantly, the adult expressed his hatred for this crying kid and wanted to get rid of him. "He's a wimp," he said, from another false belief that belonged to an earlier day. Through realistic thinking he acknowledged his loss and accepted his grieving child. He ended the scene by putting his arms around the little boy. Sarcastically, at the end of the session, he said, "what's this got to do with my difficulty finding a job?" With tongue in cheek, I responded, "now that you're looking after this sad little boy, the cause of your morning depression, you can get out of bed and look for a job."

Discovering False Beliefs in Context

Psychiatry is noted for its analytical introspection, through left brain intellectualization. Words without feeling are almost useless. The lyrics have to fit the music. Mental imagery and hypnotherapy allow rapid access to the sensory emotional experiences laid down in the right brain. Going back to the events and reliving them is the way to emotionally discover the false belief system. These scripts are thoughts and decisions laid down at the time of abuse by a distraught and terrorized child. Their rediscovery, in the context of the traumatic event, make it a moving, total experience that registers in both sides of the brain and resonates throughout the total self. Now there is a window of opportunity for effective change and the remaking of a new life, decisions and beliefs.

Can False Beliefs be Protective?

An accomplished, professional woman was successful in every area of her life, except love relationships. Not only did they turn out badly, they were self destructive. She was always getting hurt. As she looked back on these relationships her usual good judgment was severely impaired. "Why?", she asked. During a mental imagery session she unexpectedly went back to an experience at age twelve that she had forgotten. She was sexually assaulted while eating lunch at school by a group of male friends. The group swarmed her and began grabbing her breasts and body. She was shocked and dumbfounded. There was a noise and the boys stopped and ran away. Somewhat dazed by this, she began to think, "it's okay for them to hurt me." Today in the therapy session we looked back. She began to cry and feel the pain of the assault by her friends. She recognized this strange belief system, "it's okay for them to hurt me," as a form of protection. Not only a protection from the pain of humiliation and terror, but a way of avoiding the loss of her friends. Blocking out the experience was achieved by this false belief system so she could carry on as if nothing had happened. Today in therapy, she's reliving the long dissociated emotions of the assault. Reowning her feelings and healing the twelve year old's trauma presents an opportunity for building a realistic belief system. It's crucial that she does, for the past self destructive program is still operating in all her adult love relationships.

False belief systems are the bottom line of all mental distortions. Whenever I hear the past regrets of "poor me," "ain't it awful" and the future worries of "what if," I interject to correct the unrealistic thinking. "Avoid the paralysis of 'can't,' and shift to the action of 'will,' or respect the decision of 'won't'." Don't strikeout with three "yes, buts." Avoid the sort of exaggeration and generalization that can take disaster to catastrophe. Self blame, inappropriate to an external event, not only produces depression but like a fallen tree across a road, blocks the journey. Stop judging yourself; don't let the critical parent ego state stay in your mind rent free. Pick a loving parent ego state, an advocate or cheerleader to help urge you on. Give the realistic adult ego executive power over your internal committee of ego states. Let the adult hear all the voices, guide you sensibly, and take responsibility for decisions and actions. This V.I.P. knows that if you try and fail you may be disappointed, but if you fail to try, you miss an opportunity. Removing thinking distortions and adding new life programs lowers anxiety, and lifts depression, so you can act, move and tolerate the natural, realistic stress of change, separation or loss.

Learning From The Past versus Past Regrets

"Ain't it awful," "poor me," "if only I had — or didn't — I would be —." These major thinking distortions, when compounded by self blame, shift anxiety to depression. When past regrets are propelled into future failures of "there I go again," the overwhelming distress leads to paralysis. The circular thinking becomes a whirlpool of stagnation that can pull you under, drowning you in your self fulfilling prophecies.

Learning from the past is rewarding. The proverb, "If you forget the past, you're bound to repeat it," is true socially, politically, historically and personally. A young man beginning therapy was obsessed with this proverb. He continually reflected on past memories and images of childhood abuse in order to avoid beating his own son. He said, "It works. I cannot beat my child. You have to learn from experience." He came from a physically abusive home, beaten by his mother, who in turn was physically abused by her father. Her mother had died in childbirth and her father blamed her for the death. My patient did not want to continue the generational pattern of violence. At this time he had no insight into his lifestyle as a loser. Though bright and talented, he had never made it, never completed his university course, and always moved from job to job to job. His string of life failures culminated with the loss of a marriage. He was sent to therapy as a condition of probation after a recent criminal offense. He covered his anger with an overly nice personality style. Obsessing over childhood memories of abuse, and failure in life, was a heavy price to pay for suppressing the anger necessary to resolve his early childhood abuse. Hopefully, rage will be experienced at the appropriate subjects, and he'll find better ways of preventing the socially inherited pattern of child abuse that keeps the past alive in the present.

One of the problems with past trauma was described by Pierre Janet over a hundred years ago. "DE-REALIZATION", consists of partial memories, or incomplete experiences, which still ring the alarm of the Amagdylla in the brain, and erupt into anticipation anxiety. A present event may trigger the painful past experience. If you can see the difference between then and now, and anxiety drops, then you've healed the trauma.

A talented, artistic man shared his simple New Year's resolution, "I should lose weight and stop smoking, but I don't. Ha, ha, ha, ha." He hit the bell at the top of the scale with a huge gallows laugh. Finding lyrics to his music he heard the "fuck you" voice of his inner child rebelling at his authoritarian shoulds. Repeating the "fuck you", he laughed almost uncontrollably. Yet he knew it wasn't funny. Now he recognized that his frustrated goals were the constant bickering of his internal "should" parent, and the passively resistant child. Of course, it was helpful to protest, if he could emancipate. Subconsciously, his was the interminable duel of one thrust forward, one step back. When placed in context, with the image of a five year old child as chairman of his adult corporation, he imagined an inner cabinet with all his ego states. Grown up children with a small stubborn kid at the head of the table. At this point he turned red. The insights of his left brain had united with the experience and feelings of his right brain and energy radiated through his body, through his parasympathetic system and nervous system, dilating the vessels in his face and opening his mind. The past was now fully conscious in the present. Now, with full awareness, he is free to choose.

Emotional Reasoning versus Realistic Thinking

"Feelings in my heart may not be factual." Right brain experiences need left brain understanding to be more realistic. True insights are an integration and balancing of both sides of the brain. Emotional reasoning alone is distorted thinking. When I attended the European Hypnosis Convention in Vienna, I was awed by the magnificent architecture, the aura of culture and the intelligencia, and the music of Beethoven, Mozart and Strauss. My thoughts turned to the 1938 annexation by the Nazis, who had been welcomed with open arms by Austrian citizens. The deportation of the Jews in cattle cars to concentration camps began shortly after. I pushed the painful feelings of the Holocaust away and returned to the conference, only to find them returning in strange human ways.

I met a German surgeon who suddenly apologized to me for the Holocaust. He shared the troubling questions he had asked his father. In our brief encounter, he shared his ill health, for the next week he was undergoing major cancer surgery. We spent a few hours together and I used hypnosis for positive visual imagery, a rehearsal to aid him in a successful operation and immune system enhancement for recovery.

At the conference, I was irritated by an overly exuberant older woman who kept invading my personal space. At the Wine Garden banquet she invited me to her table where wandering musicians were playing popular Viennese music. She sang along with gusto, knowing all the music. Something clicked. I knew she was Jewish and a Holocaust survivor. She told me her story. She was sixteen years old when her parents put her on the last train out of Austria for Palestine. Her parents, with her younger siblings, were shipped to a concentration camp and killed in the gas chambers by the Germans. "How can you be so happy," I asked. She responded,

"I've done my grieving over the years and today I'm celebrating the good life me and my family had growing up in Vienna."

The next morning the convention arranged a tour of the Sigmund Freud Museum. This stately apartment where Freud lived and practiced had finally been converted into a museum, long after the world had honored the famous Jewish father of modern psychiatry. The curator, welcoming us as Freud's disciples, gave us a privileged and comprehensive tour. He described the historical background of Freud's family. When the Nazis had declared their goal of exterminating the Jews, Freud's children urged him to leave Vienna as they had done. He resisted. He could not accept that genocide would shortly follow, but at the last moment he fled for England.

Freud's waiting room was filled with the original furniture, right down to the last detail, including a cabinet filled with antiquities. Many were gifts from his patients. Even the original analytical couch was there. Puzzled, I asked how it had survived and the curator explained, "It had all been sent to England. Freud took everything with him." When the museum was opened many years later the original furniture was sent back from the London Museum. I was surprised that while fleeing from the Nazis he was able to take everything. At the end of the tour we were shown old movies of Freud and his family. His sisters were in the movie sharing the family joys. At the end of the film it was noted that his sisters had died in the Holocaust. I felt a rush of anger and again questioned the curator. "Freud took every piece of furniture but left his sisters!?" I exclaimed. "He speculated that the Germans wouldn't let them leave." In my eyes the explanation failed and my anger persisted.

When I returned home I talked to a friend, a professor of Jewish history, who reviewed the historical facts with me. He said that in the early years of the war the Germans wanted to get rid of all the Jews. They wanted all the Jews to leave the country. The official extermination plan, headed by Eichman, did not begin until the early forties. The problem was that no country would take the Jews. The Canadian Minister of Immigration said, "None is too many." My rage at Freud switched to anger at the world and a deep sadness overcame me. Historical fact shifted my emotional reasoning and I grieved again the massacre of six million Jews. When would the grieving end? Could it ever?

During the next high holiday, during the Yom Kippur service, I was restless and left the synagogue. I went to a park and sat in front of a Holocaust memorial. It was a tree cut off at its base, with human forms clambering up the sides. I walked by and looked at the plaques from each concentration camp. I finally stopped at one that said, "A million five hundred thousand children were murdered by the Nazis." I burst out crying. I sat on the bench and in my mind's eye, my son appeared with his new baby. My cry became a happy/sad. This baby was a symbol of the continuation of the Jewish race, in fact, of all mankind. This was God's plan for humanity. As a young boy I blamed God. How could he stand by while his chosen people were destroyed? Spinoza's words finally rang true, "God gave man the greatest gift of all, free will." It was man, not God, who abused it. Paradoxically, when my emotional reasoning shifted to factual reality, true emotions of sadness replaced my anger to Freud. My grieving had taken another turn, another step forward, a step closer to the end. I had regained a sense of spirituality.

The State of Israel is painfully, slowly, coming to terms with the past and finishing its mourning over the Holocaust. Now it is freer to risk its security by giving Palestinians land for peace. In the ancient Jewish tradition, it is a duty to get on with life. Getting on with life shows honor and respect for those who died.

Beating the Beaten Child

In the continuing psychotherapy of a young man who had grown up in an alcoholic home, emotionally abused and physically beaten by his father and older brothers, this was one of the many times that he had relived the abuse by his father and felt intense rage at him, and a deep sadness for his own aloneness. There was no one there for him. When I suggested a healing image for his damaged child, his mind went blank. When I suggested that the adult who had survived this abusive childhood go back in time and do something for this child, his mind went blank again. Finally, an image flashed. He was taking a gun and shooting this kid, yelling his head off, "You fucking wimp." He could understand the child's realistic anger and sadness, but the strongest feeling and recurrent fantasy in time of stress, was of beating this child again. Of course, he's grown up as a self-blaming, critical adult with chronic depression and suicidal wishes. His immediate response to any difficulty is to sit back and beat the beaten child.

A young woman was overtaken by unexplainable bursts of rage. Simply following a slow, elderly driver in the left hand lane of a highway and swerving to the right around him, she felt an almost explosive rage. As we worked, using the rage in the present, going on a journey into the past, she discovered herself as a nine year old girl, who was being taken down the street by an elderly man. The little girl was quiet and non responsive. The woman began to scream her rage at this little girl, calling her stupid, didn't she know what was happening, stupid, stupid. Did she not realize that this man wanted to do something to her? She yelled and screamed with uncontrollable rage as she despised this little girl within her. After a few moments, reviewing the situation, she realized that this little girl was terrorized by this man and was literally frozen. In fact, she had dissociated, clicked out. That's the way she learned to handle terror anyway, especially with her brutal father who verbally and physically threatened her. Her only escape was emotionally disconnecting, not being there. Of course, she had to pay the price of being robot-like or frozen, but this was the only way she could escape from her father's abuse. She had nowhere else to go. Strangely enough, as she relived this little nine year old's experience with this man's sexual threat, she sensed him putting his arm around her as they walked down an abandoned street. Suddenly this little girl clicked in and ran away. At that moment, the adult woman looked back and realized that this was not a stupid little girl, that she was handling terror in her usual way, clicking out. Fortunately, she was able to click in to the anxiety of the situation, enough to run away and protect herself. At this point, she burst out crying with compassion for this part of herself that she had been rejecting. She could see herself kneeling at the feet of this little girl as the little girl put her arms around her and they both cried together, then walkedoff holding hands.

Re-victimization

The chances of an abused child being abused again as an adult is much higher than normal. Attachment may be part of the answer. The abused child, when placed in a protective and loving foster home, runs home as soon as he can. The emotional connection is to the abusing parent, not the new safe one. Feelings win out, overriding reason Perhaps it's Pavlovian conditioning. If a dog hears a ringing bell each time its fed then eventually it's conditioned to salivate to the bell alone. Painful human bonding resembles Pavlovian conditioning. When pain begins the glue of attachment binds. One patient said, "Nice guys don't attract me! But why can't I learn from experience?" The answer lies in the question, for if there is partial dissociation to past sexual, physical, or emotional abuse, part of the experience is not available. It has been dissociated, detached, forgotten or repressed. If the Amygdala screams out "danger", and it may not, for the pain may be the part that has been disconnected, leaving a lack of past memories and the patient vulnerable to recurrent assault. Even with complete awareness of past distress, the false belief systems developed at the time of assault invade the present, and judgment is impaired. The patient vows to do it better this time, negating the obvious external danger. With a poor self concept, how can they expect any better? They often choose partners much below their own true worth. The vulnerability of the victims of repeated childhood abuse is not a volitional act of suffering, but often a naiveté from dissociation and an inability to learn from experience.

Here and Now / Mindful Meditation

"Stay with your feelings. Feel the moment. What's happening right now?" These are my constant remarks to my patients. Frequently, past regrets and future worries follow an experience crowding out the present. What is the fleeting moment now? If it's so painful, why would you want to stay there? Get out, run away as fast as you can!

Fritz Perls" Gestalt therapy shifted the patient's preoccupation with the past with the empty chair experience. Imagine your mother, father, lover, in the chair and tell them what you think or feel. A major change occurs with a dramatic shift in emotion, perhaps from rage to love, or a rush of new insights or thoughts. Through the use of visual imagery the Gestalt experience has transformed past reflections into an unexpected experience in the present.

Dr. Eugene T. Gendlin's theory of focusing is an expansion of the present. Accepting the body's wisdom, focusing on the physical center of distress, allows movement, expansion, or a significant shift. Like feeling the pain in your head, may switch to the sadness in your eyes, followed by an image of personal loss.

Dr. John Schaffer's transformational imagery uses the body center as symbolic stages. Looking for blocks or connections between different body centers opens a dramatic conflict in search of resolution.

A woman with constant knots in her stomach saw an image of entangled rope. As she unties the knots there is a release in the chest and an instant shift to tightness in her throat. Focusing, she sees the tightness in the muscles in her neck, constricting the opening, shutting off the air. Short of breath, she labors to breathe. "Put a sound to the tightness" I say. Quiet at first, grunting and groaning, she finally yells, "NO," with a total body release. Her smiles of relief quickly shifted to anger at her troubled marriage. Her left brain insights immediately followed the right brain imagery as she stayed focused on the now.

A patient was seen in the midst of a panic attack. It began as he was talking to a friend about a sick older brother. With left brain reflection he shared the recent death of another brother and was now upset about the life-threatening illness of his last remaining sibling. With sadness he said "I'll be the only one left." This was the extent of his left brain understanding. As he explored his panic attack through mental imagery he felt the panic in his head, and saw the image of himself drowning. The panic increased. "Use your dimmer switch" I said and turn down the intensity of the feelings. "Stay with your drowning". He finally called out "help." Immediately the image shifted. The water suddenly drained away through a funnel and he was relieved. In the conscious processing that followed, he explained that as the only survivor of the family, the burdens would all be on his shoulders and it would be too much. His cry for help was difficult to accept for it filled him with shame as being "weak" and "needy."

If you said you're sad, what else is there to say? Where is the sad center in your body? If you focus on that place or imagine yourself there, something moves or shifts in a process of discovery, revelation and possible journey, of resolution. For a tidal wave of sadness soon flows into a trough of tranquillity and you end up closer to shore.

If you stay with your feelings and listen to your automatic thoughts you find the lyrics to the music, and the negative thoughts that cause the sadness. Now you can change your distorted thinking and false belief systems. A shift to realistic thinking offers the hope of a return to pleasure.

Try a simple "now" test. Place a few raisins in your hand. Look at them. Feel the texture. Now place one in your mouth. Don't bite it. Feel the contact with your lips, your cheeks, roll your tongue around it. Slowly bite down and taste the sweetness. Feel the urge to swallow the raisin and resist it. Now make a decision when to swallow it. You have now empowered yourself. Rather than being reactive, you are now proactive, in charge, in control, decisive.

If then and there, is here and now, you can uncover the past by expanding the present. Avoid past regrets and future worries for they will produce overwhelming anxieties that paralyze. Preoccupation with the past and the future obliterates the present. Focus on the now and discover yourself. True love can follow, for the formula for a happy relationship is I and Thou, Here and Now.

Back to the Present

A patient was once again in the doldrums of a Christmas depression. She had a flashback to Christmas at the age of six. Her father, in a drunken rage, was burning the presents. Shouting with religious fervor, "How can you enjoy yourself when all those children are starving." The mother stands paralyzed, and the six year old is terrified. Exploring this as a scene in a movie, a dramatic conflict emerged. Initially tempted to get rid of her father, she exclaimed, "But I love him. When he was not drunk he was kind and loving." In the imagined next scene, her father fell asleep from the alcohol, and she and her mother went to her grandparent's home for Christmas. Here she felt safe and peaceful. She enjoyed the presents, the Christmas tree and the Christmas cheer. Coming back to the present she felt calm and at peace. The Christmas depression had lifted and now with future rehearsal she saw her family having a marvelous Christmas, opening all their wonderful presents under the Christmas tree.

When trauma and conflict resolution of the past is accomplished, it's crucial to come back to the present. Bring back the healing experience, the new insights and feelings. With conscious processing make new decisions from what you've learned. Convert and adapt them to today's living.

A mature social worker was having one major complication at work. She was unable to complete her charts. Perplexed, she enjoyed her work, but the tediousness of the administrative part immobilized her. All the left brain insights failed to mobilize her. Through mental imagery and hypnotherapy she went into an imaginative state and saw the charts piling up on a table. She covered them with a large lead box and then unexplainedly felt like embracing them. As she did so she felt a deep sense of disgust and choking in her throat. Through a somatic bridge focusing on the body sensation, she went back to an early childhood experience of about age seven in the dining room of her home, where her father is yelling at her to eat her vegetables as she stubbornly resists. Coming back to the present and bringing in her adult realistic part, she said, "Whenever I'm pushed into something, I obviously resist." The connection to the present is obvious. The charts are representative of an authoritarian "should" and her stubborn child was protesting. She called out to me, "Help me. What can I do?" It was immediately obvious that if I told her what to do I would now be part of the authoritarian "shoulds" and her rebellious child would protest and resist. With this instant awareness she went back to the understanding of her childhood and she said, "It's not only stubborn resistance, this was a way of getting attention, for my father rarely recognized me for anything positive. In fact, he never recognized me at all. The only time I existed was when I was doing something wrong and he was shouting at me. I guess negative attention was better than none at all." Now back to the present: What had this to do with her inability to complete the charts? Well, in a way this was getting negative attention too, complaints from her superiors. This child of the past was somehow still present in her work as a social worker, wanting attention through negative stroking. Then her adult came in and spoke up, "And yet I enjoy my work and I get recognition for the good things I do." How could she now balance her realistic adult awareness with this child of the past, coming back to the present refusing to do the charts. The insight alone will motivate, for certainly the adult's awareness of today's satisfactions from within and without were enough recognition and she could now hear the voice of the hungry child as it came back to the present.

CHAPTER SEVEN

Positive Self Imaging

Whenever my clients have any degree of success, even a small step, I react intensely and say, "Let's celebrate!" I need to talk faster because one of my patients responded before I could complete the sentence, "I'm busy today. I don't have time." I quickly explained that therapeutic celebration means taking a picture. Now, they look pleasantly puzzled and smile. I ask if they have a camera and they say, "No, not with me. Do you have a camera?" "No, I don't," I reply. "Then how are we going to take a picture?" "Well, you have a great camera, in your mind's eye." "Sit back and relax," I say, "don't let your thoughts intrude. Open your imagination and see a picture of yourself that represents your recent achievement." As they're searching I go over some of their accomplishments. I even use their words of success. I add a few of my own to strengthen the direction of their growth. When they have a clear picture I ask whether it's black and white, or in color, and suggest they focus clearly. "Look at this image in your mind's eye, and see if it brings back the good feeling." If it doesn't we search for another image or alter the one they have. "Now let's put a title to the picture, the name of your new script, a few words that describe your positive change, like "winner"." Now for background music. What song fits? "Sing it out loud," I suggest. Most refuse to do so, they're too embarrassed to sing. Occasionally, I accompany them to lower the discomfort. Sometimes they sing it quietly inside. How about lyrics to the song? Quite spontaneously magic words appear like "whoopee, I made it" or "wow!" accompanied by an observable physiological change, like a glow that conditions the image. Now we have a full package, a whole new experience, involving all the senses. Some patients produce a collage of many images from childhood to adulthood or from different areas of their life, perhaps a video of success.

"Now, look inside your body and find your center of self for storing these pictures." Sometimes it's the brain or the heart or the whole body; more often the center of self is in the middle of the stomach. Look at the internal image and check out your good feelings again. "Continue regular deep breathing and experience the good feelings from this positive self center radiating all over." As you spend a few moments filling up with the emotions, notice any blocks in the body that don't let the good feeling through. If they find obstructions we do further mental imagery resolution therapy. Once the body has fully accepted the pleasure, I suggest future rehearsal, "Look into the immediate future and do future planning. See yourself getting on with living in this rewarding, successful way. For this picture of yourself is universal and can permeate every area of your life from work, play, love, to friends and family. Do one small scene at a time. With this future planning you are training your unconscious mind to take this positive self image with you always. You don't have to think about it, although you can sit back and consciously review this self portrait anytime. There is always anxiety of change and one step at a time avoids overload and keeps the pleasure going.

"Your unconscious mind will keep the positive self active day after day and hour after hour." (A time distortion hypnotic technique to enhance the experience). "Now take a step into the distant future, four or five years down the road. Imagine yourself having achieved some personal goal. Now ask the future successful self to look back to the present and give you some suggestion or advice to achieve your goal." Usually it's simple yet moving advice.

Looking Back from the Future [2]

I've been treating a freelance businessman whose main job is trouble shooting in his industry. He's successful and renowned for his ability to figure out all the things that can go wrong. He was a very conscientious, hard working, perfectionist, driven man, and a compulsive personality who had converted his work ethic into his personal life. His file was one constant future worry. The anxiety of vigilance impeded his personal development, as a bachelor yearning for a love relationship he was a dismal failure. The need to control is the basic script of obsessive compulsive personality types. The bottom line is control of their own emotions, especially rage. In treatment, he quickly recognized that future worries in personal living only increased anxiety to a state of paralysis which finally led to withdrawal. When he looked back from the future he had rarely picked the catastrophes that actually happened. With amazing decisiveness he began living for today, free to explore and expand himself. An imagery journey back home revealed a distant, unemotional, unaffectionate family life. Memories of childhood games with his friends came back and he found his original playful child. In his positive mental imagery he saw himself as a young child riding his new bike and smiling with joy. The updated picture of the adult today riding his bike filled him with the same excitement. Shortly after, he did a celebration ritual and bought a bike that he continues to enjoy today. He stored both pictures in his stomach, his self center. Focusing on the internal visualization he breathed deeply as the good feeling radiated throughout his body. The heart area was blocked and would not let the good feelings in. Strange, for the heart symbolized his yearning for companionship. As we focused on his heart using mental imagery an automatic thought popped up and he heard, "I don't deserve it." This was a script of "don't enjoy" that subtly, nonverbally permeated his entire childhood. With determination he said, "I will enjoy," and the good feelings spread through his heart and his whole body filled with joy. In the future rehearsal of day to day living he was having a rewarding love relationship and a healthy family life. The successful person from the distant future looked back and gave him simple advice, saying, **"Do it."**

A bright young woman ravaged by anxiety attacks which overflowed into depressions was able to tune in to her automatic thoughts. These messages are just below consciousness. She had to listen to the voice in her head. After every opinion or idea there was critical judgment of her behavior. The harsh judge, an internalization of her mother, was constantly attacking the internal child for every activity in the past, and action in the present. The internal child reacted with fear, insecurity, loss of confidence and often bouts of melancholy. The critical parent ego state is on top and a child on the bottom in Eric Berne's model of Transactional Analysis. The adult ego state, that is realistic, thinks logically, and deals only with the facts, is in the middle. Dysfunctional, this young lady lived a life of parent and child ego state battlings with the dominant critical parent wreaking havoc on the inner child. As we worked on in therapy the child finally stood up and protested. Squashed previously by the overbearing parent, the contaminated adult began to emerge, gradually accepting the child and joining it in the battle against the critical parent, now a formidable team that could block the attack of her oppressive judge ego. Eventually, a reshuffling of her internal executive board occurred and the adult became executive in charge of all these ego states. With this accomplishment we took a picture of the new president of her board, dressed in a business suit, carrying an elegant briefcase, standing on top of a mountain, yelling, "Wow!" Five years down the road she saw herself managing her own business. Looking back to the present she told herself, "You're on track, keep going." With patients who are discouraged at their progress and don't have a positive self image I explain that the camera in their mind is capable of taking future success pictures. This has been proven in a study on sports psychology. One basketball team meditated, while another practiced regularly. Studies showed that the imagery team did as well or better than the team that practiced.

Collapsing Anchors

In the exercise of positive mental imagery occasionally a negative image appears bringing painful emotions. This may also occur as people review their success, and spontaneously reflect back on scenes of failure. Collapsing anchors is an unknown neuropsychological reaction that can change a visual imprint in the brain through the imagery technique of split screen viewing. Place the negative picture on the bottom screen and the positive picture on the top screen. Now gently pull down the top screen, letting the positive self image slowly pass over the negative one. Let your imaginative mind complete the photographic process. You may be pleasantly surprised with the new picture that emerges. Frequently, the positive image dominates in a new and colorful way. Should the pictures get worse, it's time for more hypnotherapy.

After the photographic session I go through my good news/bad news routine. "Don't be upset if the old behavior comes back, for it will, briefly." It's like your personal computer, when you first turn it on, the old program may pop up immediately and fill the screen. If this happens, don't worry about it. Don't kick yourself. Press your positive self image re-entry key to bring your new way of living back into the present.

Celebration Ritual

After positive mental imagery I recommend a therapeutic ritual, basically a celebration of the patient's achievement. Years ago I thought rituals were silly, superficial and unrealistic. I've certainly changed my mind, for rituals and ceremonies positively condition life achievements. Do something to acknowledge who you are. "Go out and celebrate." Like birthdays, marriages or graduations, it's time to recognize personality growth. I leave them with a last double bind. "This is a great beginning," which leaves the door open for ongoing progress.

In all psychotherapy there is a natural and healthy resistance, like the child rebelling against the parent to emancipate and become independent. One way to rebel is to prove the psychiatrist wrong by demonstrating that changes are much more than a new start, they're an entrenched process of maturation.

With the end of a love relationship or the death of a loved one, the therapeutic ritual is painful, yet serious healing. "Go back to the cemetery and say goodbye," or "write a goodbye letter to the person you've lost." For personal change I recommend writing a short story of the childhood trauma they've just resolved and stress the need for an ending. On the next visit they share the ritual. If they give me their letter or story to read, I quickly refuse, explaining, "I couldn't to it justice." I act as an editor as they read their writing. I, as their editor, accentuate or add a final touch, perhaps note a part they've left out and frequently suggest they write an additional paragraph that will come from our sharing.

The goodbye rituals are paradoxical, for the catharsis of tears and anger are so painful you want to escape. Stay with your feelings, for the only way to the light at the end of the tunnel is through it. The waves of grief flow into the shallows of relief and recovery. It may take two or three writing sessions to complete your goodbye, but then you're free to live in the present!

CHAPTER EIGHT

Death Imagery

A young man wants to die, having lost yet another career. He had returned to university as a mature student and was soon overwhelmed by the volume of work. Self critical over realistic stress, he labeled it another failure, adding to future hopelessness, leading to a serious depression. Tragedy sometimes comes in threes, as his beloved grandmother died and his lover abandoned him. The pain was too much to bear and he wanted to die. Working with him in group therapy I applied the Eriksonian principle of accepting where he was, and helping him to find the next step. I suggested a death imagery experience. Step by step imagine your own suicide. He drove into the garage, closed the door, left the car running and crawled into the back seat. As he smelled the fumes he became sleepy and died. His young nephews found him and cried, calling for their mother. The initial concern was short lived, as he experienced his relief from suffering. Even at the funeral his mother's cries soon passed as the earth covered him, lulling him into peacefulness. Death imagery here only confirmed this patient's strong suicidal impulses.

Other group members shared earlier suicidal experiences. One man told of his addiction to cocaine and how close he came to death, standing on a bridge ready to jump. The image of his only caring "mother", his grandmother, flashed through his mind and he stepped back, deciding to live and never touching cocaine again. A woman in the group relived her teenage suicide attempt brought on by depression and alcoholism. Her death imagery, much to her surprise, revealed an intense love for her older sister whom she saw crying over her grave. As she spoke the tears flowed and she vowed never to hurt herself for it would destroy her sister. Another woman in the group pleaded with the young man not to kill himself as she recalled the suicide attempt of her brother. She then shared her own suicide attempt and hospitalization as a teenager. Her depression had been overwhelming and she couldn't have imagined or believed how happy she would be today. There were no material gains or great successes, but intense satisfaction with her own life and personal growth was rewarding. As each patient talked I interacted and stroked them for growth, recognizing their courage and strengths. Hitting the bottom of the barrel left one place to go - up. I congratulated them as I repeated their successes in coping with pain and depression. I shared the reality that depressions are self limiting, with or without treatment. They all lift, even though some appear to go on forever. Everyone recovers from depression, without residual damage to the personality. As members of this group had shown so clearly, all had grown from previous pain. The suicidal young man become more alert and optimistic as he heard their stories. While he said little, he was obviously involved, listening intently. The Principle of Universality, acknowledging that he wasn't alone, touched him deeply.

To honour and acknowledge the achievement of the patients in the group who had survived tragedy, we began an exercise of positive self imagery. I asked each of them to find in their mind's eye a positive image of themselves. For those who were not there yet and still living with the turmoil of their pain, the camera in their mind's eye could take positive future planning images. The woman who survived her suicide attempt now saw the distressed teenager holding hands with the surviving adult and both smiling. At the end of the session the young man gave me a "no suicide" contract, he promised he would contact a professional if he felt overwhelmed. When I have a bond with a patient the "no suicide" contract works. In addition, we re-established life lines with his family and began daily therapeutic sessions, for he had refused a brief stay in the Crisis Unit of a psychiatric hospital. The death imagery he described that night was so powerful. It proved to me once again that facing your demons and going through the pain, grieving your losses and disappointments, will lead to the light at the end of the tunnel, and a stronger more complete self image. I am more convinced that ever that "the truth shall set you free!"

Mirroring - How We See Ourselves Through Others

The young child is initially right brained and visual before the language skills of the left brain develop. He or she learns by mirroring. Looking in the face of the warm, playful, smiling, loving mother the child learns he is loved and experiences himself as worthwhile. The converse is true, for the harsh tones of a rejecting caregiver only instill feelings of fear and a sense of inadequacy.

As psychoanalysis advanced from transference resolution, to "self psychology" it opened the therapeutic value of mirroring as a therapeutic healing process. The psychoanalyst, shifting from his stoical, distant approach, became warmly responsive to the patient. At times of conflict resolution, the therapist, recognizing the patient change, reflected a new image of self worth. This empathic interpretation was seen as the therapeutic mirroring and the creative healing process of psychoanalysis. In the group work I do the relief through sharing, the Principle of Universality emerges, for we all have common pain, conflicts, joy and pleasure. Healing occurs by seeing ourselves in others. In the sharing of the death imagery, the suicidal impulses of the patient, reflected in others with relief and hope for recovery.

Positive self mirroring is insightful. Looking inside at all our ego states, seeing and feeling their growth from early childhood to the present, protecting, respecting and reowning each one, leads to wholeness and integration. By seeing the other person in our eyes, we can rise above narcissism, to genuine love and empathy. Finally, we can answer the age old question - *if not for me, who will be, if only me, who am I?*

CHAPTER NINE

The Expanding Self

Maturing and growing as a person, is the process of fulfilling our human potential and becoming more of who were are. Emancipation from the past and emotional separation from parents are necessary for survival. The theory of evolution suggests that the continuation of the species depends upon the young surviving after the parents die. They must be strong and independent, capable of caring for themselves and the generation to come.

Reaching your potential means filling up the personality pie with more and more of your ego states, being able to flow from one to another spontaneously and appropriately to changing life experiences.

Accepting the polarities of personality makes us whole. In our goal to be independent, self sufficient and strong, we need to accept the opposite, our weakness, dependency, and need for nurturing. It is only through the free flow of opposite ego states through the figure eight of polarities that we can become complete and love another. If we don't emancipate into our separate selves, we become enmeshed or over attached and risk falling into the painful triangle of rescuer/persecutor/victim. With clear cut individual boundaries we can touch and bond to each other intensely, lovingly, caringly, yet still remain free to explore beyond the boundaries of our relationship.

The fence around healthy intimacy is open and permeable with unlocked doors. Full trust gives each lover freedom to explore life independently and return with new discoveries. Flexibility of movement allows for change and stimulates continued excitement in long-term relationships. The childhood curiosity of the inner child is flourishing in the grown up adult of each partner.

A Healthy Love Relationship

When the right and left brain work together you can be logical and imaginative, blend realism with fantasy, and put feelings to our words. When music and lyrics play harmoniously with the images of life, the movie of personal living flows like a river. Stagnation and stuckness of life is painful, yet comfortable, for it avoids the natural anxiety of movement. Take the risk of the unfamiliar journey, stimulated by the excitement of discovery. You can avoid the overwhelming anxiety that causes paralysis by putting aside the future worries of "what if," and the past regrets of yesterday's mistakes or pain. In the thought distortions of past and future you miss the present. Go one small step at a time, for new beginnings are pleasant stopovers in the journey. Negative thinking, self criticism or self blame, turns disappointment into anxiety and depression, becoming a huge boulder in the road ahead.

Eric Berne, in his work on Transactional Analysis [7] developed his ego state concepts of parent, adult and child. He opened our field of view to see, hear and experience parts of ourselves, moment to moment. The parent ego state has its critical and caring parts and speaks in domineering "shoulds," "musts," and "got tos." With the pointed finger of authority it becomes the conscience and ethics of past generations and judgmental behavior. It motivates behavior by obligation and duty. The adult ego state deals with information and facts in a logical, realistic manner, appropriate to life's situations. The child ego state, the center of emotions, divided into a natural free part and an adapted part, includes all of the feelings of the young children we once were. This natural child is still present in the adult today, needy, hungry, friendly, playful, loving, scared, angry, mischievous, even sexy, while the adapted child is trying to please. All these ego states need to be discovered, reowned, protected and upgraded into adult living today. Hopefully, your adult can become the CEO, in charge of the inner cabinet, accepting and recognizing all members. Your adult ego state can guide each ego state to express itself in useful ways that resolve conflict and complete the Gestalts of life experiences and set you free. Face past disappointments and lost dreams or opportunities. Mourn your losses. Go through the sadness and the anger. Complete your grieving and say goodbye to the past, and free yourself to live in the present and plan for tomorrow.

The Hanging Judge

I believe the internal critical parent ego state is over active in most of the psychiatric conflicts I see. It beats the internal child into depression. Posing as a realistic and reasonable adult, it speaks with "shoulds" and "shouldn'ts", "musts" and "ought tos" rather than the "wills" or "won'ts" or "want" or "don't want." It disguises itself by invading adult space and contaminating the factual, realistic ego. The resulting stress and free floating anxiety of constant pressure on the internal child boils over into burn out or secondary depression.

A handsome middle aged man has had a chronically non productive life. His life has ranged from pacifity to depression, affecting his love life. He has a broken marriage and many failed relationships and a career that is stagnant. With psychological insight he became aware of a critical parent yelling "shoulds" at his internal child who's always rebelling with, "fuck you." While he is a bright adult who is very knowledgeable about life and has a number of university degrees, he is ineffective in altering the system. There's a continual argument between the big critical parent and small "fuck you" child. It goes back and forth in many combinations. The critical parent eventually becomes frustrated with the obnoxious child and beats it into depression. When it recovers the child starts fighting back in its rebellious passive/aggressive way, defeating every initiative of progress. This bright adult watches ineffectively, while the passive/aggressive angry child takes over executive control. Could you imagine a major corporation being run by a small child?

This internal cabinet drama offers you many possibilities for resolution. Could the effective adult become more powerful and be voted into executive control? If the rebellious child begins taking over the meeting, could it be asked to keep quiet with the promise that it would get something it wants after the meeting. Quid Pro Quo works quite well. You can't get rid of any ego states. Reown all your parts. Have them negotiate. Reshuffle the inner cabinet until the blocks are removed and the process continues. Let the passive/aggressive with its stuckness shift its anger into action and its curiosity into exploration in day to day living.

I was often surprised to find the origins of this unrelenting judge to be more severe than the actual parents. Why? For protection or motivation? Do you need to beat yourself to learn or work or achieve? Is there no natural curiosity, the urge to discover, or the pride of accomplishment? The critical parent's role as protector was obvious, especially in the obsessive/compulsive person, for the whole structure is devoted to control. The bottom line though, was to control his own anger. The boiler concept of hostility, the suppression of aggression without adequate release, builds intense internal pressure until a trivial event erupts in a rage attack. The critical parent stands righteous and firmly taking control, suppresses the anger, only to have it build up pressure again. As in so many life experiences, here the attempted solution is the problem, the suppression of the aggressive energy, not the explosion of hostility. The solution, of course, is to build safety valves for affective assertion. But here the critical judge would lose his job, for the sole purpose of control would be obsolete.

A young man had a near miss car accident. While driving on the highway his car skidded over black ice and did a 360 degree turn, ending up on the other side of the road, going the wrong way. Fortunately, he escaped with only minor damage to his car and no injury to others. While initially relieved, a few hours later he began to imagine his death in the accident and became panic stricken. In the therapy after questioning this irrational, catastrophic projection, we did an affect bridge to the past. Initially, he went back to a grade one experience. He was sitting in class and was terrified of going home because he had been told by his parents that they would be away for the afternoon. He was preoccupied with the future anxiety of being home alone. Lifting the next layer off this experience he relived an early childhood scene. He was standing in his bed, crying for his mother, who was away. He was not alone for his father and an older sister where there. With conscious processing of these events he shared the excruciating pain of being scared and wanted to get away from it. He wanted to rid himself of this frightened child. At this time he realized that his whole personality structure was top heavy. He had a pushy parent ego state emphasizing independence and self reliance. It was an attempt to hide, or suppress the polarity of his personality, the opposite of his strength, the terrified dependent child who wanted his mother. This child not only emerged after the accident, but was unconsciously, subtly invading his life. He realized that staying in a love relationship that was obviously over was a fear of future aloneness and a resurgence of his dependent, frightened child.

Another woman was crying in the group and had been stuck for a long time in the internal, ongoing battle between critical parent and scared child. She finally understood her reluctance to shift the paradigm. The judge was the only one strong enough to manage her inner terror. We've now proven the obvious, that the harsh hanging judge is a self creation, to protect and control unacceptable inner feelings. It had been constructed at a much earlier age and today served a primitive, obsolete system still operating in the grown up. How can we update or improve the system? We need to accept all our emotions fully. If it's overwhelming, let a little out at a time. Free the realistic, mature adult from the grips of the critical judge and let it take executive control. Sometimes the parent has been so big and powerful that a conglomerate of other ego states needs to combine to make an effective executive team that can manage the self. Occasionally, you need to make a deal with the critical parent, perhaps for early retirement, or bring in a loving parent ego state.

A patient, in brief intensive imagery therapy, discovered a very critical parent that was constantly criticizing her and keeping her in deep depression. As well, her "all or nothing at all" thinking was restrictive and mostly negative, again a major factor in her depression. In mental imagery therapy she was able to focus on the "all or nothing" thinking and see as it as black or white thinking, which quickly transposed into rainbow thinking. The colors brightened her up and she began to smile, feeling happy and content. The critical judge kept interfering, telling her she didn't deserve to feel good and therefore her body couldn't accept the positive feelings. But she began to deal with the judge in a very creative way. Initially she wanted to get rid of him. Finally, she accepted that the judge might have some usefulness, but would be better at something else. During the imagery journey she asked him if he would go into the other room. This allowed her to take a very free and spontaneous journey into the joys of positive thinking, with a positive mental image. While we were discussing her imagery journey she became aware that her judge had returned and was criticizing her. She thought it would be nice to give him an occasional break. Maybe he's been working too hard, twenty-four hours a day. I remarked that judges take a recess. She imagined a judge's chamber where he could take a rest and let her explore her life.

Contamination

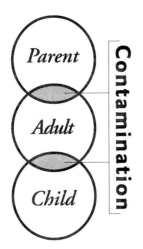

The words of the critical parent ringing in your head are frequently misinterpreted as the voice of the realistic adult. The life time habit of judgmental thinking is a contamination of the adult ego, which may be distorted beyond recognition.

Contamination of Ego States

Through years of habit, the *shoulds, musts, got tos, have to* words of the parental ego state are erroneously accepted as the voice of the factual adult. With insight they can be distinguished, freeing the submerged adult. The adult may be underdeveloped, but its potential for realistic thinking is there. Nurture, guide and educate the adult, for its eventual role as president of your inner cabinet.

The obsessive/compulsive personality disorder is the extreme of left brain processing, where analysis of life's events becomes excessively detailed, obsessive, and ruminative. Constant pros and cons over every issue leads to stagnation, with future worries, indecision and failure to act. Waffling back and forth leads to anxiety, exhaustion and depression. The personality is rigid, driven and perfectionistic. The excessive high code of personal ethics and work addiction eventually causes burn out. The judge ego state is masquerading as the adult, even deceiving itself that the words and thoughts are realistic and factual. The difficulty distinguishing the distorted automatic thoughts of the judge, from the realistic thinking of the adult ego state, can be facilitated by a right brain exercise. Imagine a group of ten to twelve people observing the event. What would most of them say? How would they describe what they saw? What would be their realistic, factual correction of your distorted judgmental thinking? Don't be discouraged with the difficulty in shifting your thinking, for old belief systems are deeply rooted in the past.

As you can see from the diagram similar processes occur in the rebellious child ego state. The rage at authorities appears logical, justified and valid, until you hear the voice of the raging child, pretending to be the grownup. Separation of the child from adult contamination allows freedom and expansion of the personality.

The histrionic personality disorder, spontaneous, outgoing, attractive and self centered, is the extreme of the right brain processing.

Emotional thinking supersedes realistic thinking. Life issues are exaggerated to high drama, over attachment and the excessive need for attention destroys relationships. Emotions erupt and change, like the movements of a roller coaster, to self deception. The person believes they are totally factual and thinking logically. That inner child state has contaminated the adult, and acts as if it's grown up. It's easy to see the confusion of the real self, if both the parent and the child alternate masquerading as the realistic adult ego state. With the next life crises the old distorted thoughts of the contaminated ego states come back first, hopefully followed by realistic correction.

Writing helps. Keep a diary. On one side of the page write your automatic thoughts, on the other side your realistic corrections. Your anxiety or depression will drop if your corrections are valid. Putting your thoughts on paper is a blending of right brain visualization and left brain thinking, a simple exercise for integration and cognitive retraining.

Game Plan

The therapeutic game plan I recommend in therapy is an internal cabinet of a personal corporation. If you went down to the dissociative workroom and imagined all your ego states sitting around the table negotiating some present business and saw the critical parent at the head telling *"shoulds,"* and the internal child rebelling with *"fuck you,"* we would certainly have a stalemate. Perhaps there is a bright, educated adult who knows everything that is going on but he seems to be either off at the sidelines or sitting down at the other end of the table. Of course, the continual argument back and forth leads to extended frustration. You don't want the critical parent running the internal cabinet, and you certainly don't want the rebellious child defeating every initiative of progress. We need to promote this bright adult. Perhaps elections are in order. If the rebellious, angry child takes over the meeting, he can be asked to be quiet with the promise of a reward. He would get a special treat for cooperating. You can honor the parent by making him Chairman of the Board, providing this does not cause major problems for the others.

Some of my patients developed clever game plans for their ego states, a reorganization of the team positions of their inner self to produce a winner. A psychologically sophisticated man who had gained great insight from many years of therapy was still troubled by social withdrawal and recurrent depression. He discovered an overbearing, critical parent and a rebellious, sneaky inner-child. The constant internal battle left a stalemate. With all his insights, he remained impotent and failed to move. He found a powerful part that periodically exploded in sports that were physical, a part that sought revenge on his opponent. Fortunately, he kept this under control in day-to-day life by his internal judge.

He visualized his ego states as a hockey team and decided to use the powerful parent as the goalie, where his angry protective strength could be used against the opponent. But something was missing. He realized his bright, knowledgeable adult was only a spectator, an outside observer, all knowing, but without power. He made him the coach and restored him to executive control. Plays developed and emerged and the strong killer part was used as defense to shoot the puck to his weaker forward for an easy goal. This fascinating imagery removed the block and opened a new route in the journey of change. The new team, unfamiliar with the new roles, would need much experience and many games before it become a winner.

Ego State Maturation

A young woman, recently recovered from alcohol addiction, came to psychotherapy for her post-alcohol depression. We worked through her early childhood trauma of major psychological abuse by an older brother who dominated and controlled her. He continually negated any of her opinions, threatening her if she did not follow his dictates. She grew up terrified. In psychotherapy, the conflict emerged in the transference. At times when I interacted she felt I was trying to control and dominate her like her brother. In one session she confronted me and despite trepidation, continued to negotiate until she succeeded in expressing her viewpoint and having me listen. In the next session, feeling very good, she said she felt like a fighter, which in the past sounded negative. Today she felt the excitement of confrontation, something she never did with her threatening brother. As she glowed, I asked her to sit back and take a positive self image. We were going to take a picture and celebrate the discovery of her fighter. She came up with the image of the Greek goddess, Athena. She saw herself as Athena, dressed in a business suit and yet having Athena's shield, able to confront, negotiate and fight for her rights. She had a tremendous glow of pleasure and satisfaction as she saw this part of herself, Athena the fighter.

At first she was going to store it in her shoulder, but it didn't feel right. The aggressive fighter part belonged in her lower back and as she imaged this picture of herself, she could feel a surge of energy up the back, throughout her entire body, from the tips of her toes to the top of her head. The crown opening at the top of her head was open to the universe. There was no blockage within the body that resisted her becoming Athena, the warrior. She smiled and glowed, and felt alive with the energy of a fighter part that could negotiate and debate in socially acceptable ways. In a future rehearsal she saw herself in different life situations, one scene at a time, where Athena the warrior was effectively asserting herself, at work or play, and in personal relationships. She was training her unconscious mind to do this automatically. It would take practice, and the old, frightened, depressed person would come back, but this image would always be there to refresh her memory. She came out of the hypnotic experience, talking about this surge of energy and went home to celebrate in her own personal way the development of Athena.

Ego State Transplant

A woman lost her job and became depressed. As she discussed the conflict at work she felt an internal rage, but felt helpless to fight back. Using this as an affect bridge to the past, she saw a picture of her mother's face, looking disapprovingly at her as a seven year old child. This began the homework of writing her childhood movie. When she came to the next session, she described the childhood scene of mother's rejection. Doing transformational imagery work she looked into her body and saw her heart burning as red hot lava, which was a weight in her chest. Suddenly this big ugly thing smashed to pieces. The scene switched to an open sunny field. In the conscious processing of this image she was pleasantly surprised and asked the question, "What is my power?"

In the next session, somewhat embarrassed, she described a Chinese mythical figure, a cherub, dressed in red ribbons who moved on rings of fire. This cherub was a hero that she saw in movies and it redressed social injustices using all sorts of magical weapons, energized by fire. As she talked about this Chinese mythical figure, called La Cha, she felt excited and cried with an ecstasy experience. This was her power, how could she integrate it into the adult? Recently, she was becoming more effectively assertive and forthright. We then decided to take a positive mental picture of her new personal power and in the process she saw a video of La Cha coming towards her. It was her face on La Cha, but eventually she was able to integrate and fuse with her. She glowed and smiled with this vivid experience which she stored in her stomach, her self center.

With future rehearsal she imagined a new sense of personal power and affective assertiveness evolving into every area of daily life. After the imagery experience, with a new set of skills, she was beaming and no longer depressed. She had an aura of self confidence. She would never let anyone push her into a corner again. Now, the homework, a celebration ritual of her new found personal power.

If you lack an early prototype for a new ego state, adopt one, or create one from one that you have admired in others. Seeing and feeling the love you receive from a friend, a favorite aunt, or a doting grandparent, can be the source of a internal loving parent ego state. Through the process of mirroring, you can transplant a healthy self-caring ego state into your self center.

Playing with a young child can help you to awaken and develop the embryonic, curious child within. Mythical figures or real life heroes can be interjected for strength and courage. Psychological transplants are bloodless but need time and practice to be synthesized with the rest of you. Through trial and error they mature and become ego syntonic (feel like you). Protect, nurture, comfort, reward and use your new ego state. Let it radiate and permeate throughout your living.

Integration

Through the wonderful, imaginative aspects of the right brain you can see, feel and experience these ego states, rather than simply intellectualize their presence. Many of my patients recognize themselves in very personal ways, and act like a cheerleader urging themselves on, rather than a critic who harasses, blames and demands perfection. They accept the inner child, even if it's scared or needy. One of my patient's protested, "I've dealt with my needy child. Why am I still tormented? I know my mother was sick and unavailable and I had to look after her. I know my father beat me, but I've forgiven him. He's great today. I've accepted the hurt, needy child and grieved my past pain. But he still rages on. I want to stop it." "Yes," I responded, "You had healed the painful past but your needs still exist. How are you filling those needs today, for the past is in the present?" One patient described a forest child who left the home to survive the abuse, as well as a sneaky avenger who manipulates for survival and gets revenge. As you find the embryo of an ego state you've ignored, subdued, or rejected, reown and accept it. Nurture this new ego state. Give it time to grow and become part of the inner grown up self.

The integration of a previously dissociated ego state requires processing. Facing and re-experiencing the original trauma. Feeling the pain you suffered and possibly the guilt, shame, embarrassment and humiliation over your own behavior. To heal you must grieve your losses. The childhood pain, the wasted years, the lost dreams. Grieving is healing and ending the grief frees and energizes the ego state to live again in the grown up adult.

If you see a missing part of yourself in another, use the reflection from that mirror to develop your self. You can always create another part of yourself and integrate it into your personality. Give it history if you wish and it will become your own. If you've been too serious, develop a sense of humor and adapt it to all aspects of your life. Take it to work and develop a warm repartee and share absurd life experiences. The payoff of fun easily out weighs the risks of embarrassment and humiliation. Interact, listen, share and cross over the internal boundary of narcissism to empathy.

Each ego state is a "persona," some are like a small individual within each of us and appear to have a full complement of behaviour, emotions, sensation and knowledge. Others are less complete,

269

fragment or specific purpose states, i.e., one created solely to be present for verbal put-downs. Leave the boundaries between each distinct but open, able to flow from one to another with awareness and ease, for thick walls keep you a distant and fragmented person. Now you can respond to life's events appropriately, rewardingly and decisively. The Personality Pie is now like a wheel on an axle that turns and responds to people in context, appropriately and realistically to external life issues. The vast range of responses can be liberating and rewarding. You now have choice and free will.

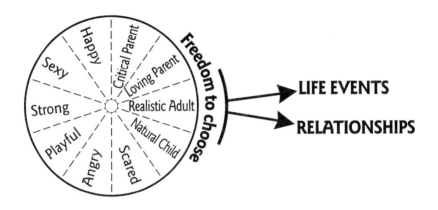

Let the adult take charge and accept and use all parts in a realistic way for effective and creative action. Avoid contamination; don't let the judgmental parent sneak in under the guise of realistic thinking. One woman creatively responded to her mother's criticism by saying, "I never make mistakes. All my past behavior and decisions were made with the knowledge I had at the time and were the best I could do. When things changed I responded with what I had learned." Don't let the child, run by emotions, contaminate the adult and assume executive control of the personality, for it will gallop into instability and bolt out of control. Let the adult recognize and guide these emotions with full acceptance and acknowledgment of all ego states, the ones you like as well as the ones you don't. The whole total self, more than an end point, is a process sparked by curiosity of the surrounding world, turning exploration anxiety into the excitement of discovery. Function on "wants" and "likes" or "don't wants" and "don't likes," when deciding action. Let your ego states flow and respond effectively and harmoniously to the outside world. The pleasure of a genuine, totally full person is a supreme satisfaction and one of the unsung rewards of living. Your self worth, motivated more by yourself rather than by others, can now take genuine personal action. Standing alone, initially scary and unfamiliar, quickly leads to a unique, powerful individual, capable of action and filled with the joy of personal freedom. Now you can live as Shakespeare said, *"This above all, to thyne own self be true."*

We need all our ego states to manage realistic stress, to cope and survive, and to tolerate disappointment, grieve our losses and overcome embarrassment and humiliation. Transfer self ridicule into absurd life humor and blend seriousness with playfulness. Convert anger into self assertion. Switch anxiety to excitement. Enjoy success and the rewards of achievement. Nurture yourself and be empathetic. Relate, trust, interact, share and love. Grow, change and create.

Hemispheric Asymmetry

Before I bring you up to date on right brain/left brain research I would like to clarify the basic concepts again. I focused on hemispheric specialization as a model for my clinical work in mental imagery and hypnotherapy. The left brain, dominant in 85% of usually right handed people, contains the speech center, while the right brain, has been described as the imagery hemisphere. Through auto-hypnosis, or self hypnosis, my patients have bypassed their auditory, rational side into the visual and imaginative. Recent studies in hemispheric specialization have advanced the original model describing hemispheric asymmetry. Simply, each hemisphere processes information with ideas and feelings, however the left hemisphere is the positive thinker, resulting in positive mood and attitude. The right side is a more negative thinker, followed by more negative moods. In interactions and discussions the left tends to be more agreeable, while the right is disagreeable.

A group of normal subjects were shown an ambiguous picture. When directed at the right brain, the participants responded with negative thoughts of death and danger. When the picture was directed to the left brain, it stimulated stories of adventure and excitement. Studies show that the right hemisphere was the original site of early language processing. The left hemisphere took over later as language skills increased. Perhaps in my work accessing early childhood trauma the pain was more accessible through the right brain. The treatment may involve processing incomplete past traumatic memories from the right brain into a complete narrative of the left. The completed experience with resolution extends beyond the painful event into more positive thoughts. As an example, when grief is over the memories and feelings of sadness might be replaced with pleasant memories of the lost one, free of emotional pain and now centered in the left brain.

One patient's description of her thinking was a revelation. An extremely bright, highly educated career woman had resolved her childhood neglect by an alcoholic mother and an absent father who left the family when she was quite young. Nevertheless, excessive anxiety responses continued in minor events. She was quite aware of catastrophic thinking which revealed future worrying. Her attempts at realistic correction, which usually failed to lower her distress, were, "You shouldn't worry about the future until in happens." When I pointed out this was her parent/judge talking, not a realistic here and now adult assessment of the problem, she was surprisingly moved. At the next visit she shared a simple but powerful insight. "When I'm working," she said, "I'm always logical and realistic. But in my personal life, when my inner child is upset, I respond with a critical parent." For the first time she was aware of different informational processing from each side of her brain. Something clicked and she was now integrated. In the past the right brain processing had been suppressed and isolated from awareness. Now the inhibition had been removed and she has synthesized both systems into one. This feeling of oneness and wholeness was very powerful. Finally she was in her right mind.

Graduation Picture

As you finish this chapter, sit back, relax and meditate. Do an integration imagery video. Imagine all your ego states, whether special purpose of a complete persona, integrating with each other. Is there a special setting where this occurs? As the fusion takes place feel the ecstasy of wholeness and let the good feeling fill you up from the tips of your toes to the top of your head with the joy and contentment of self. Let each player respect, accept and protect each other. Imagine them participating in all of life's events together. Do a future rehearsal. See yourself in each situation of your life, active, involved, relaxed and free, caring for yourself while you empathize with others. (Some may prefer to do this exercise in the presence of their therapist.)

When my patients complete their therapy, I recommend a Graduation Picture. One young man, who was an anxious, analytical, perfectionist left-brain personality, found his right brain. During therapy he had discovered his primary visual track and was able to see the big picture of his life and feel a full range of emotions from anger to love and caring. Through hypnotherapy he resolved his childhood trauma of emotional abandonment from an alcoholic father and a mother preoccupied with her marriage turmoil.

Now full of excitement, and looking forward to a new career, he said goodbye to the group. In his graduation picture he saw himself as a powerful eagle, soaring through the sky, seeing the whole world below. As a strong wind approached he changed directions and flew above it. Glowing with excitement he carried his symbol of strength, confidence and freedom in his heart and in his head.

Mending Fences

Now that you've resolved your past trauma, grown, integrated and matured, how do you live in the present with the people from your past?

Paradoxically, over attachment was the relationship between the abused child and the abuser. Why, you ask? Harlow's monkey experiments demonstrated this phenomenon. Monkeys separated from their mothers and placed in cages with cloth monkeys would hang on more intensely to the cloth monkeys when there was danger. When cold air was blown through the cloth monkey to frighten the infant it only intensified its grip on the transitional mother, for this was its only security. Frightened children do the same thing. In times of danger they hold on tighter to their only security, their parents, even if they were the perpetrators of abuse.

After healing of the past, when confidence and personal powers have developed, the person is now able to detach from the emeshement and reattach, if they wish, with more distant and separate boundaries. One of my patients, after facing her rage at her mother's neglect, forgave her. Today she feels a genuine concern and a care for her mother, as they re-established a new, pleasant relationship, with mutual caring. Finally they have become friends with more openness and sharing than ever before. Mending their fences now has a statute of limitations on the past, for they both live now, in the present. Conflicts still arise, usually focusing on differences of opinion. Occasionally, the past gets in their eyes, but only briefly. The new boundaries have "No Trespassing" signs. Both avoid the drama triangle of victim/persecutor/rescuer. This woman is now free to be herself and relate to her parents, not from old "shoulds," but from "wants or don't wants." Most of the time you mend fences, for only a few homes are so dirty that you need to move out.

CHAPTER TEN

The Hypnotherapist

Psychoanalysts rarely talk because they fear contaminating the transference. I talk. I interact quickly and intensely with the patient. Doing brief intensive individual therapy followed by group therapy requires rapid attachment. I need to get on the patients wave length and initiate a bond of trust. We need to decide if we can work together or if we cannot. We may not like each other, but the patient and I need to connect in some meaningful way. The patient has to sense that I am competent and that I care and am on his/her wave length. I need to sense that the patient is motivated to change and learn and has the potential for personal psychological awareness and the honesty and openness to share his/her inner pain.

A successful middle-aged professional woman, bitter and angry in every area of her life, was continually confronting everyone she met, including me, her new psychiatrist. After a few sessions I confronted her, "You can't scapegoat me with all your anger, that is not psychotherapy." We worked it through. She understood the nature of her belligerence and was willing to take a step back and look at her life. "How do I begin?" she asked. "Go home and write out your childhood story. Do it as a movie script. Write all of the parts. Play all the different people in your life and I will be your director. One small scene at a time is a good start," I explained. We began, she wrote and relived massive childhood trauma, neglect and abandonment by alcoholic parents. Her rage was there, just where it belonged. As the anger flowed, I saw the tear in her eye and focused on her sadness. She then grieved the pain and loss of her childhood. Over the next few sessions a triple grief - the pain of her childhood, the loss of her childhood dream that should have been, and the loss of the years that followed through depression and misdirected anger. I helped her fill out each experience and accompanied her through the childhood dungeons sharing her pain. The real distress was overwhelming and more painful than the defensive neurosis. I was there to support her, acknowledge her distress and the validity of her pain, and share my strength with her to help her accept the whole trauma. Dr. J. Watkins describes this as "resonating." The therapist experiences, suffers and celebrates with the patient. It's similar to how we identify with the hero or heroine of a movie, experiencing their emotions and imagining ourselves in their life situation.

Even though I cannot see the movie in their mind's eye, I imagine it in mine and go with them to relive the traumatic memories. More than just a technician inducing hypnotic trance, reforming techniques of regression, affect and somatic bridge or dissociative table, I'm a travelling companion, sharing, empathizing and giving them strength and hope.

I'm a "boundary dancer." I step into their space when it's too painful to walk alone and help them see a new pathway. I share my feelings and support theirs, or open up ones they have suppressed. I step out to voice a realistic danger or correct a false belief system that was made by a small child under duress. I step out to avoid the intensity of their pain and to function as an objective observer offering realistic observations. I step back when they need to walk alone to independence and autonomy.

In a clinical study of group psychotherapy, professional observers watched a number of therapists doing their different forms of psychotherapy. They concluded that they couldn't discern the difference between the distinct psychological models, whether Gestalt, Transactional Analysis or Analytically Oriented Therapy.

They found that the best and worst therapy followed the same psychiatric approach. The best therapy depended on the therapist. Music obviously depends on the musician, not the instrument. The great symphony is the harmony developed between patient and therapist. As Dr. Watkins said "we may study psychotherapy as a science but we practice it as an art."

Through imaginative moves of trial and error, we heal the damaged child. The patient makes the moves and the therapist/director keeps the scenes on track, encouraging harmony, synthesis and integration. When healing or growth occurs, a moment of ecstasy, a "happy sad" follows. As Eric Berne said "a painful insight or change is accompanied by Ah ha - the satisfaction of self-discovery, even though it hurts." This is the moment of boundary crossing again. I step in to positively stroke for growth, to acknowledge their achievement, and to condition it with a positive self-image. At this moment I share great detail of the psychological understanding of their shift, not to make them psychotherapists, but to condition their improvement through positive recognition.

I may invite them to cross boundaries into my space where I share a personal experience that mirrors their own. I celebrate their success and resonate with their joy for their improvement is my satisfaction. My work as a psychotherapist is never fatiguing when it is moving in a valid direction whether pain or pleasure. It is only exhausting and frustrating when resistance to change and growth persist, blocking meaningful action.

The Therapist Gets In My Eyes

Resolution of the transference is the major healing process in psychoanalysis. In fact, examining and resolving the therapeutic relationship in any model of psychotherapy is effective therapy.

Unfortunately, waiting for the patient to relive and re-enact his unfinished troubled past may take a long time. You can access this past quickly and effectively, by imaging the transference. A patient in group therapy protests to me, her therapist, "You keep cutting me off. You never let me speak. You're just like my father." "Imagine your father sitting beside me," I answer. Now tell each of us exactly what you think and feel. There was a spontaneous abreaction of rage to a long dead parent. "You never heard me. You always put me down, like I was stupid. I hate you." As the reliving of the repressed pain and anger exploded, she began to hyperventilate. "Use the emotional dimmer switch. Turn down the feelings just a little." Calming down, she continued to express the years of frustration at never being heard. After the emotion settled down, she switched to her adult ego state, who explained that while my style at times irritated her, she now felt the true rage at her father's emotional abuse. The past was in her eyes in the transference. The Gestalt imagery of putting her father in the empty chair brought him into the present and opened her door to resolution of the childhood trauma.

In the transference the past becomes alive again in the present therapeutic relationship. Now, more than an intellectualization reliving the past through mental imagery of the trauma opens all senses of feelings, seeing and thinking, a total experience necessary for the process of healing.

In counter-transference the therapist re-enacts to his past in the relationship with the patient. When my children left home I moved my practice into my home. Despite considerable anxiety of crossing personal boundaries, I was pleasantly surprised to find greater satisfaction in my work. Some of my patients remarked how relaxed I looked. Suddenly the past was in my eyes. The group meeting in my living room was my family back home again and I enjoyed it. As a therapist I had to maintain therapeutic boundaries. The coffee corner which had always been available continued. Now the fruit on the table was naturally eaten, but the door to the Frigidaire remained closed. Positive counter-transference and positive transference can be used effectively, therapeutically and realistically, even without analysis, for the good feelings between therapist and patient are a motivator for both to do good work. Many a patient has said, "I got on with my life because I liked you and I felt so good about my therapy."

CHAPTER ELEVEN

Psychoneuroimmunology
The Science of Mind / Body healing [9]

The immune system consists of one trillion white blood cells that protect us from all kinds of invaders, from environmental dust and pollen, to bacteria, viruses, and abnormal or cancerous cells. This vast army is in constant vigilance, seeking to destroy invaders. Occasionally, it mistakes itself for the enemy, which can cause auto-immune diseases like Rheumatoid Arthritis, Rheumatic Heart Disease, Systemic Lupus Erythematoses and possibly Multiple Sclerosis. An excessive response to mild intruders, like pollens, produces an over-reaction with histamine release that causes the suffering of hayfever and asthma. The immune forces have front line troops called Macrophages that engulf any debris. When it encounters a major invasion of organisms or cancer it summons the specialized forces of the T-cells. The helper T-cells are the commanders. Their release of lymphokines mobilize the killer T-cells, the big guns with highly specialized chemical weapons that can be used against specific organisms or cancer cells. B-cells are the biological arms factory that manufactures antibodies, specific to the type of invader. The forces attack and destroy until the enemy is defeated. When the war is won the suppresser T-cells halt the battle and the troops are demobilized. Memory T-cells remain on guard for they can recognize the enemy quickly in case of re-attack. In AIDS, the virus invades the helper T-cells, disabling the command post. One cancer hypothesis suggests that in the body, during the replacement of cells, some defective cells appear which are normally detected and removed by the immune system. If the prevalence of abnormal cells is excessive, or the immune system impaired, cancer develops.

Stress and the Immune System

Mental stress and depression are major suppressers of the immune system. In grief and bereavement studies it was found that the health of sixty-seven percent of widowers declines within one year of the death of a spouse. Forty-five percent of all bereaved suffer a major depression. Depression and a pessimistic personality show impaired immune responses with subsequent poor health. Seventy-five percent of cancer patients referred for psychotherapy had a previous grief experience and sixty percent were suffering from unresolved grief. During stress large amounts of steroids called cortisol secretions suppress the Macrophage response to infection impairing the immune system. It's not surprising then that mental stress can actually make us physically ill. If the mind can contribute to physical illness, can it help us recover from serious illness as well? With this thinking, clinicians like Dr. Carl Symington and Dr. Bernie Segal [10] have developed a psychological aid to cancer treatment to improve the immune response with a positive mental outlook and positive mental healing imagery.

Exercise produces endorphins (the body's internal narcotics), endo-morphines, which reduce anxiety and depression and create a sense of well being. They may also increase the Macrophage and T-cell production with their chemicals, interlukins and interferon.

A Revelation in Psychoneuroimmunology

In 1989 I presented a workshop titled, *Adding Imagery to Psychotherapy* at the World Conference on Mental Imagery outside Washington, D.C. As usual, I learned more than I taught. Some of the lectures brought in exciting new findings that substantiated the validity of mental imagery. Laboratory tests were confirming the effects of positive mental imagery on the immune system. There was an increase in adherence, or stickiness of the white blood cells, as well as an increase in their number. Imagining an increase in one kind of cell could stimulate a specific increase in that cell itself. Gamma globulin, a biological chemical of the immune system, was measured in the saliva and showed increases with positive mental imagery. These researchers shared with me the beginnings of the revolution in psychoneuroimmunology, developments that would be published in the June, 1989 edition of the Smithsonian magazine. After the conference, on my way to Washington airport I picked up a few copies of the Smithsonian magazine to take to Israel. As I read it on the plane I was extremely excited. The Chief of the Brain Chemistry Section at the National Institute of Mental Health, Bethesda, Maryland, Candice Pert, was the leader of the revolution. This began with her landmark discovery in 1973, identifying the opiate receptor in the brain where morphine-like substances would attach, like a key that fits a lock. Strange, she pondered, that the body would have a receptor site for an external opiate, simply for the purpose of getting high. She deduced that there must be internal body opiates. This sent the world on a search and in 1975 endogenous opiates, endorphins were discovered. They were many times more potent than heroin. The opiate receptor discovery lead to a pharmacological factory of many peptides or neurotransmitter substances that interacted with specific receptors to become the biochemistry of emotions. With the use of Positive Emission Tomography, PET-Scans, using radioactive molecules, sites in the brain and the body where these receptors were found were mapped out. The brain, the immune system, and the endocrine system all had similar receptor sites, sharing common neurotransmitters, "informational substances."

In 1981, Edwin Blaylock, of the University of Texas, found a biological molecule where it wasn't supposed to be. The hormone called ACTH was known to be secreted by the pituitary gland in the brain and belonged to the endocrine system. Blaylock kept finding this hormone in laboratory flasks filled only will human cells belonging to the immune system. He began to wonder if the ACTH, a hormone, was made by the white blood cells as well. He found the informational link between the Immune and Endocrene Systems, each producing the same chemicals.

High density receptor sites were found in three areas of the brain: the frontal cortex, the Hippocampus, and the Amygdala. These correlate with sites of known emotional centers. The breathing centers of the brain stem and sexual areas of the body had high densities of neurotransmitter concentration. They were obviously areas of emotions and all necessary for human survival.

The traditional medical model of the separation of the brain and the nervous system, from the hormonal endocrine system and the immune system is outdated. The mind is now seen as an internal internet with communications by shared neurotransmitter or informational substances. Each system is actively communicating to each other. The seat of the mind is no longer only in the brain, but all over the body. Now there is a scientific explanation for the concept of psychosomatic disease. The mind/body healing of cancer described by Symington and expanded by Segal now has validity. I was very excited to bring these discoveries from America to Israel, where I shared them with my cousin, Dr. Michael Schlesinger, a renowned cancer researcher. He showed me some personal research that had been published a few months earlier describing the effect of psychosocial stress on natural killer cell activity. He had completed a study on Kibbutzniks (individuals living in agricultural settlements in Israel). The participants of the study were divided into two groups. Copers who functioned well with stress, were compared to non-copers who withdrew under stress, stopped working, and had dysfunctional families. The non-copers showed a significant reduction in natural killer cells compared to the copers. The way we handle stress, rather than the stress itself, seemed to be the major depressor of the immune system.

I conducted lectures throughout Israel. In Be'er Sheva I presented my work on imagery and psychotherapy and shared these exciting discoveries again, only to find that some of the people I was talking to had done some of the original research on neurotransmitters. I was bringing coal to Newcastle and was pleased to find the small country of Israel as technically advanced as the United States. I returned home and began to review some of the studies on mind/body healing. Dr. David Spiegel, a psychiatrist at Stanford University was initially a skeptic over the mind/body healing work of Dr. Bernie Segal. He reviewed many years of group therapy work with 86 breast cancer patients and compared it with a control group of similar patients who had not undergone psychotherapy. Much to his surprise he found that the group having psychiatric treatment lived a year and a half longer than the control group. Dr. Spiegel was now a believer.

Further psychological research into cancer patients revealed that there appeared to be a predisposing psychological profile to cancer patients. Notably, there was emotional denial of problems and repression of the conflicts, a complete denial of all the emotional turmoil, terror and upsets that are realistically there. Suppression of hostility was an almost universal finding. These people were simply too nice, rarely expressing anger. In most cases there had been a major personal loss through death within the last year.

The science of psychoneuroimmunology stimulated my interest and I wondered if the mental imagery conflict resolution work I was doing could be useful. Dr. Symington and Dr. Spiegel focused on positive self mental imagery and positive attitudes and practiced guided imagery healing of the cancer through visualizations or drawings. My goal was to expand their premise into imagery conflict resolution. I organized group therapy for cancer patients over the period of one year. This was accompanied by testing before and in the middle of therapy for killer cell activity. Unfortunately, the laboratory results were defective and rendered the results useless. The psychotherapy that evolved was different than I expected.

My patients all had advanced disease with metastases and most of them were suffering from a reactive depression. A few were exceptional patients who had made positive lifestyle changes when the cancer was discovered, determined to live each day to its maximum.

The therapy initially focused on positive self imagery and ego strengthening, looking at each patient's past achievements and successes and their resources in coping with their present illness. The immune system enhancement imagery began with presentations of colored pictures from an electron microscope of killer cells fighting cancer. (Color images from the National Geographic, June 1986, Vol. 169, No. 6). After viewing these pictures I would encourage the patients to go into their imagination to see their own immune system fighting. There were many unique and varied ways the patients approached it, some with war imagery with high tech laser beams in the hands of highly trained soldiers that were increasing in numbers and efficiency. Some patients were offended by the violence of such concepts and developed gentler approaches, using color or butterflies as ways of removing or dissolving the cancer. My attempts at doing insight therapy emphasizing mental imagery resolution were limited. Only one patient, who was already an exceptional survivor, had a Gestalt experience by viewing his wife and boss in the empty chair. He finally experienced his hidden rage and accepted his aggressive power with great satisfaction. The remaining patients had difficulty with insight psychotherapy. Possibly their predisposing personality style, the ravages of their advanced disease compounded by the mental retardation of their depression made them poor candidates for conflict resolution work. Their interests and goals were more concrete as they excitedly talked and shared with each other their search for help. I found the bonding to each other was rapid and intense and personally rewarding. At times I felt my presence as a psychotherapist was intrusive on their intimacy and sharing. When the study was complete I concluded that the major benefit was a right brain experience of "solacing." The sharing and caring for each other gave sustenance and hope and may be one of the major factors in immune system enhancement.

Mind/body healing techniques could be an adjunct to the treatment of cancer but not a replacement for traditional medical therapy. The sooner these techniques could be used the better, which brought me back to the best treatment possible, prevention. Mental imagery therapy should be encouraged for mental and physical wellness and stress management. In times of overload deal only with one problem at a time and contain the others. Put them away in a vault, to avoid their intrusion, promising that you will deal with them one at a time when you're ready. Build a retreat in your mind's eye a retreat and go there regularly for relaxation and rejuvination. You can go to your comfortable or safe place for a daily holiday. Take advantage of the ultradian rhythm and perhaps when you're tired in the middle of the afternoon, give up the coffee break for a journey into your favourite place for relaxation, rejuvenation and strengthening. When you're down accentuate the positive, look back at some positive self imagery and perhaps you can find a resource that you can bring into the present. When life is stressful do a double or triple point dissociation. Watch it on your interactive video. Step back and look at yourself in that conflict. It will definitely reduce stress. If it doesn't, take another step backward and look at yourself looking at yourself in the stress. It definitely lowers anxiety and perhaps even gives you another view point. It may even shift a painful situation into an absurdly ridiculous one. Approach your feelings rather than withdraw, for the only way to get over pain is to go through it and there's always a light at the end of the tunnel. Express and share your emotions, rather than hide them, for keeping secrets increases stress. Respect your right brain contributions for imagination and intuition can be as valued as logic and reason. Integrating both leaves you well balanced with an immune system functioning at top efficiency.

Solace Center

The solace center in the right brain is the emotional equivalent of the hunger center. As we need food for physical energy, we need recognition, stroking, love, attachment, succor, for emotional survival. When empty we call it loneliness. While we prefer positive stroking, when hungry anything will do. You may have developed illness, rebellious behavior, or a complaining attitude, simply for attention. An underlying loser script may be its foundation, at least you're noticed when you fail or get into trouble.

Look back at the personality pie with all its different ego states. At the hub of each is the solace receptor which influences your expression of any personality trait, whether it be anger or power, dependence or independence, sexual behavior or affection. Part of any performance may be the need for recognition. That need in itself influences the way we express ourselves.

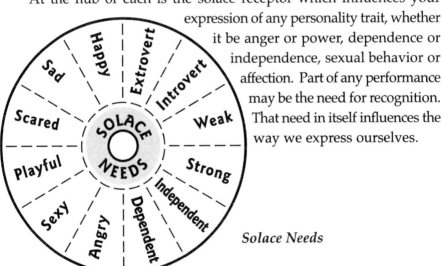

Solace Needs

If the nourishment from within is self caring and the sharing with others is rewarding, your satisfaction is complete. The whole self is filled with pleasure and your immune system is at peak performance.

Many reject the need for attention as weak or dependent, self centered or selfish. I believe it is the foundation of a good love relationship. For loneliness, beyond self love, is filled by the love of others. Personal contentment opens empathy, the ability to give love as well as receive it. A healthy love relationship fills the solace center with gourmet food.

CHAPTER TWELVE

The Violent Offender

In the early 1980s I heard a keynote speaker at a psychiatric convention talk on violence in society. He was a fascinating man, and neither a psychiatrist nor a physician. In fact, he had difficulty defining his profession for he had been on the Rand Commission, an advisor to President Kennedy and was president of a university. With tongue in cheek he remarked that if anyone read his curriculum vitae he would never be hired, for he rarely held a job for more than one to two years.

He focused on the increasing violence committed in cities by teenagers and young adults. He showed graphs of the usual causes and precursors of violence over the last fifteen to twenty years: business recession, unemployment, poverty, lack of education and social upheaval. These and many other common predisposing factors had barely changed, yet youth violence had significantly increased. "Why?" he asked and then responded with puzzling information. Violent offenders had an extremely high incidence of childhood abuse, mostly physical, often followed by sexual assault and emotional neglect. I walked out of the lecture puzzled and disturbed. Was it possible in our modern, sophisticated, ethical and democratic society that parental abuse of children was increasing? As my work in hypnotherapy developed, offering rapid access to early childhood experiences, I was shocked to discover the truth of his message. Dysfunctional, violent families, compounded by drug and alcohol abuse, were flagrant precursors to adult psychiatric illness. One of my colleagues, a forensic psychiatrist specializing in the treatment of violent street kids, found almost universal childhood trauma pathology. One of his young patients during hypnotherapy demonstrated this theme. While he had partial conscious memory of his father's violence, in a therapeutic session he regressed to an eight year old watching his father beating his mother. Hearing his mother's screams, he cowed in terror which quickly shifted to anger and a murderous rage. He wanted to kill the drunken bastard. After the abreaction he succinctly summarized his life, "No wonder I'm so angry."

Psychopaths (antisocial personality disorder) make up 30% of the criminal population. They are an extremely violent, arrogant, callous, cunning and impulsive group. They kill, mutilate, and sexually assault without conscience. Unable to love and incapable of empathy, they are driven only by the excitement of violence and the power of control. Male psychopaths are smooth, charming and manipulative and find women easy prey, even succeeding in seducing a high percentage of female therapists. The recidivism rate of psychopathic sexual offenses is almost 100%, while 80% of all violent psychopaths are recharged with an offense within five years. Psychiatric treatment of the psychopath has been a dismal failure. A job, a trade, a career, basically providing them work, has been the only effective treatment for the teenage psychopath.

A male patient had been in therapy for many years for recurrent depressions and violent behavior. His depressions responded well to treatment but the violence continued to erupt from easy provocation. Alcohol added a fine trigger while abstinence decreased the occurrence and intensity of his rage. He was a poor candidate for insight psychotherapy. He was rigid in his thinking, mistrustful of others and projected the blame for his problems on people and society. With little ability for abstraction, he was concrete in his paranoid thinking. Paradoxically, he would shift to anger and criticism at himself, precipitating a recurrence of depression. His social skills were anxious, unfriendly and irritable. People quickly avoided him. His history of love relationships was brief and empty, as he was unable to sustain any meaningful, long-term contact. During a session I observed a momentary blank period, with him staring, like a video tape that had stopped for a second. Suspecting petit mal epilepsy I referred him for a neurological consultation. The electroencephalogram demonstrated temporal lobe epilepsy. This is a known brain disorder frequently associated with violent offenders. This patient was a time bomb. Anticonvulsant treatment controlled the epilepsy but failed to deal with the rage and anger.

One day in group therapy with a minor confrontation he had a rage attack, threatening other patients. This was the final straw. With his inability for psychological insights, his organic brain disorder and a propensity for violence, I discontinued my treatment and referred him to a rage disorder center. Over the following years he came back for consultation, complaining of the lack of progress. I would usually refer him to another treatment center where trials of different therapies and medication failed. Surprisingly, he always came back, asking for help. On the last visit, I was developing my right brain psychotherapy with mental imagery and hypnotherapy. I recognized that his rigid, angry thinking tapes in his left brain were impenetrable. Surprisingly, his right brain was available, like a blank video tape and I invited him back into therapy. I believed that we had much better prospects of helping him by discovering resources through his right brain. Through the mental imagery techniques I bypassed his thoughts and through hypnotherapy began to explore.

My first therapeutic move was a regressive technique to recall a positive early experience. Much to my surprise it opened an early teenage love relationship where he relived the joys showing a capacity for pleasure I'd never seen. He then burst out crying as he described the eventual loss. This blocked grief was instant access to a reservoir of suppressed emotional experiences. I realized that we had an untapped resource for treatment and in the series of sessions that followed I continued indepth hypnotherapy. In one session shortly after he had experienced a killer rage at a driver who had cut him off, I made a decision to explore his excessive rage, and risk potential violence. It is wise to initially clarify with patients that violence of any type is unacceptable in therapy, and also to be careful to avoid any unconscious communication that I expect violence. In the past he had had fights with strangers with little provocation and was occasionally beaten by stronger opponents into unconsciousness. Using an affect bridge, I had him focus on the killer rage in the present, and then go back to the past. He regressed to a ten year old boy and burst out crying as he relived beatings by his older brother. The explosion of pain was overwhelming. He turned down the intensity with his dimmer switch. Staying with his pain, he relived the repeated beatings that lasted for years. He was angry that there had been no parental protection. His rage quickly shifted to his parents who he wanted to kill.

In full consciousness he filled in the story. His older brother was his hero, athletic, tough and generally protecting him from other bullies in the street. Yet he would periodically turn and beat him up. He was filled with ambivalent feelings toward his only protector, his violent abuser. His occasional protests to his parents fell on deaf ears. The source of his present rage was more than temporal lobe epilepsy, it was a reaction to childhood physical abuse and the unfinished past was in his eyes. We now had tools for repair and a right brain that was amenable to treatment.

The improvement has been slow, but steady. His rage is

settling down with a more realistic adult ego state now in charge. He is growing as a person and opening feelings of joy, playfulness, warmth and intimacy, even empathy. Developing more interactive skills with a great sense of humour will help him make friends and possibly a healthy love relationship. Insights into his childhood abuse have given him strong motivation to change. Most violent offenders lack this insight and their aggression is still directed towards society. They justify their violent behavior using a personal belief system that makes the other bad and nothing wrong with themselves.

We are developing effective therapies to treat the violent offender through right brain mental imagery and hypnotherapy, offering rapid access to early childhood trauma and creative therapeutic intervention. With personal insights motivation increases, a far cry from the courts forcing a felon into psychiatric treatment. Prevention becomes our best approach in treating violence. Educating young parents in child care, helping them recognize and manage the stress of child rearing, offering help and respite. Early childhood social programs like Head Start for Children, may rescue them from dysfunctional, impoverished homes. Early recognition of the abuse of children and rapid intervention may save society from the adult violent offender's wrath. This may also save the offender from himself and self-destruction. Improved psychological training for teachers is necessary for they can become transitional surrogate parents or positive role models, or detect signs of childhood abuse.

CHAPTER THIRTEEN

For New Beginnings

When:

- Childhood trauma is resolved.
- Dissociation is lifted.
- Your personality pie is full.
- You've healed, reowned, respected and accepted every one of your ego states.
- Integrated all your ego states into a whole self.
- Grieved your losses and disappointments.
- Said goodbye to the past.
- Replaced distorted thoughts and false beliefs with positive, realistic thinking.
- Blended feelings and thoughts, like lyrics to a song.
- Integrated right brain experiences with left brain understanding.

You are now ready to:

- Tolerate the realistic anxiety of change.
- Switch to the excitement of discovery.
- Open creativity.
- Make new beginnings

Your psychological growth through the maturity and expansion of all your ego states can go on as long as you live.

"To Althea from Prison"

Stonewalls do not a prison make

Nor iron bars a cage

Minds innocent and quiet take that for a hermitage

If I have freedom in my love

And in my soul am free

Angels alone that soar above

Enjoy such liberty.

REFERENCES

PART ONE - *In Your Right Mind*

(1)   **Stitches**, January 1996 - Volume 49

(2)   **Dear Abby** - Syndication - January 14, 1996 - Toronto Sun

(3)   **Dr. Bessel van der Kolk** - 14th Annual Convention of Clincial
        Hypnosis San Diego, California
        Lecture: *Trauma, Memory and Dissociation, June 27/97*

(4)   **Be You Own Healer**, John T. Shaffer, D.Min
        Published by Well Being Center, Jacksonville, Illinois, 62650 USA

(5)   **Dr. Brian & Shauna Moench**

PART TWO - *The Past gets in My Eyes*

(1)   **Canadian Journal of Psychiatry**, volume 41, #4 - May, 1996 - A
        Critical Review of Recovered Memories in Psychotherapy (part
        1 trauma and memory, part II trauma and therapy) by Dr. Joel
        Paris, M.D.

(2)   **Back From The Future**
        Workshop presented at the 11th International Conference of
        Dissociative States by Dr. Moishe Torem

(3)   **The Dissociative Table Technique in the Treatment of
        Multiple Personality and Ego-State Therapy**
        Dr. George A. Fraser
        Journal of Dissociation, Vol. IV, No. 4, December, 1991

(4)   **Diagnosis and Treatment of Multiple Personality Disorder**
        F.W. Putman The Guilford Press, N.Y.

(5)   **Myer Williams**

(6)   A Reader's Guide to Pierre Janet on Dissociation: A
        Neglected Intellectural Heritage
        Otto Van Der Hart, Barbara Friedman, Journal of Dissociation,
        Vol. 1. No. 1, March, 1989

(7)   Games People Play Eric Berne, M.D. Grove Press, N.Y., 1966

(8)   The Intrusive Past: The Flexibility of Memory and the
        Engraving of Trauma
        The Tenth International Conference for the Study of Dissociation
        Bessel van der Kolk

(9)   A Molecular Code Links Emotions, Mind and Health
        Stephen S. Hall
        Smithsonian Vol. 20, Number 3, June, 1989

(10)   Love, Medicine and Miracles
        Bernie Siegel
        Harper and Row, N.Y., 1986

READING LIST

Mental Imagery

Imagery in Healing
Jeanne Acterberg
Boston New Science Library 1985

Head First: The Biology of Hope
Norman Cousins
Published by E.P. Dutton, N.Y. 1989

Focusing
Eugene Gendlin, Ph.D.
Bantam Books 1988

Effects of Psychosocial Stress on Natural Killer Cell Activity
Michael Schlesinger, M.D. and Y. Yodfat, M.D

Psychosocial Factors & Cell Mediated Immunity
M. Schlesinger, M.D. and Y. Yodfat, M.D.
Clinical Immunology Newsletter 9.10 85

Be Your Own Healer
John T. Shaffer, D.Min.
Published by Well Being Center,
1926 Cedar St.
Jacksonville, Illinois, 62650 USA

Hemispheric Specialization
Psychiatric Clinics of North America
Vol. 11 # 3 September 1985

Death Imagery
Edited by Anees A. Sheikh and Katharina S. Sheikh
Published by American Imagery Institute

READING LIST

Hypnotherapy

Going Back In Time
Nicholas E. Brink. Ph.D.
202 S. Second St. Lewisberg. P.A. 17837 USA

My Voice Will Go with You
Sydney Rosen
The Teaching Tales of Milton Erickson
W. Norton and Company, N.Y and London

Techniques for the Management of Abreactions
K. Steele, R.N.M.N.
Atlanta Georgia

The Affect Bridge (1971)
J.G. Watkins
International Journal of Clinical and Experiential Hypnosis
19 (1) 28

Hypnosis and Ego State Therapy
John G. Watkins and Helen H. Watkins
Hypnoanalytic Techniques 1990 J.G. Watkins
Clinical Hypnoses Vol. #2, New York Irvingston

The Handbook of Hypnotic Suggestion and Metaphors
C.D. Hamond (Ed) 1990
Washington, D.C.

A Teaching Seminar with Milton Erickson
Edited by Jefffrey K. Zeig, Ph.D.
Brunner Mazel, New York, 1980

Future Focussed Therapy
Moshe S. Torem, M.D.
ISSMP & D Vol. 12 #1 February 1994 P. 89

Disorganized/Dissociated Attachment in the Etiology of Dissociative Disorders
Journal of Dissociation, Volume 5 #4
Gioanni Liotti, M.D.
December, 1992 196-205

Dr. Bessel van der Kolk
Director Trauma Clinic, Mass General Hospital
Harvard Medical School

> 1) Inescapable Shock Neurotransmitters and Addiction to Trauma
> Biological Psychiatry 1985 March, Vol. #20 (3) 314-325
>
> 2) Dissociative Disorders in Psychaitric Inpatients
> American Journal of Psychiatry 150 (76) 1037-42 1993 July
>
> 3) Childhood Trauma in Borderline Personality Disorders
> American Journal of Psychiatry 1989
> Vol. 146(4) 490-495
>
> 4) The Compulsion to Repeat the Trauma
> Re-enactment, Revictimization and Masochism
> Psychiatric Clinics of North America 1989
> June Vol. 12(2) 389-411

READING LIST

General

Cognitive Therapy for Personality Disorders
Aaron Beck, M.D. & Arthur Freeman, Ed.D.
The Guilford Press 1990

Attachment & Loss
Attachment Vol. I - Hogarth Press 1969
Separation Vol. II - Hogarth Press 1973
Loss Vol. III - Basic Books, 1980
Bowlby, John

Feeling Good
David Burns, M.D.
William Morrow and Co. In. N.Y., N.Y., 1980

Gestalt Therapy Verbatim
Fredrick S. Perls, M.D. Ph.D.
Real People Press 1969

Postscript

While writing this book has been a labor of love I truly miss the interaction of the reader. Your comments, ideas, and opinions would be greatly appreciated.

FAX Number 416-972-0768
e.mail address: jbmd@intradigital.com